ARIS AND PHILLIPS CLASSICAL TEXTS

Greek Orators VIII

Isaeus: Orations 1, 2, 4 and 6

Edited with an Introduction, Translation and Notes by

Brenda Griffith-Williams

LIVERPOOL UNIVERSITY PRESS

First published 2022 by
Liverpool University Press
4 Cambridge Street
Liverpool
L69 7ZU

www.liverpooluniversitypress.co.uk

Copyright © 2022 Brenda Griffith-Williams

The right of Brenda Griffith-Williams to be identified as the author of this book has been asserted by her in accordance with the Copyright, Designs and Patents Act 1988.

All rights reserved. No part of this book may be reproduced, stored in a retrieval system, or transmitted, in any form or by any means, electronic, mechanical, photocopying, recording, or otherwise, without the prior written permission of the publisher.

British Library Cataloguing-in-Publication data
A British Library CIP record is available

ISBN 978-1-802077-13-1
eISBN 978-1-802078-95-4

Typeset by Tara Evans

Printed and bound by CPI Group (UK) Ltd, Croydon CR0 4YY.

Cover image: The grave stele of an Athenian cavalryman, Dexileos (394/393 BC) in Kerameikos Archaeological Park (site of the largest cemetery in classical Athens)

CONTENTS

Acknowledgements	v
Abbreviations	vii
General Introduction	1
Isaeus 1: On the Estate of Cleonymus	
Introduction	14
Text and translation	25
Commentary	42
Isaeus 2: On the Estate of Menecles	
Introduction	65
Text and translation	75
Commentary	92
Isaeus 4: On the Estate of Nicostratus	
Introduction	121
Text and translation	129
Commentary	142
Isaeus 6: On the Estate of Philoctemon	
Introduction	161
Text and translation	175
Commentary	200
Bibliography	237
Index	243

ACKNOWLEDGEMENTS

This book would not have been possible without the help, support, and encouragement of many friends and colleagues. My warmest thanks are due, in particular, to the following. Professor Chris Carey (University College London) and Professor Mike Edwards (Royal Holloway University of London), have both generously sent me copies of published and unpublished papers. Dr Janek Kucharski (University of Silesia in Katowice) assisted me with references and comments on Athenian judicial punishment (especially death sentences) for the commentary on Isaeus 4. Dr Jakub Filonik (University of Silesia in Katowice) provided information on Athenian military service for the commentary on Isaeus 2. I am also extremely grateful to Clare Litt of Liverpool University Press for her sympathetic help and support, and to the series editor, Professor Alan Sommerstein, whose insightful comments on my manuscript have significantly enhanced the finished work. Any remaining errors or omissions are, of course, entirely my own responsibility.

ABBREVIATIONS

Ancient authors and works

Aesch.	Aeschines
Andoc.	Andocides
Ant.	Antiphon
Arist.	Aristotle
NE	*Nicomachean Ethics*
Rhet.	*Rhetoric*
Ath. Pol.	*Athēnaiōn Politeia*
Dein.	Deinarchus
Dem.	Demosthenes
Diog. Laert.	Diogenes Laertius
Hyp.	Hyperides
Isae.	Isaeus
Isoc.	Isocrates
Lyc.	Lycurgus
Lys.	Lysias
Men. *Sam.*	Menander *Samia*
Plaut. *Merc.*	Plautus *Mercator*
Plut. *Alc.*	Plutarch *Alcibiades*
Thuc.	Thucydides

Modern works

IG	*Inscriptiones Graecae*
KA	*Poetae comici graeci*, eds R. Kassel and C. Austin, Berlin, 1983–2001.
LGPN	*Lexicon of Greek personal names*
OCD	*Oxford Classical Dictionary*

General

c.	*circa*
dau.	daughter
ed./eds	editor/edited
esp.	especially
fr(r).	fragment(s)
Gk.	Greek
lit.	literally
m.	married
ms(s).	manuscript(s)
n.	note
trans.	translator/translated

GENERAL INTRODUCTION

The four speeches in this volume were delivered by litigants involved in disputed inheritance claims in the Athenian courts of the fourth century BC. They were written by Isaeus, a logographer (professional speechwriter) who apparently specialized in this area of the law.

These speeches are worth reading because they illustrate various aspects of Athenian law and procedure, and the stories told by the litigants offer a unique insight into the lives and values of fourth century Athenians (although we should not assume that the situations they describe were typical). They can be read and enjoyed as rhetoric or social history, but a fuller understanding and appreciation of their value requires some knowledge of the legal context in which they were written. The primary aim of my translations and commentaries is, accordingly, to explain the legal framework of each case and show how the logographer's rhetorical strategy was designed to achieve the desired legal outcome for his client. The introduction to each individual speech sets out the basic 'facts' of the case (according to the speaker), identifies the legal issues, and (where relevant) explains the historical background.

This General Introduction provides some basic background information about Isaeus and the Athenian legal culture within which he worked, and introduces some of the topics of scholarly debate which are explored in greater depth in relation to the individual speeches. The coverage of the Athenian legal system is by no means comprehensive. Griffith-Williams (2013, 1–31) provides a more detailed account of Isaeus's work and of the Athenian inheritance system. Readers who would like to find out more about the Athenian legal system in general are advised to consult one of the standard works such as Harrison (1968 and 1971). MacDowell (1978) provides a simpler and (especially for the Greekless reader) more accessible account, which is still a reliable introduction to the subject. Todd (1993) offers a more sophisticated (and not uncontroversial) analysis, but is also a reliable source of information.

Isaeus and his work

Isaeus is one of the so-called 'Attic orators', canonized in late antiquity, whose speeches (or some of them) have survived through the mediaeval manuscript tradition. Very little is known about his life. He is not mentioned in any surviving fourth century sources, and biographical information from later antiquity is sparse and sometimes contradictory. According to Hermippus (third century BC) he was born in Athens, but Demetrius of Magnesia (first century BC) says that his birthplace was Chalcis. There is no evidence that he was ever involved in litigation himself, or that he participated in Athenian politics, so, although this is not conclusive proof, it seems more likely that he lived in Athens as a metic (resident alien) than as a citizen. He was reputed to have been a pupil of Isocrates and teacher of Demosthenes.

The work attributed to Isaeus in later antiquity includes a rhetorical handbook and 64 forensic speeches, of which 50 were accepted as genuine. Of the 12 extant speeches, the first 11 (known from the mediaeval manuscript tradition) are all concerned with disputes about inheritance. Isaeus 12, from a case of disputed citizenship. survives in the form of a substantial fragment preserved by Dionysius of Halicarnassus (first century BC) in his critical essay on Isaeus. Evidence of some of the lost speeches survives in the form of shorter fragments, while others are known from titles recorded by grammarians such as Harpocration in late antiquity. Forster (1927, 445–81) includes the text and translation of existing fragments, with explanations of their subject matter. Edwards (2007, 199–210) includes translations with brief comments.

Isaeus apparently had a long career: the earliest of his extant speeches (Isaeus 5) was probably written in 389 BC, while the latest (Isaeus 12) may be as late as 344/3. Some of the other speeches, including two in this volume (Isaeus 2 and 6) can be dated with reasonable accuracy from internal evidence. Wevers (1969) suggests dates for the remaining speeches based on a stylometric analysis. Further information can be found in the introductions to the individual speeches in this volume.

Athenian family structures and inheritance laws

The basic principle of Athenian inheritance law is that a legitimate son had an absolute right to inherit his father's estate, and the inheritance was partible (i.e. if there was more than one son they all had an equal share).[1] A legitimate son was one whose parents were legally married to each other,

---

1 See commentary on 6.25.

and in a society where remarriage after divorce or the death of a spouse was common, there were many families where the paternal inheritance had to be shared among half-brothers by different mothers. Athenian men enjoyed considerable freedom to engage in informal relations with mistresses or prostitutes, but illegitimate children from such relationships were not legally members of their father's family (*oikos*) and had no right to inherit from him. In practice, the distinction between legitimate and illegitimate offspring could be uncertain, and recognition of legitimate status depended crucially on the father's willingness to acknowledge the child. Public recognition took place in two stages. A legitimate son was first introduced to his father's phratry (a kinship-based religious organization), and, when he reached adulthood, registered in the father's deme (administrative division of the Athenian state) as a citizen.

Partible inheritance, combined with the exclusion of illegitimate children, inevitably created a source of rivalry between half-brothers when it came to the division of the paternal estate, and it was an obvious tactic for the sons of one mother to accuse their rivals of being illegitimate. Although the specific facts of the case are complex and obscure, this type of conflict is at the heart of the dispute in Isaeus 6.

The inheritance rights of natural legitimate sons are implicit in a law attributed to the renowned sixth century legislator, Solon:

> Those citizens who had not been adopted and thereby may neither renounce [the inheritance] nor claim their rights in an *epidikasia*[2], when Solon entered on his archonship shall be allowed to bequeath (*diathesthai*) their own property as they wish, *as long as they do not have male legitimate children*, and their intellect was not disturbed by insanity, senility, drugs, sickness or by the manipulation of a woman, or forced by necessity or imprisonment. (Cited at [Dem.] 46.14: Leão and Rhodes 2016. fr. 49a, emphasis added.)

The wording of this law, known as Solon's 'law on wills', is vague. By the fourth century it was interpreted as permitting a man without natural legitimate sons to adopt a son as his heir and successor, either during the adoptive father's lifetime (adoption *inter vivos*) or in a will, so that the adoption would come into effect only after his death (testamentary adoption). In the case of an adoption *inter vivos*, the adoptive father would

---

[2] See p. 5 below.

complete the formalities of the adoption by introducing his new son to his phratry and enrolling him in his deme, giving him exactly the same inheritance rights after the father's death as a natural legitimate son. A testamentary adoption, on the other hand, required the approval of the court, and the formalities of phratry introduction and deme enrolment were not carried out until this had been obtained. Isaeus 2 provides an example of adoption *inter vivos*, while both Isaeus 4 and Isaeus 6 are concerned with disputed testamentary adoptions. The other speech in this selection, Isaeus 1, is also from a dispute about a will, but, unusually, one that does not involve adoption.

Another Solonian law (modified in the late fifth century) dealt with the disposition of a dead man's property if he left no legitimate sons, natural or adopted, or descendants through a male line:

> If a man dies without having made a will, if he leaves daughters, the property shall be to them; if not, the following relatives shall be entitled to the property: if there are brothers of the same father or legitimate children of brothers, they shall take the part of the father; if there are no brothers or children of brothers, then ‹the cousins on the father's side and the children› of them shall inherit in the same way. The male relatives and their male descendants shall take precedence, if they are from the same ancestors, even if they are of remoter affinity. If there is nobody on the father's side to the degree of children of cousins, the relatives of the deceased on the maternal side shall inherit in the same way. And if there is nobody on both sides covered by these degrees, then the next of kin on the father's side shall inherit. Neither an illegitimate son nor an illegitimate daughter shall have rights of kinship, either in sacred or in secular affairs. (Effective from the archonship of Eucleides.) (Cited at [Dem.] 43.51; Leão and Rhodes 2016. fr. 50b.)

The first situation envisaged by this law, where a man died leaving a daughter or daughters but no sons, does not arise in any of the speeches selected for this volume. But it is discussed as a hypothetical scenario in Isaeus 1 and 6, and explanations can be found in the commentary on those speeches.

As to the order of succession among the dead man's collateral relatives, some of the details in the law are obscure or ambiguous, but its most significant feature is its patrilineal structure: kinsmen who were related to the deceased on his father's side had priority over those related to him through his mother. Within each degree of kinship, in accordance with the principle of male precedence, a woman could inherit only if there was no surviving male who was equally closely related to the deceased.

The majority of attested inheritance disputes from classical Athens involved a contest between the dead man's closest relative or relatives (next of kin) and someone claiming to be his adopted son or the beneficiary of his will. Three of the speeches in this selection fall into that category. The speakers of Isaeus 1 and 4 claim to be the next of kin of, respectively, Cleonymus and Nicostratus, while their opponents base their claims on wills. The speaker of Isaeus 2 defends his status as the son adopted *inter vivos* by Menecles.

Athenian court procedures
Most trials in the Athenian courts were adversarial, with one party (the prosecutor) accusing the other (the defendant) of a specific violation of the law. There was no office equivalent to that of a modern public prosecutor, and in a so-called 'private action' (*dikē*) it was up to the victim of an alleged offence to initiate and pursue a prosecution. In a public action (*graphē*), which was deemed to be of interest to the *polis* as well as the individual victim, it was open to any citizen to act as 'volunteer prosecutor' (Greek *ho boulomenos*, literally 'he who is willing').

The legal basis of an inheritance dispute was different: there was no inherent allegation of wrongdoing, but rather a contest between two (or more) rival claimants to an estate. When a dispute went to court, the winner would be the one who could persuade the judges that he had the best legal claim to the estate (in most cases either as the dead man's adopted son or his next of kin). So the procedure, too, was different from the adversarial model. Anyone claiming a dead man's estate as his next of kin or son adopted by will had to submit a formal, written claim to the appropriate official, the archon. If this was not challenged, the estate was awarded to the claimant by *epidikasia* (probably an administrative procedure with no judicial involvement). But if the archon received more than one claim, the dispute was determined judicially by means of a *diadikasia*, the special procedure used in the Athenian courts for competing claims to a benefit or to avoid performing a duty. There could, in principle, be any number of parties to a *diadikasia*, but in practice it seems that there were rarely more than two. The parties were on an equal footing, with neither formally identified as prosecutor or defendant, but their litigation tactics often resembled those of litigants in an adversarial trial, with each party attacking his opponent's case as well as defending his own. Two of the speeches in this volume, Isaeus 1 and 4, were delivered by claimants in a *diadikasia*.

A natural legitimate son, or a son adopted *inter vivos* by the dead man, was in a privileged position. He did not have to go to court to assert his claim to his father's estate, but could simply take direct possession of the property. If anyone else submitted a claim to the court, the son could block it with a *diamartyria*: a formal statement in which either the son himself or a witness on his behalf testified that the estate in question was not subject to the adjudication of the court because the deceased had left a legitimate son. If the rival claimant still wanted to pursue the claim, he had to prosecute the witness in the *diamartyria* for false testimony (*pseudomartyria*) and the case would be tried by the court as a *dikē pseudomartyriōn*. Isaeus 6 is the prosecution speech from such a trial, while Isaeus 2 is the speech for the defence.

There were no professional lawyers or judges in classical Athens. Every litigant was expected to present his own case, although he sometimes had the assistance of a friend or relative as a supporting speaker (*synēgoros*). Two of the speeches in this volume, Isaeus 2 and 4, were delivered by supporting speakers. The case for each party to the trial was normally presented in a single speech, sometimes with the addition of a shorter supplementary speech. In an adversarial trial (*dikē* or *graphē*) it was always the prosecutor who spoke first, but we do not know how the order of speakers was determined in a *diadikasia*. Speeches were subject to a time limit which varied according to the type of case, and all trials were completed within a single day.

An Athenian trial was heard by a panel of ordinary Athenians known as dicasts (the Anglicized form of the Greek word *dikastai*) who had no special training and whose functions combined those of a modern judge and jury. (Throughout this volume I have chosen to use the word 'judges' rather than 'jurors' or 'dicasts'.) At the end of the trial there was no attempt to reach a collective decision; each of the judges formed his own judgment and voted for the litigant of his choice. Voting was done by a system of placing discs with axes (Gk. *psēphoi*, lit. 'pebbles') in urns, and the winning litigant was the one who received a simple majority of votes. The details of the system changed over time, and varied for different types of procedure.[3]

Witness testimony

The most important form of evidence in Athenian trials was witness testimony. Witnesses were required to be present in court, but they were not questioned or cross-questioned by the parties and (at least from the early fourth century) they did not give oral testimony. Their written depositions were read out by the court clerk at the request of the speaker, as were other forms of documentary evidence such as laws, contracts, or wills. The reading of this evidence did not count towards the time limit for the speech.

As in the majority of other surviving speeches of the Attic orators, the text of the witness testimony produced by Isaeus's clients does not survive; the scribes who copied the speeches simply marked the point at which documentary evidence was read out, without recording its content.

Witnesses are not routinely named in Isaeus's speeches; they are sometimes identified as members of the dead man's family (who were likely to be the most credible witnesses on domestic matters) or of his phratry or deme. Often they are described in more general terms such as 'those who were present' or 'those who know the facts'. Their testimony typically relates to questions of identity or status, or the authenticity of a will. A claimant whose legitimacy had been questioned would, ideally, need witnesses to testify that he had been introduced to and accepted by his father's phratry, and that his parents had been legally married. Testimony on phratry and deme membership would also be needed by someone claiming to have been adopted *inter vivos*. A litigant claiming an inheritance on the basis of a will would be expected to produce witnesses who were present when the will was made (6.7). Further testimony might be deployed to support a range of other 'facts' mentioned by a speaker in his narrative. Examples include a quarrel between the deceased and one of his relatives (1.32), the giving of a dowry when a woman was

---

3   For a full account, see Harrison (1971, 164–66).

married (2.5), the result of an arbitration (2.34), and the conduct of a funeral (2.37).

The work of the logographer: telling a persuasive story

Many, perhaps most, inheritance disputes, ancient and modern, involve narratives of family conflict, with the rival claimants to an estate putting forward fundamentally different accounts of the 'facts', and in order to put his or her case as effectively as possible to the judge or jury, a litigant pursuing an inheritance claim in the modern courts would probably engage the services of a legally qualified advocate. The closest equivalent to a qualified lawyer in the Athenian legal system was the professional speechwriter (logographer), whose main advantage over the ordinary citizen was his rhetorical training and who, for a fee, would compose a speech for his client to learn and deliver in court.

Like the majority of contested inheritance claims, the cases featured in this book turned on disputed facts, or sometimes disputed interpretations of agreed facts. rather than disputes about the law itself. No-one questioned the legal right of a legitimate son to inherit his father's estate, or of a childless Athenian to adopt a son or make a will, but disputes could and did arise about the identity of a claimant, the authenticity of a will, or the intentions or mental capacity of a testator or adopter. Did Cleonymus want to revoke his will before he died, or simply to amend it (Isaeus 1)? Was Menecles acting under the influence of his ex-wife when he adopted her brother, or was it a free and rational choice (Isaeus 2)? Did Nicostratus leave a will in which he adopted Chariades, or was the document produced in court a forgery concocted by Chariades and his friends (Isaeus 4)? Was the boy introduced by Euctemon to his phratry really his legitimate son, or the son of an ex-slave who had beguiled the old man into treating her child as his own (Isaeus 6)? In all of these cases, the judges were faced with fundamentally conflicting stories, and their task was to decide which was true, or at least more likely to be true.

The basic facts about a will or adoption were the obvious and essential starting point for the speechwriter, in consultation with his client; but, even supported by witness testimony, the basic facts alone would not be sufficient to win a case in the face of a competing narrative from the opposing party. So Isaeus's narratives also cover a range of other matters including family quarrels (Isaeus 1, 2, and 6), friendship between families (Isaeus 2), or the conduct of the funeral for the deceased (Isaeus 2 and 4). All of these additional facts, while not in themselves conclusive, supported the speaker's claim, but they still had to be supplemented by arguments from probability (Gk. *eikos*) designed to undermine the opponent's case and persuade the judges that his story was more likely to be true than his opponent's. The use of these supplementary facts and arguments, and their relevance to the contested issues, will be explored in the commentaries and the introductions to individual speeches.

A skilled speechwriter could also enhance the plausibility of his client's case through a range of rhetorical and stylistic devices.[4] In Isaeus's case these include, in particular, repetition, rhetorical questions, and irony. A speaker can hammer home his message by repeating key words or phrases throughout the speech; he can engage the attention of his audience by making his point in the form of a question rather than a statement; or he can discredit his opponent's actions and arguments by using irony to make them seem absurd. All the speeches in this volume provide examples of these techniques, which are discussed in the individual introductions and commentaries.

Isaeus and modern scholarship

The first published translation into English of Isaeus's work was that of the 18th century barrister and antiquarian Sir William Jones (1779). This excluded the speech now identified as Isaeus 2, the Greek text of which was not published until 1785. Jones's 1779 translation was followed by those of Forster (1927) in the Loeb Classical Library, and Edwards (2007) in the *Texas Orators* series. Translations of individual speeches have occasionally featured in anthologies of the Attic orators, or in separate editions; for example, Carey (2017) includes a translation of Isaeus 4.

The only complete edition of Isaeus's speeches with a full commentary in English is that of William Wyse (1904), notable for his biased and hostile characterization of Isaeus as a devious and unscrupulous advocate, whose clients were invariably in the wrong and whose speeches are an unreliable source of Athenian law. Scholars such as Avramović (1997) and Hatzilambrou (2018b) have sought to restore Isaeus's reputation as

---

4   For a brief but useful analysis of Isaeus's style, see Hatzilambrou (2018a, 35–41).

a legal source. Griffith-Williams (2013) has provided a commentary on four of Isaeus's *diadikasia* speeches (7, 8, 9, and 10), while Hatzilambrou (2018a) offers an edition, English translation, and commentary on Isaeus 3. The latest complete edition of the speeches is that of Cobetto Ghiggia (2012) with an Italian translation and notes. Critical editions of two speeches, with Italian translations and substantial commentaries, have also been pubished separately: Isaeus 5 (Cobetto Ghiggia, 2002) and Isaeus 8 (Ferrucci, 2005).

Despite this more recent work, the influence of Wyse (1904) has remained pervasive throughout the 20th century and beyond, and some of the speeches, notably Isaeus 6, still need to be reassessed in the light of later research on the historical background. While monographs and scholarly articles devoted exclusively to Isaeus remain relatively rare, his speeches have been widely used as source material for more general studies of Athenian legal culture and social attitudes, often within the framework of scholarly debates about the nature of the Athenian legal system and the 'relevance' of the evidence used by Athenian litigants. Were Athenian judges prejudiced against wills and adoption (Isaeus 1 and 4)? How did they view the competing claims of kinship and friendship (Isaeus 1, 2, and 4)? What was the purpose of character evidence (Isaeus 4 and 6)? What (if any) was the relevance of evidence on family quarrels (Isaeus 1) or the conduct of the dead man's funeral (Isaeus 1, 2, and 4)? As is discussed in the commentaries and the introductions to the individual speeches, some of the scholars who have addressed these issues have concluded that the Athenian courts ignored the law, and that litigants relied on irrelevant or 'extra-legal' evidence to persuade the judges that they were more deserving than their opponents on moral rather than legal grounds. I hope to show that a more nuanced reading of the speeches, with due attention to context, suggests some different answers.

The text of the speeches

The principal source for the text of Isaeus's speeches is the Codex Crippsianus (A), a 13th century manuscript now in the British Library, which also contains the speeches of Andocides, Antiphon, Deinarchus, and Lycurgus. All other existing manuscripts of Isaeus are considered to be derived from A, apart from Ambrosianus, D 42 sup. (Q), which contains only Isaeus 1 and 2. Wyse (1904, i–lii) gives an exhaustive overview of the manuscript tradition, including a detailed description of A. Forster (1927, xiv–xvi) provides a brief summary.

My text is based on that of Forster's 1927 Loeb edition (also available online at Perseus Digital Library), which should be consulted for a full critical apparatus. As explained more fully in the commentary, I have departed from the Loeb text in the following places.

1.47	Ἀθηναῖοι AQ.: ἄνδρες.
4.7	ἐξ Ἀκῆς A: ἑξάκις.
4.7	εἰσηλθέτην Edwards (2002): ἠλθέτην.

ISAEUS:

ORATIONS 1, 2, 4 AND 6

ISAEUS 1: ON THE ESTATE OF CLEONYMUS

INTRODUCTION

Cleonymus died leaving a will, deposited in the office of a public official (the archon), in which he bequeathed his estate to some distant relatives. Isaeus does not say how many beneficiaries there were, and only one of them, Pherenicus, is named in the speech. Their exact relationship to Cleonymus is not specified. Isaeus's client in this case is Cleonymus's nephew (probably his sister's son) speaking on behalf of himself and his brother (or possibly brothers) who challenge the will and claim the estate as Cleonymus's next of kin. Again, the number is not specified, but for the sake of simplicity I shall assume that the speaker had only one brother (as is suggested by §16).

Nothing is known about Cleonymus or his family from external sources, and there are no historical references in the speech to provide a date. Wevers (1969, 21) suggests $c.$ 355 BC.

The speaker says that he and his brother were children when their father died, so Deinias, their uncle (father's brother) became their guardian. There was a quarrel between Cleonymus and Deinias (who, if Cleonymus was indeed the speaker's maternal uncle, were not blood relations); and Cleonymus could not bear to think that he might die while his nephews were still under age, leaving his estate under the control of his bitter enemy. To ensure that would not happen, he made the will in favour of more distant relatives, but in the event it was Deinias who died while the boys were still minors, and Cleonymus took them into his own house and helped them secure their property against creditors. Having always been well disposed towards his nephews (and, before his quarrel with Deinias, always wanted them to inherit his property) Cleonymus now became closer to them than anyone else. On the other hand, he fell out with one of the relatives named in his will, Pherenicus. Some time later Cleonymus became ill, and asked Poseidippus to fetch the archon so that he could revoke his will. Poseidippus refused, and even turned the archon away when he arrived at the door. Cleonymus was angry, and asked Diocles to summon the archon on the next day, but

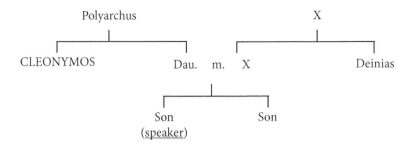

Figure 1.

it was too late; he died unexpectedly during the night. After Cleonymus's death the speaker's opponents claimed his estate under the will. Some family members, one of whom was called Cephisander, tried to negotiate a compromise between the rival claimants, proposing that they should all take a share of the property. But the opponents persisted, using unfair and aggressive tactics to pursue their claim to the whole estate.

Cleonymus's will

The most usual form of Athenian will seems to have been one in which a testator with no legitimate sons adopted a son as his universal heir and successor. There is no reference to adoption in this speech, so it appears that Cleonymus's will did not conform to this model; he evidently bequeathed his property to several individuals, but without adopting any of them. One of the beneficiaries was Pherenicus (§§31–32), and Poseidippus may have been another (§§14–15). Other individuals named in the speech (Diocles, Cephisander, Simon) appear to have been friends or relations of Cleonymus but not beneficiaries under his will.

According to MacDowell (1978, 101) there was 'not much scope for a will' in classical Athens apart from adoption. There is, nevertheless, sufficient evidence that it was possible for a childless man to make a will disposing of his property without adoption; Rubinstein (1993, 86) lists five examples of wills left by Athenians without adopting the beneficiary.[1] She concludes that testamentary adoption was an indicator

---

1 Lys. 13.41; Dem. 41.10; Isa. 7.6; [Andoc.] 4.15 and Plut. Alc. 8.4 (on the will of Alcibiades); Diog. Laert. 3.41–43 (on Plato's will).

of the importance attached by an individual to his tomb cult and the continuation of his line of descent; if he simply wanted to disrupt the order of intestate succession (that is, to leave his property to someone other than his closest relative), he could do so without adopting an heir.[2]

Cleonymus's will is also unusual in another respect; he is the only Athenian testator known to have deposited his will in the custody of the city's officials, although there are several instances in the extant speeches of wills left for safekeeping with a friend or relation of the testator,[3] The reasons for Cleonymus's action are unclear, but one possibility is that he simply did not have any disinterested friends or kinsmen whom he could trust sufficiently to take on the responsibility. It is possible, in any event, that an official witness was required for the revocation of a will (cf. Isae. 6.32) and it seems clear from both Isaeus 1 and Isaeus 6 that an Athenian testator could only revoke his will by physically destroying it, not simply by countermanding it in a later document.[4] That would be consistent with the Athenian practice of destroying public documents such as laws and decrees once they were repealed or superseded.[5]

The legal basis of the dispute and the speaker's case

The issue in dispute is the validity of Cleonymus's will: not the authenticity of the document, but the intentions of the testator, or 'the will behind the will' (Wohl, 2010, 262).[6] The speaker does not deny that Cleonymus made the will, but claims that he changed his mind and wanted to revoke it. Scholars have sometimes suggested that the speaker's claim was based on equity rather than law: he was 'arguing against the validity of

---

2 Rubinstein (1993) is ambivalent in her treatment of Isaeus 1. She includes it in a list of 'law-court speeches that have a direct bearing on adoption' (p. 4), and does not mention it in her discussion of wills without adoption (pp. 81–86). She lists it as a case of testamentary adoption in her catalogue of attested adoptions, but with the comment (p. 118) 'possibly testamentary, but it is not stated explicitly that Kleonymos adopted any of his beneficiaries. It is indeed possible that his will did not provide for adoption.'
3 Cf. Lys. 32.5; Isa. 7.1; Isa. 6.7; Isa. 9.5; Dem. 45.18; all cited by Harrison (1968, 154, n.3).
4 Cf. Harrison (1968, 154–55).
5 Cf. Thomas (1989, 51–54).
6 Cf. Sawyer and Spero (2018, 45): 'The documentary will should give expression to the testator's true "will" about what should become of their property.'

[the] will on moral rather than legal grounds, because the law was not on his side'.[7] But Isaeus's approach was actually more subtle; he was not relying on moral rights or unwritten rules, but trying to persuade the judges that the law *was* on his client's side. It was, of course, up to them to decide whether they agreed.

Cleonymus, like any Athenian who had no legitimate sons or descendants through a male line, was legally entitled to dispose of his property as he wished, provided (and the caveat is important) that his mind was not impaired by any of the factors mentioned in Solon's 'law on wills'.[8] If he had not left a will, or if the will that he did leave was found to be invalid, his property would go to his next of kin, as determined by the order set out in Solon's 'law of intestate succession'.[9]

The speaker mentions the law (or laws) six times, but he does not have any specific law read out to the court. He tells the judges they will not be acting 'in accordance with the law' if they reject his claim (§40). He bases his own claim to the estate on Solon's law of intestate succession ('the laws have given us the right to inherit in terms of our degree of kinship', §4), but he gives no details of the order of succession determined by the law – casting some doubt on his repeated statements that he and his brother are Cleonymus's next of kin and their opponents are more distantly related.

In any event, the speaker cannot rely on the law of intestate succession unless he can persuade the judges that Cleonymus's will is invalid. He describes the will as 'illegal' or 'against the law(s)' (§§26, 35) but he does not refer explicitly to Solon's law on wills or to any other law that has been violated by the will. He does, indirectly, allude to Solon's law with his repeated assertions that Cleonymus made the will while he was angry with Deinias. At first this is simply presented as a fact, part of the narrative that explains why Cleonymus made the will in favour of the speaker's opponents and why he subsequently changed his mind. Later, though, the speaker says that Cleonymus 'made his will while he was angry with Deinias and not thinking straight' (§11). Then he tells the judges that, to discover Cleonymus's true intention, they should consider his later actions, when he looked after his nephews, not what he had done in a state of anger 'in which we all make mistakes' (§13). He also

---

7   Edwards (2008, 46).
8   See General Introduction, p. 3.
9   See General Introduction, p. 4.

says that if his opponents' version of the story is true, they are accusing Cleonymus of 'utter insanity' (§19).

The language of 'madness' or 'insanity' (*mania*, §20; *paranoia*, §§19, 50) is carefully chosen to remind the judges of Solon's law on wills, implicitly inviting them to declare the will invalid because Cleonymus was not in his right mind when he wrote it. But Isaeus never explicitly claims that Cleonymus's anger with Deinias amounted to insanity under the terms of the law, perhaps because he knew that an argument along those lines would have been stretching the meaning of the law and might not have been accepted by the judges. Instead, he simply claims that the will does not represent Cleonymus's wishes at the time of his death because he had changed his mind, and wanted to revoke it because he had made it in anger against Deinias, not from any wish to disinherit his nephews. How would an Athenian court have responded to this, given that Cleonymus had not in fact carried out his supposed intention of revoking the will?[10]

It is worth pointing out that, despite differences of legal detail and procedure, establishing that a will represents the testator's true wishes is just as much a concern (and a problem) for the modern courts as it was in classical Athens. The question is not simply whether the will was genuinely written by the testator, and is not a forgery, but whether the testator was of sound mind and free from duress or undue influence at the time of writing it. Under modern English law, according to Sawyer and Spero (2018, 45), 'The testator must have the mental capacity to make a will and they must not be unduly influenced by any other person. The will must be truly the testator's – that is, they must know and approve of all parts of it that are to be admitted to probate.' Evidence of a testator's good or bad relations with the beneficiaries of his will, and with others, may be an important (albeit not conclusive) indication of his intentions.[11]

A written 'will' provides documentary evidence of the testator's 'will' (wishes) about the disposition of his property after his death. Testators frequently change or revoke their written wills, because their wishes have changed (or because external circumstances have changed, e.g. by the death of a beneficiary). But what if a testator has changed his mind, but neglected (or been unable) to revoke or change the terms of

---

10 Harris (2013c, 194–96) takes a slightly different approach, arguing that the speaker's case is based on a broad interpretation' of Solon's law on wills.

11 For modern examples, see Griffith-Williams (2012, 157–58).

his written will? A modern court would take a strictly formal approach to that question:
> If a person has a perfectly valid will but tells everybody in sight that she has changed her mind, that the last will does not say what she wants, this has no effect. She has to change the will or tear it up. Otherwise, it will govern what happens to her estate, even though we know this is not what she wanted. (Friedman 2009, 62)

But the Athenian courts were not constrained by modern formalities, and would not necessarily have rejected the speaker's case out of hand, provided they were satisfied about Cleonymus's intentions; in fact, the archon must have accepted at the preliminary hearing that the speaker had an admissible claim.[12] The written will, nevertheless, remained in force unless and until the judges could be persuaded that it should be annulled, after hearing both sides of the case. It seems to have been agreed by both parties that Cleonymus did try to retrieve his will from the archon's office on the evening before his death, but his reasons for doing so were disputed. The speaker says that Cleonymus wanted to revoke the will, while his opponents (according to the speaker) say that he wanted to confirm its provisions in their favour. So the challenge for Isaeus was to to rebut the opponents' version of events and persuade the judges that Cleonymus really did intend to revoke his will because he had changed his mind.

The narrative in this speech is remarkably short, and the information about family relationships is sketchy, leaving a number of questions unanswered. If Cleonymus made the will because he was angry with Deinias, why did he not revoke it as soon as Deinias died rather than waiting until he himself was (as it turned out) terminally ill? Isaeus is typically vague in this speech about chronology, so we cannot tell how much time had elapsed, but it seems to have been at least several years. If Poseidippus refused to summon the archon at Cleonymus's request, why did the archon arrive at the house anyway? (Was it, in fact, the speaker himself or one of his associates, rather than Cleonymus, who had sent for the archon?) Most importantly, perhaps, who exactly were the beneficiaries of Cleonymus's will, and what was their relationship to him? The speaker's reticence on this point arouses suspicion about his claim that he and his brother were Cleonymus's next of kin.

---

12   Cf. Harris (2013c, 196).

Athenian wills and attitudes to wills

Most of the speech is devoted to argumentation from probability, designed to cast doubt into the minds of the judges about the validity of the will and persuade them that – since they cannot be sure about the will – it would be safer for them to award the estate to the next of kin, the speaker and his brother.

Misunderstandings about the argumentation in this speech have contributed to a perception among some scholars that the Athenian courts were prejudiced in principle against wills in favour of claims based on blood kinship.[13] Victoria Wohl's imaginative reinterpretations of Athenian inheritance cases bring a new perspective to the debate, offering fresh and illuminating insights, but she is fundamentally mistaken in her characterization of the Athenian will as a 'tenuous document, without the clear legal force it has today' (Wohl, 2010, 259). The legal force of wills in general, as distinct from the validity of a particular will, is never challenged in the extant Athenian inheritance speeches; indeed, one of Isaeus's clients, while accusing his opponents of forging a will, acknowledges (in a clear allusion to the words of Solon's law) that 'no-one could have prevented [the testator] from giving his property to anyone he wished' (Isae. 9.11).

Particularly misleading is the statement that 'wills are ubiquitous in inheritance speeches, yet in only two cases are their contents actually read out to the judges (Wohl, 2010, 260).' First of all, wills are disputed in only four of Isaeus's 11 inheritance speeches, so they are hardly 'ubiquitous'.[14] Secondly, Wohl seems to forget that there were two parties to a dispute, only one of whom (the proponent of the will) would have been expected to have it read out at the trial. The two extant speeches

---

13 See, especially, Wyse (1904, 177): 'The judges took the greatest liberties with testaments, and did not hesitate to substitute their own sympathies and preferences in place of the intentions of the deceased.' Harrison (1968, 153) refers to a 'general prejudice against wills'. As discussed in the introduction to Isaeus 4 (p. 123) Wyse's approach is challenged by Thompson (1981, 24), For further discussion, see Griffith-Williams (2012, 149–51).

14 Disputed wills are the subject of Isaeus 1, 4, 6 and 9. Wills are mentioned in Isaeus 3, 5, 7 and 11, and in [Dem.] 43, but as part of the history of the dispute, not as the subject of the court hearing in which the speech was delivered. There is no reference at all to a will in Isaeus 2, 8 or 10.

in which a will was read (Isaeus 6 and Isocrates 19) are precisely those where the speaker is defending the will in question. In the other three speeches, Isaeus 1, 4, and 9, the speaker challenges a will which (it is safe to assume) was read out at the request of his opponent.

Arbitration, pre-trial negotiation, and private agreements

The speaker mentions several times that friends of his opponents have proposed that Cleonymus's estate should be shared between the two opposing groups of claimants. (See commentary on §§16, 28, 29, 35 and 51). Wyse (1904, 175–76) takes this to indicate that the trial was preceded by a failed attempt at arbitration, arguing that there must have been a panel of arbitrators comprising supporters of both sides, but that the speaker mentions only his opponents' friends because he does not want to admit that his own supporters have recommended compromise. It is certainly possible that the proposed compromise was supported by some of the speaker's friends – a fact that Isaues would have wanted to gloss over – but the language of formal arbitration is never used in this speech. (For more details on Athenian arbitration, see the commentary on 2.29–32.) It seems more likely that the proposal arose either from informal negotiations between friends and relatives of the rival claimants, or (as the wording of the speech suggests) a unilateral offer of settlement from the speaker's opponents.

There is, in fact, no conclusive evidence that arbitration was, or could be, used in Athenian inheritance disputes. The arbitrations mentioned in Isaeus 2 and 5 are not directly related to the inheritance claim, but to a sale of land (Isaeus 2) and an action to compel the discharge of a suretyship (Isaeus 5). The only evidence for arbitration in an inheritance claim comes from a deposition produced in [Dem.] 43, where Phylomache is said to have won her claim to the estate of Hagnias 'before the arbitrator'. The reference is obscure, and little reliance can be placed on this source, given the doubtful authenticity of the depositions interpolated in the Demosthenic corpus.

It is likely that many disputes in Athens were settled by private negotiation between the parties rather than by an adjudication of the court. A process of bargaining, perhaps involving a series of offers and counter-offers, is well suited to adversarial litigation, where the party who claims to have been wronged can decide how much or how little he is prepared to accept in compensation from the wrongdoer. It is less easy to see how this would work in the context of an inheritance dispute, given the prescriptive nature of the relevant law and the requirement for any claimant, apart from a legitimate son, or one adopted *inter vivos*, to obtain the authority of a court before he could legally enter on the estate. It may be, on the other hand, that the inflexibility of the law actually encouraged private settlements, for example in cases where the strict order of intestate succession might be seen to be unfair to one member or branch of a family. In such circumstances an informal agreement would not necessarily have been regarded as a violation of the law, provided it was acceptable to the parties involved, although it is questionable whether it would have been legally enforceable.

An offer such as the one apparently made in this case by the speaker's opponents would have been characterized by its proponents as a conciliatory gesture, but it could equally have been an act of aggression.[15] As Isaeus represents them, his clients' opponents were aggressive and unscrupulous, prepared to stop at nothing to gain an unfair advantage over the weaker party. The language of the speech is unusually adversarial for a *diadikasia*, and the opponents are even described as sykophants, a term normally reserved for an allegedly malicious prosecutor. It would be consistent with this depiction if the opponents had made the offer not as a conciliatory gesture but as an attempt to buy off a legitimate claim to the estate with the threat of all-out opposition if the offer was rejected.

That, no doubt, was how Isaeus wanted his audience to interpret the speech, but the reality may have been that it was the speaker and his brother who were the aggressors. Perhaps they knew that Cleonymus had not really wanted to revoke his will, but exploited the element of uncertainty about his intentions, hoping that the Athenians' suspicion of written documents (even if it did not amount to a prejudice against the principle of testamentary disposition) would enable them to win. In that case their opponents, also knowing that challenges to wills were often successful, might have felt pressured to make what seems like a generous offer because of their fear

---

15 Isoc. 18 illustrates how an offer to settle could be deployed as part of a dishonest litigation strategy: the speaker claims to have been maliciously sued for a sum he did not really owe, and then persuaded by his opponent's friends to settle for a smaller amount in order to avoid the uncertain outcome of litigation and the possible loss of reputation as well as money.

of losing the whole estate. Whatever the true position, Isaeus's rhetorical skill enabled him to exploit the offer to the advantage of his clients.

Witness testimony

The speaker produces witnesses to testify that Poseidippus refused to summon the archon and turned him away when he arrived (§16), but that does not explain why, if Poseidippus had refused to fetch the archon, he nevertheless arrived at Cleonymus's door. (And it would have been more convincing if the witnesses had actually spoken to Cleonymus during his last illness and could clarify his intentions.) A second piece of witness testimony confirms that Cephisander and other friends of the speaker's opponents had proposed that the estate should be shared among the rival claimants (§17). That may not have been a point of contention, and any event it was not essential for the speaker's case, although it does enable Isaeus to introduce a tendentious argument about the opponents' motivation. Finally, witnesses testify to the quarrel between Cleonymus and Pherenicus (§32) but that testimony does not cover Cleonymus's relations with his other beneficiaries, and neither does it rule out the possibility that Cleonymus had become reconciled with Pherenicus before his death. It is striking that there is no testimony about Cleonymus's quarrel with Deinias, or his protection of his nephews after Deinias's death. Despite his insistence that Cleonymus's quarrel was not with his nephews but with Deinias, and his expressions of gratitude to Cleonymus for 'rescuing' him and his brother after Deinias's death, there is no firm evidence that Cleonymus died on good terms with the nephews.

Conclusion

We do not know the outcome of this case, and we are certainly not in a position to judge whether Isaeus's client was telling the truth. Nor should we assess the legal basis of his claim from a modern perspective, and assume that an Athenian court would have rejected it because the will had not actually been revoked. We may, nevertheless, be left with the impression that his case was weak. His story, though not inherently implausible, is relatively thin, and there is no evidential support for some of the key 'facts'. Crucially, Isaeus's vagueness about family relations and chronology enables the speaker to avoid addressing some awkward questions about the timing of Cleonymus's decision to revoke his will and the claim of the speaker and his brother to be his next of kin. The Athenian judges (who, unlike us, had the benefit of hearing both sides of the case) may have been left with similar doubts, so the speaker's chances of success depended on Isaeus's skill in diverting their attention from the weaknesses in his story and casting doubt in their minds about the case put forward by his opponents.

ISAEUS 1: ON THE ESTATE OF CLEONYMUS

πολλὴ μὲν ἡ μεταβολή μοι γέγονεν, ὦ ἄνδρες, τελευτήσαντος Κλεωνύμου. ἐκεῖνος γὰρ ζῶν μὲν κατέλιπε τὴν οὐσίαν, ἀποθανὼν δὲ κινδυνεύειν περὶ αὐτῆς πεποίηκε. καὶ τότε μὲν οὕτως ὑπ' αὐτοῦ σωφρόνως ἐπαιδευόμεθα, ὥστ' οὐδ' ἀκροασόμενοι ἤλθομεν ἐπὶ δικαστήριον, νῦν δὲ ἀγωνιούμενοι περὶ πάντων ἥκομεν τῶν ὑπαρχόντων· οὐ γὰρ τῶν Κλεωνύμου μόνον ἀμφισβητοῦσιν ἀλλὰ καὶ τῶν πατρῴων, ὀφείλειν ἐπὶ τούτοις <ἡμᾶς> ἐκείνῳ φάσκοντες ἀργύριον. [2] καὶ οἱ μὲν οἰκεῖοι καὶ οἱ προσήκοντες [ἐπὶ τούτοις] οἱ τούτων ἀξιοῦσιν ἡμᾶς καὶ τῶν ὁμολογουμένων, ὧν Κλεώνυμος κατέλιπεν, αὐτοῖς τούτων ἰσομοιρῆσαι· οὗτοι δὲ εἰς τοῦτο ἥκουσιν ἀναισχυντίας, ὥστε καὶ τὰ πατρῷα προσαφελέσθαι ζητοῦσιν ἡμᾶς, οὐκ ἀγνοοῦντες, ὦ ἄνδρες, τὸ δίκαιον, ἀλλὰ πολλὴν ἡμῶν ἐρημίαν καταγνόντες. [3] σκέψασθε γὰρ οἷς ἑκάτεροι πιστεύοντες ὡς ὑμᾶς εἰσεληλύθαμεν· οὗτοι μὲν διαθήκαις ἰσχυριζόμενοι τοιαύταις, ἃς ἐκεῖνος διέθετο μὲν οὐχ ἡμῖν ἐγκαλῶν ἀλλ' ὀργισθεὶς τῶν οἰκείων τινὶ τῶν ἡμετέρων, ἔλυσε δὲ πρὸ τοῦ θανάτου, πέμψας Ποσείδιππον ἐπὶ τὴν ἀρχήν· [4] ἡμεῖς δὲ γένει μὲν ἐγγυτάτω προσήκοντες, χρώμενοι δὲ ἐκείνῳ πάντων οἰκειότατα, δεδωκότων δ' ἡμῖν καὶ τῶν νόμων κατὰ τὴν ἀγχιστείαν καὶ αὐτοῦ τοῦ Κλεωνύμου διὰ τὴν φιλίαν τὴν ὑπάρχουσαν αὐτῷ, ἔτι δὲ Πολυάρχου, τοῦ πατρὸς <τοῦ> Κλεωνύμου, πάππου δ' ἡμετέρου, προστάξαντος, εἴ τι πάθοι Κλεώνυμος ἄπαις, ἡμῖν δοῦναι τὰ αὐτοῦ. [5] τοσούτων τοίνυν ἡμῖν ὑπαρχόντων οὗτοι, καὶ συγγενεῖς ὄντες καὶ οὐδὲν δίκαιον εἰπεῖν ἔχοντες, οὐκ αἰσχύνονται καταστήσαντες ἡμᾶς εἰς ἀγῶνα περὶ τούτων, περὶ ὧν αἰσχρὸν ἦν ἀμφισβητῆσαι καὶ τοῖς μηδὲν προσήκουσιν. [6] οὐχ ὁμοίως δέ μοι δοκοῦμεν, ὦ ἄνδρες, διακεῖσθαι πρὸς ἀλλήλους. ἐγὼ μὲν γὰρ οὐχ ὅτι ἀδίκως κινδυνεύω, τοῦθ' ἡγοῦμαι μέγιστον εἶναι τῶν παρόντων κακῶν, ἀλλ' ὅτι ἀγωνίζομαι πρὸς οἰκείους, οὓς οὐδ' ἀμύνεσθαι καλῶς ἔχει· οὐ γὰρ ἂν ἐλάττω συμφορὰν ἡγησαίμην κακῶς ποιεῖν τούτους ἀμυνόμενος, οἰκείους ὄντας, ἢ κακῶς παθεῖν ἐξ ἀρχῆς ὑπὸ τούτων. [7] οὗτοι δ' οὐ τοιαύτην ἔχουσι τὴν γνώμην, ἀλλ' ἥκουσιν ἐφ' ἡμᾶς καὶ τοὺς φίλους παρακαλέσαντες καὶ ῥήτορας παρασκευασάμενοι καὶ οὐδὲν ἀπολείποντες τῆς αὐτῶν δυνάμεως, ὥσπερ, ὦ ἄνδρες, ἐχθροὺς

For me, gentlemen, the death of Cleonymus has brought about a great reversal of fortune. In his lifetime he left his property to us, but with his death he has put our claim to it at risk. In the old days we were brought up so respectably by him that we never set foot in a lawcourt even just as listeners, but now we have come here to fight for everything we have. For our opponents are contesting not only Cleonymus's estate but also our paternal inheritance, asserting that we owe money to his estate as well. (2) Even their own relatives and friends agree that we should have an equal share with them in the property undisputedly left by Cleonymus, but our opponents are so shameless that they are even trying to deprive us of our own patrimony – not, gentlemen, in ignorance of what is right, but because they have seen that we are completely isolated.

(3) Consider on what grounds each of the claimants has come before you. Our opponents, on the one hand, are relying on a will that Cleonymus made not because he had any quarrel with us but because he was angry with one of our relatives, and which he revoked before his death, sending Poseidippus to the archon's office. (4) We, on the other hand, make our claim both as his next of kin and as those who were on the most intimate terms with him. The laws have given us the right to inherit on the basis of our degree of kinship, and Cleonymus himself gave it to us through his affection. And so did Polyarchus, Cleonymus's father and our grandfather, when he told Cleonymus to leave his property to us if he should die childless. (5) Despite such weighty factors on our side, our opponents, although they are our kinsmen and have no lawful claim, are not ashamed to bring us to court about such matters as it would be shameful even for people who were completely unrelated to dispute. (6) And I think, gentlemen, that we don't have the same feelings towards one another, since I believe the worst of my present difficulties is not being unjustly put at risk, but being involved in a dispute with relatives, against whom it would be discreditable even to defend oneself. For I would consider it no less a disaster to inflict an injury on my relatives while defending myself against them than to have suffered an injury from them in the first place. (7) But they don't take the same view, gentlemen; they've summoned their friends and procured speakers and done everything in their power to attack us, as if they were going to punish enemies rather than harm

τιμωρησόμενοι, καὶ οὐκ ἀναγκαίους καὶ συγγενεῖς κακῶς ποιήσοντες. [8] τὴν μὲν οὖν τούτων ἀναισχυντίαν καὶ τὴν αἰσχροκέρδειαν ἔτι μᾶλλον γνώσεσθε, ἐπειδὰν πάντων ἀκούσητε· ὅθεν δ' οἶμαι τάχιστ' ἂν ὑμᾶς μαθεῖν περὶ ὧν ἀμφισβητοῦμεν, ἐντεῦθεν ἄρξομαι διδάσκειν. [9] Δεινίας γὰρ ὁ τοῦ πατρὸς ἀδελφὸς ἐπετρόπευσεν ἡμᾶς, θεῖος ὢν ὀρφανοὺς ὄντας. Κλεωνύμῳ δ' οὗτος, ὦ ἄνδρες, διάφορος ὢν ἔτυχεν. ὁπότερος μὲν οὖν αὐτῶν ἦν τῆς διαφορᾶς αἴτιος, ἴσως οὐκ ἐμὸν ἔργον ἐστὶ κατηγορεῖν· πλὴν τοσοῦτόν γε ἂν δικαίως αὐτοῖς ἀμφοτέροις μεμψαίμην, ὅτι καὶ φίλοι τέως ὄντες καὶ προφάσεως οὐδεμιᾶς γενομένης ἐκ λόγων τινῶν οὕτως εἰκῇ πρὸς ἀλλήλους ἔχθραν ἀνείλοντο. [10] τότε γοῦν ἐκ ταύτης τῆς ὀργῆς Κλεώνυμος ταύτας ποιεῖται τὰς διαθήκας, οὐχ ἡμῖν ἐγκαλῶν, ὡς ὕστερον <ἐσώθη> ἔλεγεν, ὁρῶν δὲ ἡμᾶς ἐπιτροπευομένους ὑπὸ Δεινίου, καὶ δεδιὼς μὴ τελευτήσειεν αὐτὸς ἔτι παῖδας ἡμᾶς καταλιπὼν καὶ τῆς οὐσίας ἡμετέρας οὔσης γένοιτο κύριος Δεινίας· ἡγεῖτο γὰρ δεινὸν εἶναι τὸν ἔχθιστον τῶν οἰκείων ἐπίτροπον καὶ κύριον τῶν αὐτοῦ καταλιπεῖν, καὶ ποιεῖν αὐτῷ τὰ νομιζόμενα τοῦτον, ἕως ἡμεῖς ἡβήσαιμεν, ᾧ ζῶν διάφορος ἦν· [11] ταῦτα διανοηθεὶς ἐκεῖνος, εἴτ' ὀρθῶς εἴτε μή, τὰς διαθήκας ταύτας διέθετο. καὶ εὐθὺς ἐρωτῶντος τοῦ Δεινίου παραχρῆμα εἴ τι ἡμῖν ἢ τῷ πατρὶ ἐγκαλεῖ τῷ ἡμετέρῳ, ἀπεκρίνατο πάντων τῶν πολιτῶν ἐναντίον ὅτι οὐδὲν πονηρὸν ἐγκαλεῖ, καὶ ἐμαρτύρησεν ὡς ὀργιζόμενος ἐκείνῳ καὶ οὐκ ὀρθῶς βουλευόμενος ταῦτα διέθετο. πῶς γὰρ ἂν εὖ φρονῶν, ὦ ἄνδρες, κακῶς ποιεῖν ἡμᾶς ἐβουλήθη, τοὺς μηδὲν αὐτὸν ἠδικηκότας; [12] ὕστερον δὲ τούτων, ὃ μέγιστον ἡμῖν τεκμήριον ὅτι οὐδὲ ταῦτα ἔπραξεν ἡμᾶς βλάπτειν βουλόμενος· τελευτήσαντος γὰρ Δεινίου καὶ τῶν πραγμάτων ἡμῖν πονηρῶς ἐχόντων οὐδὲ περιεῖδεν ἡμᾶς οὐδενὸς ἐνδεεῖς ὄντας, ἀλλ' αὐτοὺς μὲν εἰς τὴν οἰκίαν τὴν αὐτοῦ κομισάμενος ἐπαίδευε, τὴν δ' οὐσίαν ἀφελέσθαι τῶν χρήστων ἐπιβουλευσάντων ἔσωσεν ἡμῖν, ἐπεμελεῖτό τε ὁμοίως τῶν ἡμετέρων ὥσπερ τῶν αὐτοῦ πραγμάτων. [13] καίτοι χρὴ θεωρεῖν αὐτοῦ τὴν ἔννοιαν ἐκ τούτων τῶν ἔργων μᾶλλον ἢ ἐκ τῶν διαθηκῶν, καὶ τεκμηρίοις χρῆσθαι μὴ τοῖς μετ' ὀργῆς πραχθεῖσιν, ἐν οἷς ἅπαντες πεφύκαμεν ἁμαρτάνειν, ἀλλ' ἀφ' ὧν ὕστερον φανερὰν τὴν αὐτοῦ ἔννοιαν ἐποίησεν. ἔτι γὰρ μᾶλλον ἐν τοῖς τελευταίοις ἐδήλωσεν ὡς εἶχε πρὸς ἡμᾶς. [14] ἤδη γὰρ ἀσθενῶν ταύτην τὴν νόσον ἐξ ἧς ἐτελεύτησεν, ἐβουλήθη ταύτας τὰς

family members and kinsmen. (8) You will have an even better idea of their shamelessness and greed when you have heard the whole story, so I'll begin from the point where I think you will most quickly understand what our dispute is about.

(9) Our uncle Deinias, our father's brother, became our guardian when we were orphaned, but, gentlemen, he happened to be in dispute with Cleonymus. Which of them started the quarrel is perhaps not for me to judge, but I could rightly blame both of them equally since they had previously been friends and they took up their mutual enmity so rashly, on the basis of a few words and with no real justification. (10) At any rate, it was then, under the influence of this anger, that Cleonymus made this will – not to spite us, as he explained later, but because he saw that Deinias was our guardian and he was afraid that if he himself died while we were still minors and his property came to us, Deinias would get control of it. For he thought it would be terrible to leave his worst enemy as the guardian of his relatives and in control of his property, and for Deinias, with whom he had been at odds during his lifetime, to be left to perform the customary rites for him until we grew up. (11) Rightly or not, it was with that in mind that he made this will. And when Deinias immediately asked him whether he had anything against us or our father, he replied in the presence of all the citizens that he had no grievance against us, thus testifying that he had made his will while he was angry with Deinias and not thinking straight. For how could he have wanted to harm us, gentlemen, if he had been in his right mind, since we had done him no harm? (12) What he did later is the strongest indication in favour of our contention that he did not act out of any desire to injure us. When Deinias had died and things were going badly for us, he did not allow us to be in need of anything but took us into his own house and brought us up, rescued our property from creditors scheming to deprive us of it, and looked after our affairs exactly like his own. (13) You need to consider his intentions in the light of these actions rather than the will, and not rely on the evidence of what he did in anger (in which we all naturally make mistakes) but of his later actions, by which he made his intention clear. And he revealed even more clearly how he felt towards us in his last actions. (14) For while he was already suffering from the illness that caused his death, he wanted to revoke the will and told Poseidippus

διαθήκας ἀνελεῖν καὶ προσέταξε Ποσειδίππῳ τὴν ἀρχὴν εἰσαγαγεῖν. ὁ δὲ οὐ μόνον οὐκ εἰσήγαγεν, ἀλλὰ καὶ τὸν ἐλθόντα τῶν ἀρχόντων ἐπὶ τὴν θύραν ἀπέπεμψεν. ὀργισθεὶς δὲ τούτῳ Κλεώνυμος πάλιν ἐς τὴν ὑστεραίαν Διοκλεῖ καλέσαι τοὺς ἄρχοντας προσέταζε, καὶ οὐχ οὕτως ὡς ἀσθενῶν διακείμενος· ἀλλ᾽ ἔτι πολλῶν οὐσῶν ἐλπίδων, ἐξαπίνης τῆς νυκτὸς ταύτης ἀπέθανεν. [15] πρῶτον μὲν οὖν ὑμῖν παρέξομαι μάρτυρας ὡς οὐχ ἡμῖν ἐγκαλῶν ἀλλὰ Δεινίᾳ πολεμῶν ταύτας τὰς διαθήκας διέθετο, ἔπειτα ὡς ἐκείνου τελευτήσαντος ἐπεμελεῖτο τε τῶν ἡμετέρων ἁπάντων, καὶ αὐτοὺς ἐπαίδευεν εἰς τὴν οἰκίαν τὴν αὑτοῦ κομισάμενος, πρὸς δὲ τούτοις ὡς Ποσείδιππον ἔπεμψεν ἐπὶ τὸν ἀστυνόμον, οὗτος δ᾽ οὐ μόνον αὐτὸς οὐκ εἰσεκάλεσεν, ἀλλὰ καὶ ἐλθόντα ἐπὶ τὴν θύραν [ἀρχονίδην] ἀπέπεμψεν. [16] ὡς οὖν ἀληθῆ λέγω, κάλει μοι τοὺς μάρτυρας.

ΜΑΡΤΥΡΕΣ

ἔτι τοίνυν ὡς οἱ τούτων φίλοι καὶ Κηφίσανδρος ἠξίουν νείμασθαι τὴν οὐσίαν καὶ τὸ τρίτον μέρος ἡμᾶς ἔχειν ἁπάντων τῶν Κλεωνύμου, καὶ τούτων μοι κάλει μάρτυρας.

ΜΑΡΤΥΡΕΣ

[17] ἡγοῦμαι μὲν τοίνυν, ὦ ἄνδρες, πᾶσι τοῖς τῶν κλήρων ἀμφισβητοῦσιν, ὅταν ἀποφήνωσι σφᾶς αὐτοὺς ὥσπερ ἡμεῖς καὶ τῷ γένει προτέρους ὄντας καὶ τῇ φιλίᾳ τῇ πρὸς τὸν τετελευτηκότα, περίεργον εἶναι τοὺς ἄλλους λόγους λέγειν· ἐπειδὴ δὲ τούτων οὐδέτερον ἔχοντες οὗτοι τολμῶσι τῶν οὐ προσηκόντων ἀμφισβητεῖν καὶ ψευδεῖς παρασκευάζονται λόγους, βούλομαι βραχέα καὶ περὶ τούτων αὐτῶν εἰπεῖν. [18] ἰσχυρίζονται γὰρ ταῖς διαθήκαις, λέγοντες ὡς Κλεώνυμος μετεπέμπετο τὴν ἀρχὴν οὐ λῦσαι βουλόμενος αὐτὰς ἀλλ᾽ ἐπανορθῶσαι καὶ βεβαιῶσαι σφίσιν αὐτοῖς τὴν δωρεάν. ὑμεῖς δὲ σκοπεῖσθε τὰς διαθήκας τὰς μετ᾽ ὀργῆς γενομένας πότερα εἰκός ἐστι βουληθῆναι Κλεώνυμον ἀνελεῖν, ἐπειδὴ πρὸς ἡμᾶς οἰκείως ἔσχεν, ἢ σκοπεῖν ὅπως ἔτι βεβαιότερον ἡμᾶς ἀποστερήσει τῶν αὑτοῦ. [19] τοῖς μὲν γὰρ ἄλλοις κἀκείνων ὧν ἂν ὀργισθέντες τοὺς οἰκείους ἀδικήσωσιν ὕστερον μεταμέλει· οὗτοι δὲ ἐκεῖνον ἀποφαίνουσιν, ἐν ᾧ πρὸς ἡμᾶς οἰκειότατα διέκειτο, μᾶλλον βεβαιοῦν τὴν διαθήκην βουλόμενον, ἣν

to bring the archon. Yet Poseidippus not only didn't bring him, but when one of the archons arrived at the door he actually sent him away. Cleonymus was angry with him, and this time it was Diocles whom he told to summon the archons on the next day, even though he was in no fit state because of his illness. But although there were still good hopes of his recovery, he died suddenly during the night.

(15) I will produce witnesses to testify, first, that Cleonymus did not make this will because of a grievance against us but because of his enmity towards Deinias; next, that after Deinias's death he looked after all our affairs, took us into his own house, and brought us up; and, in addition, that he sent Poseidippus for the official, but that Poseidippus not only failed to summon him, but even sent him away when he arrived at the door. (16) Please call the witnesses to prove that I am telling the truth.

WITNESSES

Please also call witnesses to testify that our opponents' friends, including Cephisander, thought it appropriate for us to share the estate and have a third of all Cleonymus's property.

WITNESSES

(17) Well now, gentlemen, I think that in any dispute about an inheritance, whenever the claimants can demonstrate (as we can) that they were closer to the dead man in terms of both descent and affection, any other argument is superfluous. But our opponents, who have no claim on either of these grounds, have the temerity to enter into dispute about what does not belong to them and have concocted mendacious arguments, so I want to speak briefly about precisely those points. (18) They rely on the will, saying that Cleonymus didn't send for the official because he wanted to revoke it, but to amend it and confirm his bequest to them. Consider, though, whether it is more likely that Cleonymus wanted to revoke the will, having made it in anger but later become intimate with us, or that he wanted to confirm his intention to deprive us of his property. (19) Others who have done wrong to their relatives in anger change their minds later, but my opponents portray Cleonymus as wanting, while he was on the friendliest terms with us, rather to confirm the will that he made while

ὀργιζόμενος ἐποιήσατο. ὥστ᾽ εἰ καὶ ἡμεῖς ὁμολογήσαιμεν ταῦτα καὶ ὑμεῖς αὐτοὶ πιστεύσαιτε, ἐνθυμεῖσθε ὅτι παράνοιαν αὐτοῦ τὴν μεγίστην οὗτοι κατηγοροῦσι. [20] τίς γὰρ ἂν γένοιτο ταύτης μανία μείζων, ἢ τότε μὲν ὅτε Δεινίᾳ διάφορος ὢν ἔτυχεν, ἡμᾶς κακῶς ποιεῖν τε καὶ διατίθεσθαι τοιαύτας διαθήκας, ἐξ ὧν οὐκ ἐκεῖνον ἐτιμωρεῖτο ἀλλὰ τοὺς οἰκειοτάτους ἠδίκει· νυνὶ δὲ χρώμενος ἡμῖν καὶ περὶ πλείστου ποιούμενος ἁπάντων, μόνους ἐβουλήθη τοὺς ἀδελφιδοῦς, ὡς οὗτοί φασιν, ἀκλήρους ποιῆσαι τῶν ἑαυτοῦ. καὶ τίς ἂν εὖ φρονῶν, ὦ ἄνδρες, τοιαῦτα περὶ τῶν αὑτοῦ βουλεύσαιτο; [21] ὥστ᾽ ἐκ τούτων τῶν λόγων ῥᾳδίαν ὑμῖν τὴν διάγνωσιν πεποιήκασι περὶ αὐτῶν. εἰ μὲν γὰρ ἀνελεῖν τὰς διαθήκας βουλόμενος μετεπέμπετο τὴν ἀρχήν, ὥσπερ ἡμεῖς φαμεν, οὐδεὶς ἔνεστι τούτοις λόγος· εἰ δ᾽ οὕτω παραφρονῶν ἔτυχεν ὥσθ᾽ ἡμᾶς ἀεὶ περὶ ἐλαχίστου ποιεῖσθαι, τοὺς γένει πρωτεύοντας καὶ χρωμένους αὐτῷ πάντων οἰκειότατα, δικαίως ἂν δήπου τὰς τοιαύτας διαθήκας ἀκύρους ποιήσαιτε. [22] ἔτι τοίνυν ἐνθυμεῖσθε ὅτι φάσκοντες καλεῖν τὴν ἀρχὴν Κλεώνυμον, ἵνα βεβαιώσῃ τὴν αὑτῶν δωρεάν, προσταχθὲν αὐτοῖς οὐκ ἐτόλμησαν εἰσαγαγεῖν, ἀλλὰ καὶ τὸν ἐλθόντα τῶν ἀρχόντων ἐπὶ τὴν θύραν ἀπέπεμψαν. καὶ δυοῖν τοῖν ἐναντιωτάτοιν θάτερα μέλλοντες, ἢ τὴν οὐσίαν ἕξειν βεβαιοτέραν ἢ ἐκείνῳ μὴ ποιήσαντες ἀπεχθήσεσθαι, τὴν ἀπέχθειαν εἵλοντο μᾶλλον ταύτης τῆς δωρεᾶς. καίτοι πῶς ἂν ἕτερα τούτων γένοιτο ἀπιστότερα; [23] τοὺς μὲν τηλικαῦτα μέλλοντας ἐκ τοῦ πράγματος κερδαίνειν, ὥσπερ ζημιωθησομένους, φυλάξασθαι τὴν διακονίαν, Κλεώνυμον δ᾽ ὑπὲρ τῆς τούτων ὠφελείας τοσαύτην ποιήσασθαι σπουδὴν ὥστε Ποσειδίππῳ μέν, ὅτι κατημέλησεν, ὀργισθῆναι, Διοκλέους δὲ ταὐτὰ πάλιν ἐς τὴν ὑστεραίαν δεηθῆναι; [24] εἰ γὰρ δή, ὦ ἄνδρες, ὡς οὗτοί φασιν, ἐν ταῖς νῦν γεγραμμέναις διαθήκαις ἔδωκεν αὐτοῖς τὴν οὐσίαν, καὶ τοῦτ᾽ ἄξιον εἶναί μοι δοκεῖ θαυμάζειν, ὅ τί ποτε ἐπανορθώσας κυριωτέρας αὐτὰς ἡγεῖτ᾽ ἂν ποιῆσαι· τοῖς γὰρ ἄλλοις οὗτος ὅρος ἐστίν, ὦ ἄνδρες, τῶν δωρεῶν. [25] ἔτι δὲ καὶ εἴ τι προσγράψαι τούτοις ἐβούλετο, διὰ τί οὐκ ἐν ἑτέρῳ γράψας αὐτὰ γραμματείῳ κατέλιπεν, ἐπειδὴ τὰ γράμματα παρὰ τῶν ἀρχόντων οὐκ ἐδυνήθη λαβεῖν; ἀνελεῖν μὲν γάρ, ὦ ἄνδρες, οὐχ οἷός τ᾽ ἦν ἄλλο γραμματεῖον ἢ τὸ παρὰ τῇ ἀρχῇ κείμενον· γράψαι δ᾽ ἐξῆν εἰς ἕτερον εἴ τι ἐβούλετο, καὶ μηδὲ τοῦθ᾽ ἡμῖν ἀμφισβητήσιμον ἐᾶν. [26] εἰ τοίνυν καὶ τοῦτο συγχωρήσαιμεν, ὡς ἐκεῖνος ἐπανορθῶσαι τὰς διαθήκας ἐβούλετο, πᾶσι δήπου

he was angry. So, even if we were to accept that, and you yourselves were to believe it, you must conclude that they are accusing him of utter insanity. (20) For what greater madness could there be than this: that when he happened to be in dispute with Deinias, he wronged us and made this will, not punishing Deinias but injuring his closest relations, whereas now that he was on friendly terms with us and esteemed us more highly than anyone else, he wanted (as my opponents say) to disinherit us, his nephews, alone? Who in his right mind, gentlemen, would make such plans about the disposition of his property? (21) So through these arguments they have made it easy for you to decide the case. For if, as we say, Cleonymus sent for the official because he wanted to revoke the will, there is no sense in their arguments. If, on the other hand, he was so deranged that he always held us, his closest kinsmen and most intimate associates, in the lowest esteem, then I suppose you would be justified in invalidating the will.

(22) What's more, bear in mind that they say Cleonymus summoned the archon so that he could confirm his bequest, yet in spite of his orders they dared not admit the archon when he arrived, but sent him away from the door. Faced with two alternatives – either to have their inheritance confirmed or to offend Cleonymus by not doing what he asked – they chose his hostility rather than the bequest! What could be more incredible than this? (23) Those who were set to gain so much by carrying out his instructions avoided doing so as if they were going to lose by it, while Cleonymus was so eager for their advantage that he was angry with Poseidippus for not heeding his wishes and repeated the instruction to Diocles for the following day.

(24) Really, gentlemen, if, as my opponents say, he left them his property in the current version of the will, I can't help wondering how he thought he could make it more valid by amending it, since for everyone else, gentlemen, this is the ultimate form of bequest. (25) What's more, if he wanted to make some addition to it, why did he not write this in a separate document and leave it behind, since he could not get the original will back from the officials? For the only document he could revoke, gentlemen, was the one deposited in the archon's office, but he could have written whatever he wanted in another one, and not left the matter in dispute between us. (26) If we did concede that he wanted to amend the will, then I suppose it would be clear to all of you that he didn't

φανερὸν ὑμῖν ἐστιν ὅτι οὐκ ὀρθῶς αὐτὰς ἔχειν ἡγεῖτο. καίτοι σκοπεῖτε καὶ ἐντεῦθεν τὴν ἀναισχυντίαν αὐτῶν, οἵτινες ταύτας τὰς διαθήκας ἀξιοῦσιν εἶναι κυρίας, ἃς ὁμολογοῦσι αὐτὸν τὸν διαθέμενον [ταῦτα] ὀρθῶς ἔχειν ἡγεῖσθαι, καὶ πείθουσιν ὑμᾶς ἐναντία καὶ τοῖς νόμοις καὶ τῷ δικαίῳ καὶ τῇ τοῦ τετελευτηκότος γνώμῃ ψηφίσασθαι. [27] ἔτι τοίνυν τούτων ἁπάντων ἀναιδέστατος τῶν λόγων ἐστίν, ὅταν τολμῶσι λέγειν ὡς Κλεώνυμος οὐδὲν ἡμᾶς τῶν αὑτοῦ λαβεῖν ἐβούλετο. καίτοι, ὦ ἄνδρες, τίνας ἂν ἄλλους ταῦτα ἔχειν ἐβουλήθη μᾶλλον ἢ τούτους, οὓς καὶ ζῶν ἐκ τῶν αὑτοῦ πλεῖστα τῶν οἰκείων ὠφέλει; [28] πάντων δ' ἂν εἴη θαυμασιώτατον, εἰ Κηφίσανδρος μὲν ὁ τούτων οἰκεῖος δίκαιον ἡγεῖτο εἶναι μέρος ἕκαστον ἡμῶν ἔχειν τῆς οὐσίας, Κλεώνυμος δ' ὃς ἦν ἡμῖν οἰκειότατος καὶ ἡμᾶς εἰς τὴν οἰκίαν τὴν αὑτοῦ λαβὼν ἐθεράπευε καὶ ἐπεμελεῖτο τῶν ἡμετέρων ὥσπερ τῶν αὑτοῦ πραγμάτων, οὗτος μόνος ἐβούλετο ἡμᾶς ἀκλήρους εἶναι τῶν αὑτοῦ. [29] καὶ τίς ἂν ὑμῶν πιστεύσειεν εὐνουστέρους καὶ μετριωτέρους τοὺς ἀντιδίκους ἡμῖν εἶναι τῶν οἰκειοτάτων; κἀκεῖνον μέν, ᾧ καὶ ἀναγκαῖον εὖ ποιεῖν ἡμᾶς καὶ αἰσχρὸν ἡμῶν ἀμελῆσαι, μηδὲν τῶν αὑτοῦ ἡμῖν δοῦναι· τούτους δέ, οἷς οὔτ' ἀνάγκη ἐστὶν οὔτ' αἰσχύνην οὐδεμίαν φέρει, τῶν οὐ προσηκόντων, ὥς φασιν, ἡμῖν μεταδιδόναι; ἀλλὰ ταῦτα μέν, ὦ ἄνδρες, πολλὴν ἀπιστίαν ἔχει. [30] ἔπειτα, εἰ μὲν καὶ νῦν οὕτω πρὸς ἀμφοτέρους ἡμᾶς ἔχων ἐτελεύτησεν, ὥσπερ ὅτε τὰς διαθήκας ταύτας ἐποιήσατο, εἰκότως ἄν τις ὑμῶν πιστεύσειε τοῖς λόγοις τοῖς τουτωνί· νυνὶ δὲ πᾶν τοὐναντίον εὑρήσετε. τότε μὲν γὰρ ἔτυχε Δεινίᾳ, ὃς ἡμᾶς ἐπετρόπευε, διάφορος ὢν ἡμῖν τε οὔπω χρώμενος τούτοις τε ἅπασιν ἐπιτηδείως διακείμενος· νῦν δὲ τούτων μέν τισι διάφορος ἐγένετο, ἡμῖν δὲ πάντων ἐχρῆτο οἰκειότατα. [31] καὶ ἐξ ὧν μὲν αὐτῷ πρὸς τούτους ἐγένετο ἡ διαφορά, περίεργόν ἐστι λέγειν· σημεῖα δ' ὑμῖν ἐρῶ μεγάλα, περὶ ὧν καὶ μάρτυρας ἕξω παρασχέσθαι. πρῶτον μὲν γὰρ θύων τῷ Διονύσῳ, καὶ τοὺς οἰκείους ἅπαντας καλέσας καὶ τῶν ἄλλων πολιτῶν πολλούς, Φερένικον οὐδαμοῦ παρεστήσατο. ἔπειτα μικρὸν πρὶν τελευτῆσαι βαδίζων εἰς Πάνορμον μετὰ Σίμωνος, καὶ συντυχὼν αὐτῷ, προσειπεῖν οὐκ ἐτόλμησεν. [32] ἔτι δὲ πρὸς τούτοις πυνθανομένου τὴν διαφορὰν τοῦ Σίμωνος τήν τ' ἔχθραν διηγήσατο, καὶ προσηπείλησεν ὅτι δηλώσειέ ποτ' ἂν τούτῳ ὡς διάκειται πρὸς αὐτόν. καὶ ὡς ἀληθῆ λέγω, κάλει μάρτυρας.

think it was right as it was. But then consider their shamelessness in accepting this will as valid, when they agree that even he himself, the testator, didn't think it was correct, and are trying to persuade you to vote against the laws and justice and the dead man's intention. (27) And the most shameless of all their arguments is when they dare to say that Cleonymus didn't want us to get any of his property. And yet, gentlemen, who else would he have wanted to have it rather than those to whom, in his lifetime, he gave more help from his own means than to any of his other relatives? (28) And it would be most astonishing of all if Cephisander, their relative, thought it right for each of us to have a share of the property, while Cleonymus alone, who was on the most friendly terms with us and took us into his house and cared for us and looked after our affairs as if they were his own, wanted to disinherit us. (29) And how could any of you believe that our opponents are more well-disposed and reasonable towards us than our closest relatives? And that he, who was obliged to treat us well and for whom it would have been disgraceful to neglect us, didn't leave us any of his property, whereas they, who have no obligation to us and for whom neglect brings no disgrace, offered us a share of the property to which, as they say, we are not entitled? All of that, gentlemen, is completely unbelievable. (30) Again, if Cleonymus's feelings towards both us and our opponents had been the same at the time of his death as when he made the will, some of you might reasonably believe what they say; but, as it is, you will find exactly the opposite is the case. At that time, on the one hand, he happened to be in dispute with Deinias, our guardian, and not yet on friendly terms with us but well disposed towards all of our opponents. Now, on the other hand, he had fallen out with some of them, and was on more affectionate terms with us than with anyone else. (31) And I don't need to explain the substance of their disagreement, but I will mention some significant signs that it existed, to which I shall also be able to produce witnesses. First of all, when he was sacrificing to Dionysius, and had summoned all his relatives as well as many other citizens, he did not invite Pherenicus. Then, shortly before his death, while he was on the way to Panormus with Simon, they met Pherenicus, but Cleonymus couldn't bear to speak to him. (32) What's more, when Simon asked him about the disagreement, he told him all about their enmity and threatened that one day he would show Pherenicus how he felt about him. Please call witnesses to prove that I am telling the truth.

<ΜΑΡΤΥΡΕΣ>

[33] οἴεσθε οὖν, ὦ ἄνδρες, τὸν οὑτωσὶ πρὸς ἑκατέρους ἡμᾶς διακείμενον ἡμῖν μέν, οἷς οἰκειότατα ἐχρῆτο, οὕτω ποιεῖν ὅπως μηδὲ λόγον ὑπολείψει, τούτοις δέ, ὧν τισι καὶ διάφορος ἦν, σκοπεῖν ὅπως ἅπασαν βεβαιώσει τὴν οὐσίαν; καὶ τούτους μὲν νῦν περὶ πλείονος ποιεῖσθαι ταύτης ὑπούσης τῆς ἔχθρας, ἡμᾶς δὲ τοσαύτης οἰκειότητος καὶ φιλίας γενομένης πειρᾶσθαι μᾶλλον κακῶς ποιεῖν; [34] ἀλλ' ἔγωγε, εἰ κατηγορεῖν ἐβούλοντο τῶν διαθηκῶν ἢ τοῦ τετελευτηκότος, οὐκ οἶδ' ὅ τι ἂν ἄλλο πρὸς ὑμᾶς εἶπον, οἵ γε τὰς διαθήκας μὲν ἀποφαίνουσιν οὔτ' ὀρθῶς ἐχούσας οὔτ' ἀρεσκούσας τῷ διαθεμένῳ, τοῦ δὲ τοσαύτην μανίαν κατηγοροῦσιν, ὥστε φασὶν αὐτὸν περὶ πλείονος ποιεῖσθαι τοὺς αὐτῷ διαφερομένους ἢ τοὺς οἰκείως χρωμένους, καὶ οἷς μὲν ζῶν οὐδὲ διελέγετο ἅπασαν δοῦναι τὴν οὐσίαν, τοὺς δ' οἰκειότατα κεχρημένους οὐδὲ πολλοστοῦ μέρους ἀξιῶσαι. ὥστε τίς ἂν ὑμῶν ταύτας εἶναι κυρίας τὰς διαθήκας ψηφίσαιτο, [35] ἃς ὁ μὲν διαθέμενος ὡς οὐκ ὀρθῶς ἐχούσας ἀπεδοκίμασεν, οὗτοι δ' ἔργῳ λύουσιν ἐθέλοντες ἡμῖν ἰσομοιρῆσαι τῆς οὐσίας, πρὸς δὲ τούτοις ἡμεῖς ὑμῖν ἀποφαίνομεν ἐναντίας οὔσας καὶ τῷ νόμῳ καὶ τοῖς δικαίοις καὶ τῇ τοῦ τετελευτηκότος διανοίᾳ; [36] οἶμαι δ' ὑμᾶς τὸ περὶ ἡμῶν δίκαιον σαφέστατ' ἂν παρ' αὐτῶν τούτων πυνθάνεσθαι. εἰ γάρ τις αὐτοὺς ἔροιτο διὰ τί ἀξιοῦσι κληρονόμοι γενέσθαι τῶν Κλεωνύμου, τοῦτ' ἂν εἰπεῖν ἔχοιεν, ὅτι καὶ γένει ποθὲν προσήκουσι καὶ ἐκεῖνος αὐτοῖς χρόνον τινὰ ἐπιτηδείως διέκειτο. οὐκ ἂν ἄρα ὑπὲρ ἡμῶν μᾶλλον ἢ ὑπὲρ σφῶν αὐτῶν εἶεν εἰρηκότες; [37] εἴ τε γὰρ διὰ τὴν τοῦ γένους ἀγχιστείαν δεῖ γενέσθαι τινὰς κληρονόμους, ἡμεῖς ἐγγυτέρω γένει προσήκομεν· εἴ τε διὰ τὴν φιλίαν τὴν ὑπάρχουσαν, ἴσασιν αὐτὸν ἅπαντες ἡμῖν οἰκειότερον διακείμενον. ὥστ' οὐ χρὴ παρ' ἡμῶν, ἀλλὰ [καὶ] παρ' αὐτῶν τούτων πυνθάνεσθαι τὸ δίκαιον. [38] πάντων δ' ἂν εἴη δεινότατον, εἰ τοῖς μὲν ἄλλοις ψηφίζοισθε, ὅταν θάτερα τούτων ἀποφαίνωσι σφᾶς αὐτούς, ἢ γένει προτέρους ὄντας ἢ τῇ φιλίᾳ τῇ πρὸς τὸν τετελευτηκότα, ἡμᾶς δ' οἷς ἐστιν ἀμφότερα ταῦτα παρὰ πάντων ὁμολογούμενα, ἀξιώσετε μόνους ἀκλήρους ποιῆσαι τῶν ἐκείνου.

WITNESSES

(33) Do you think, gentlemen, that Cleonymus, disposed as he was towards us and our opponents, would have treated us, with whom he was on the most affectionate terms, in such a way as to leave us without a word to say for ourselves, while considering how to make the entire property more secure for our opponents, even while he was in dispute with some of them? And that, despite this enmity, he now thought more highly of them and was trying to injure us, despite the strength of the intimacy and affection between us? (34) For my part, I don't know what else they could have said to you if they had wanted to denounce the will and the dead man, since on the one hand they have shown that the will was not correct and did not satisfy the testator, while on the other hand they have accused him of such madness that they are saying he thought more highly of those who were in dispute with him than of those who were on the most affectionate terms with him, and that he bequeathed his whole property to people he didn't speak to while he was alive, considering his most intimate associates unworthy of the smallest part. (35) So how could any of you vote to confirm the validity of this will, when the testator himself rejected it as incorrect and our opponents are in practice willing to annul it and share the estate with us – in addition to which, we have shown you that the will is against the law and justice, and the dead man's intention?

(36) I think you can understand the justice of our case most clearly from our opponents themselves. For if one were to ask them on what grounds they thought they should become Cleonymus's heirs, they could say that they are somehow related to him by descent and that he was for a time well disposed towards them. But would they not have spoken in our favour rather than their own? (37) For if the right to inherit is based on the degree of kinship, we are more closely related to him, and if it's a matter of existing affection, everyone knows that he was on more affectionate terms with us. So you don't need to learn the justice of the case from us, but from our opponents themselves. (38) It would be very strange if in all other cases you were to vote, whenever you were faced with the choice, for those who show themselves to have been closest to the deceased in either kinship or affection, but in our case alone you denied us his estate, even though it's agreed by everyone that we qualify on both grounds.

[39] καὶ εἰ μὲν Πολύαρχος ὁ πατὴρ ὁ Κλεωνύμου, πάππος δ᾽ ἡμέτερος, ζῶν ἐτύγχανε καὶ τῶν ἐπιτηδείων ἐνδεὴς ὤν, ἢ Κλεώνυμος ἐτελεύτησε θυγατέρας ἀπορουμένας καταλιπών, ἡμεῖς ἂν διὰ τὴν ἀγχιστείαν καὶ τὸν πάππον γηροτροφεῖν ἠναγκαζόμεθα καὶ τὰς Κλεωνύμου θυγατέρας ἢ λαβεῖν αὐτοὶ γυναῖκας ἢ προῖκα ἐπιδιδόντες ἑτέροις ἐκδιδόναι, καὶ ταῦθ᾽ ἡμᾶς καὶ ἡ συγγένεια καὶ οἱ νόμοι καὶ ἡ παρ᾽ ὑμῶν αἰσχύνη ποιεῖν ἠνάγκαζεν ἄν, ἢ ταῖς μεγίσταις ζημίαις καὶ τοῖς ἐσχάτοις ὀνείδεσι περιπεσεῖν· [40] εἰ δ᾽ οὐσία κατελείφθη, δίκαιον ἡγήσεσθ᾽ εἶναι ταύτης ἑτέρους ἡμῶν μᾶλλον κληρονομεῖν; οὐκ ἄρα δίκαια οὐδ᾽ ὑμῖν αὐτοῖς συμφέροντα οὐδὲ τοῖς νόμοις ὁμολογούμενα ψηφιεῖσθε, εἰ τῶν μὲν συμφορῶν τοὺς ἐγγυτάτω γένει κοινωνεῖν ἀναγκάσετε, χρημάτων δὲ καταλειφθέντων πάντας ἀνθρώπους κυριωτέρους ἢ τούτους ποιήσετε. [41] χρὴ δέ, ὦ ἄνδρες, καὶ διὰ τὴν συγγένειαν καὶ διὰ τὴν τοῦ πράγματος ἀλήθειαν, ὅπερ ποιεῖτε, τοῖς κατὰ γένος ψηφίζεσθαι μᾶλλον ἢ τοῖς κατὰ διαθήκην ἀμφισβητοῦσι. τὴν μὲν γὰρ τοῦ γένους οἰκειότητα πάντες ἐπιστάμενοι τυγχάνετε, καὶ οὐχ οἷόν τε τοῦτ᾽ ἔστι πρὸς ὑμᾶς ψεύσασθαι· διαθήκας δ᾽ ἤδη πολλοὶ ψευδεῖς ἀπέφηναν, καὶ οἱ μὲν τὸ παράπαν οὐ γενομένας, ἐνίων δ᾽ οὐκ ὀρθῶς βεβουλευμένων. [42] καὶ νῦν ὑμεῖς τὴν μὲν συγγένειαν καὶ τὴν οἰκειότητα τὴν ἡμετέραν, οἷς ἡμεῖς ἀγωνιζόμεθα, ἅπαντες ἐπίστασθε· τὰς δὲ διαθήκας, αἷς οὗτοι πιστεύοντες ἡμᾶς συκοφαντοῦσιν, οὐδεὶς ὑμῶν οἶδε κυρίας γενομένας. ἔπειτα τὴν μὲν ἡμετέραν συγγένειαν εὑρήσετε καὶ παρ᾽ αὐτῶν τῶν ἀντιδίκων ὁμολογουμένην, τὰς δὲ διαθήκας ὑφ᾽ ἡμῶν ἀμφισβητουμένας· οὗτοι γὰρ τὸ ἀνελεῖν αὐτὰς ἐκείνου βουλομένου διεκώλυσαν. [43] ὥσθ᾽ ὑμῖν, ὦ ἄνδρες, πολὺ κάλλιόν ἐστι ψηφίσασθαι κατὰ τὸ γένος τὸ παρ᾽ ἀμφοτέρων ἡμῶν ὁμολογούμενον μᾶλλον ἢ κατὰ τὰς διαθήκας τὰς οὐ δικαίως γεγενημένας. πρὸς δὲ τούτοις ἐνθυμήθητε ὅτι αὐτὰς ἔλυσε μὲν Κλεώνυμος εὖ φρονῶν, διέθετο δὲ ὀργισθεὶς καὶ οὐκ ὀρθῶς βουλευόμενος· ὥστε πάντων ἂν εἴη δεινότατον, εἰ κυριωτέραν αὐτοῦ τὴν ὀργὴν ἢ τὴν διάνοιαν ποιήσετε. [44] οἶμαι δ᾽ ὑμᾶς καὶ λαμβάνειν παρὰ τούτων ἀξιοῦν καὶ μὴ τυγχάνοντας ἀγανακτεῖν, οἷς ἂν ὑπάρχῃ καὶ παρ᾽ ὑμῶν τῶν αὐτῶν τυχεῖν. εἰ τοίνυν συνέβη Κλεωνύμῳ μὲν ζῆν, ἐξερημωθῆναι δὲ τὸν ἡμέτερον οἶκον ἢ τὸν τούτων, σκέψασθε ποτέρων ἐκεῖνος ἐγίγνετο κληρονόμος· δίκαιον γάρ ἐστι τούτους ἔχειν τὰ ἐκείνου, παρ᾽ ὧν ὠφείλετο καὶ λαβεῖν αὐτῷ. [45] εἰ μὲν τοίνυν

(39) And if Polyarchus, Cleonymus's father and our grandfather, were still alive and happened to be lacking in the necessities of life, or if Cleonymus had died leaving daughters who were not provided for, then in view of our degree of kinship we would be obliged both to support our grandfather and either to marry the daughters ourselves or give them to other husbands with dowries. Kinship, the laws, and public shame would have forced us to do this, or submit to the heaviest penalties and extreme disgrace. (40) And now that property has been left, do you think it would be right for others to inherit it rather than us? You would not be voting justly, or in your own interests or in accordance with the law, if on the one hand you forced the next of kin to share misfortunes, but on the other hand, when money has been left, gave everyone else a stronger claim to inherit.

(41) So, gentlemen, it is right that you should vote (as you do) on the basis of kinship, and the truth of the matter, in favour of those whose claim is based on descent rather than a will. For you all understand what blood relationship is, and it's impossible to lie about it to you. Many people, on the other hand, have produced false wills, some of which are complete forgeries and others written by men who were not in their right mind. (42) And now you all understand our kinship, and intimacy, on which we base our claim, but none of you knows that the will with which our opponents are maliciously pursuing us is valid. Moreover, you will find that our kinship is acknowledged even by our opponents themselves, but the will is disputed by us because these men prevented him from revoking it when he wanted to. (43) So, gentlemen, it is much better for you to vote in accordance with descent, which is agreed by both sides, rather than the will, which was not rightly made. And in addition to this, bear in mind that Cleonymus was in his right mind when he revoked the will, but when he made it he was angry and not thinking straight. So it would be really extraordinary if you gave greater weight to his anger than to his rational intention.

(44) I think you yourselves expect to inherit from those who are entitled to inherit from you, and that you would be annoyed if that did not happen. Well then, if Cleonymus were still alive, and our family or our opponents' had been left without heirs, consider from which of them Cleonymus would inherit, since it is right that the people who take his property should be the ones from whom he was entitled to inherit.

Φερένικος ἢ τῶν ἀδελφῶν τις ἐτελεύτησεν, οἱ παῖδες οἱ τούτων, οὐκ ἐκεῖνος ἐγίγνετο κύριος τῶν καταλειφθέντων· ἡμῶν δὲ τοιαύτῃ τύχῃ χρησαμένων Κλεώνυμος ἁπάντων ἐγίγνετο κληρονόμος. οὔτε γὰρ παῖδες ἡμῖν ἦσαν οὔτ᾽ ἄλλοι συγγενεῖς, ἀλλ᾽ ἐκεῖνος καὶ γένει προσήκων ἐγγυτάτω καὶ τῇ χρείᾳ πάντων ἦν οἰκειότατος· [46] ὥστε διὰ ταῦτα καὶ οἱ νόμοι δεδώκασιν αὐτῷ, καὶ ἡμεῖς οὐδέν᾽ <ἂν> ἄλλον ἠξιώσαμεν ταύτης τῆς δωρεᾶς. οὐ γὰρ δήπου ζῶντες μὲν οὕτως ἂν ἐνεχειρίσαμεν αὐτῷ τὴν οὐσίαν, ὥστε περὶ τῶν ἡμετέρων κυριωτέραν εἶναι τὴν ἐκείνου διάνοιαν τῆς ἡμετέρας αὐτῶν, ἀποθνῄσκοντες δὲ ἄλλους κληρονόμους ἐβουλήθημεν <εἶναι> αὐτῶν μᾶλλον ἢ τὸν πάντων οἰκειότατον. [47] ὥσθ᾽ ἡμᾶς μὲν ἐν ἀμφοτέροις, ὦ Ἀθηναῖοι, καὶ ἐν τῷ δοῦναι καὶ ἐν τῷ λαβεῖν οἰκείους ὄντας εὑρήσετε, τούτους δὲ νῦν μὲν ἀναισχυντοῦντας καὶ τὴν οἰκειότητα καὶ τὴν ἀγχιστείαν λέγοντας, ὅτι λήψεσθαί τι προσδοκῶσιν· ἐν δὲ τῷ δοῦναι πολλοὺς ἂν καὶ συγγενεῖς καὶ φίλους ἐκείνου προείλοντο οἰκειοτέρους. [48] κεφάλαιον δὲ τῶν εἰρημένων, ᾧ πάντας ὑμᾶς προσέχειν δεῖ τὸν νοῦν· <ἐν> ὅσῳ γὰρ ἂν ταῦτα λέγοντες ἀποφαίνωσι καὶ πειρῶνται πείθειν ὑμᾶς ὡς ἐκεῖνος διέθετο ταύτας τὰς διαθήκας καὶ οὐδὲ πώποτε ὕστερον αὐτῷ μετεμέλησε, <ἀλλὰ> καὶ νῦν ἐβούλετο ἡμᾶς μὲν μηδὲν τῶν αὐτοῦ λαβεῖν, σφίσι δ᾽ αὐτοῖς βεβαιῶσαι τὴν δωρεάν, [49] καὶ ταῦτα πάντα λέγοντες καὶ διισχυριζόμενοι μηδέτερον ἀποφαίνωσι μήθ᾽, ὡς ἐγγυτέρω τῷ γένει προσήκουσι μήθ᾽ ὡς οἰκειότερον ἡμῶν πρὸς Κλεώνυμον διέκειντο, ὑμεῖς ἐνθυμεῖσθε ὅτι ἐκείνου κατηγοροῦσιν, ἀλλ᾽ οὐχ ὡς δίκαιόν ἐστι τὸ πρᾶγμα διδάσκουσιν ὑμᾶς. [50] ὥσθ᾽ ὑμεῖς ὅταν μὲν τοῖς τούτων λόγοις πιστεύητε, οὐ τούτους προσήκει ποιῆσαι τῶν ἐκείνου κληρονόμους, ἀλλὰ παράνοιαν Κλεωνύμου καταγιγνώσκειν, ὅταν δὲ τοῖς ἡμετέροις, ἐκεῖνόν τε νομίζειν ὀρθῶς βεβουλεῦσθαι λῦσαι τὰς διαθήκας βουλόμενον, ἡμᾶς τε μὴ συκοφαντεῖν ἀλλὰ δικαίως τούτων ἀμφισβητεῖν. [51] ἔπειτα, ὦ ἄνδρες, ἐνθυμεῖσθε ὅτι οὐχ οἷόν τε ὑμῖν ἐστι κατὰ τοὺς τούτων λόγους γνῶναι περὶ αὐτῶν. πάντων γὰρ ἂν εἴη δεινότατον, εἰ τῶν ἀντιδίκων γιγνωσκόντων ἡμᾶς δίκαιον εἶναι τὸ μέρος αὐτῶν λαβεῖν, ὑμεῖς ἅπαντ᾽ αὐτοὺς ἔχειν ψηφιεῖσθε, καὶ τούτους μὲν ἡγήσεσθε χρῆναι πλείω λαβεῖν ὧν αὐτοὶ σφᾶς αὐτοὺς ἠξίωσαν, ἡμᾶς δὲ μηδὲ τούτων ἀξιώσετε ὧν οἱ ἀντίδικοι συγχωροῦσιν ἡμῖν.

(45) If Pherenicus or one of his brothers had died, it would have been his sons, not Cleonymus, who took control of the property he left. But if, on the other hand, we had met with the same fate, Cleonymus would have inherited all our property. For we had no children or other kinsmen, but he was both our next of kin and on the most intimate terms with us. (46) Because of this not only have the laws given him the right to inherit our property, but we, for our part, would not have considered anyone else worthy to receive it. For I don't suppose that, having entrusted him with our property in our lifetime and given his judgment about our affairs priority over our own, we would have wanted anyone other than our closest relation to inherit it after our death. (47) So, Athenians, you will find that we are attached to Cleonymus in both respects, giving and receiving. Our opponents, on the other hand, are shamelessly talking about relationship and degrees of kinship because they expect to receive something, but in the matter of giving, they would have preferred many other kinsmen and friends as being closer to them.

(48) Here is a summary of what I have said, to which you should all pay attention. However hard my opponents try to persuade you by their arguments that Cleonymus made this will and never changed his mind about it, but still wanted us to have none of his property and to confirm his bequest to them, (49) and however firmly they insist on all this, they cannot prove either that they were more closely related to Cleonymus than we were, or that they were on more affectionate terms with him. You should remember that their accusations about him do not prove that justice is on their side. (50) So even if you believe what they say, it would be more appropriate to convict Cleonymus himself of insanity than to make them his heirs. If, on the other hand, you believe what we say, you should conclude that he was in his right mind when he wanted to revoke the will, and that we are not pursuing a malicious action but a legitimate claim to the inheritance. (51) Finally, gentlemen, remember that it's impossible for you to understand the matter on the basis of their arguments. It would be really extraordinary if, while our opponents understand that it's right for us to receive part of the inheritance, you voted for them to have all of it, thinking they should receive more than they considered themselves entitled to, while you did not think we deserved to receive even as much as our opponents conceded.

COMMENTARY

1–8. Introduction
The introduction includes a biased and selective summary of the speaker's case, combined with a fierce attack on the litigation tactics of the opponents. Using language that would be more appropriate to adversarial litigation than to a *diadikasia*, the speaker presents a pathetic picture of himself and his brother as the helpless victims of powerful and aggressive 'prosecutors'.

1 gentlemen: A direct address to the judges in the vocative case is a conventional feature of Athenian forensic oratory (equivalent to 'members of the jury' in modern court cases). In private cases, including inheritance claims, the most common forms of address were 'gentlemen' (*ō andres*) and 'judges' (*ō andres dikastai*), while the ethnic addresses 'Athenians' (*Athēnaioi*) and 'men of Athens' (*andres Athēnaioi*) predominate in public cases. In his 11 speeches concerned with inheritance disputes, Isaeus shows a marked preference for 'gentlemen', which occurs 17 times in this speech, in addition to one instance of *andres Athēnaioi* (§47). (The only form of address used in Isaeus 12, from a case of disputed citizenship, is 'judges'.)

Nearly all the extant forensic speeches of the Attic orators start by addressing the judges, to solicit their attention. Subsequent addresses may mark a transitional point in the speech, or the resumption of the speech after the reading of witness testimony or other documentary evidence. Elsewhere, an address may have a more meaningful function, drawing the judges' attention to a particularly significant point or engaging them in the speaker's argument. On addresses to the judges in Isaeus's speeches, cf. Griffith-Williams (2013, 41–42); and in the Attic orators generally, Martin (2006) and Dickey (1996, 177–81).

left his property: The statement that Cleonymus 'left his property' to the speaker and his brother is exaggerated. At most, if the speaker's story is true, Cleonymus intended to annul his will, which would have had the effect of leaving his nephews as intestate heirs, but he did not actually do so. At this stage, when the judges have not yet heard the full story, the effect is to present the speaker and his brother as the legitimate claimants to the estate, whose entitlement is wrongfully challenged by their opponents.

we were brought up: The information that the speaker and his brother were brought up by Cleonymus gives an early hint of the intimacy between them to which he later attaches so much importance, without at this stage disclosing any details of their relationship.

never set foot in a lawcourt: The 'plea of the inexperienced litigant' was a commonplace of Athenian forensic oratory, designed to engage the good will of the judges. For examples and discussion, see Harris (2013a, 70–71). In this case the speaker makes his point emphatically, claiming that he had never even attended a trial as a spectator, let alone participated as a litigant.

asserting that we owe money: The speaker passes quickly over the allegation, which he makes no attempt to rebut, that he and his brothers were debtors to the estate of Cleonymus. He makes no further direct reference to the debt, but cf. on 'rescued our property…', §12.

2 Even their own friends and relatives: At this early stage in the speech Isaeus introduces the claim that supporters of his clients' opponents have proposed a division of the estate by way of compromise. He makes effective rhetorical use of the offer, arguing that it would be wrong for the judges to deprive his clients of the estate if even their opponents are willing to share it. (Cf. §§16, 28, 29, 35 and 51.)

gentlemen: The address to the judges emphasizes the speaker's point and invites them to sympathize with his point of view.

3 are relying: The Greek verb translated here as 'rely' (*ischurizesthai*) is used by Athenian litigants who appeal to laws or contracts as 'sources of precise … information … and assert that they should be regarded as authoritative … and binding (*ischuros*)' (Christ, 1998, 219). But, as Christ goes on to point out, appeals to such documents are 'ultimately constrained by the public's discomfort with rigid appeal to written authority: litigants can characterize inflexible appeals to contracts, as to laws, as insisting on (*ischurizomai*) fine points and inconsistent with what is right (*ta dikaia*) in a particular case'.

because he was angry: Isaeus here plants the seed for a prominent theme of the speech: that Cleonymus's motive for disinheriting his nephews in his will was not hostility towards them but 'anger' with their guardian, Deinias. This enables the speaker not only to deny any personal animosity between Cleonymus and the nephews, but also to cast doubt on the validity of the will under Solon's law by implying that it did not represent Cleonymus's true wishes. (See on 'what greater madness', §20.) At this stage, when he is summarizing his case, the speaker does not mention Deinias by name; he introduces him at the beginning of the more detailed narrative (§9) and identifies him as the object of Cleonymus's anger at §11.

one of our relatives: The Greek *oikeios* (plur. *oikeioi*) is one of a range of terms used in this speech to denote relatives or family members. More inclusive than *sungenēs* (plur. *sungeneis*, used at §§5, 7, 45, and 47), it does not necessarily imply a blood relationship. To preserve the distinction I have translated *sungenēs* as 'kinsman' and *oikeios* as 'relative', although in practice the Greek usage overlaps. Cf. on 'we became his relatives', 2.5.)

revoked before his death: This gives the impression that Cleonymus actually succeeded in revoking his will, but the speaker does not repeat the claim in the narrative, saying only that Cleonymus intended to do so but was thwarted by Poseidippus's refusal to fetch the archon.

sending Poseidippus: Poseidippus's refusal to fetch the archon may suggest that he was one of the speaker's opponents, none of whom is identified by name apart from Pherenicus (**§31**).

4 next of kin: The speaker claims that he and his brother were Cleonymus's closest surviving relatives (next of kin), but he never specifies the relationship between his opponents and Cleonymus. His evasiveness about relationships in general raises the suspicion that he may be suppressing information that would be detrimental to his case. Cf. on 'Cleonymus's father and our grandfather', below, and 'his nephews', §20.

on the most intimate terms with him: The antithesis paves the way for the later, detailed argument that since Isaeus's clients were closer to Cleonymus *both* in kinship *and* in intimacy, he cannot have wanted to leave his property to their opponents.

the laws: The speaker repeatedly claims that the law is on his side, but the only law to which he explicitly refers is that on intestate succession (see following note), which would be irrelevant if Cleonymus left a valid will.

our degree of kinship: The Greek word *anchisteia*, here translated as 'degree of kinship' has a more precise legal significance than other kinship terminology such as *sungeneia* (on which see §39). The right to inherit a dead man's estate, if he had left no legitimate sons and not made a will, was determined by one's position in the *anchisteia*, as prescribed by a law of Solon (cited at [Dem.] 43.51 and discussed at Isae. 11.1–3; Leão and Rhodes, 2016, fr. 50b. The dead man's relatives on his father's side, up to the degree of 'children of cousins', took precedence over those related to him through his mother. (For the text of the law, see General Introduction, p. 4.)

through his affection: I have translated *philia* in this speech as 'affection' rather than 'friendship', because it reflects Cleonymus's subjective feelings towards his nephews rather than an objective state of relations between them.

Oration 1

Cf. Konstan (1996, 87–88): 'the young speaker of [Isae. 1] will have had no intention of representing himself as a friend or *philos* of the deceased'.

And so did Polyarchus, Cleonymus's father and our grandfather: The speaker presumably hoped to add authority to his claim by invoking the wishes of his grandfather, but he produces no corroboration for the view he attributes to Polyarchus and it would have had no legal force. Wohl (2010, 263) aptly describes this as 'a mysterious and seemingly gratuitous detail that is never mentioned again'.

We learn at this point that Cleonymus and the speaker were uncle and nephew, although the word 'nephew' (Gk. *adelphidous*) occurs only once in the speech (see on 'his nephews', §20). It has generally been assumed that Cleonymus was the speaker's maternal uncle, but there is no really conclusive evidence of this in the speech.

5 although they are our kinsmen: In this and the following sections the speaker emphasizes his kinship with his opponents, whom he accuses of dishonouring family ties, yet he does not specify the relationship between them. If he is right in his assertion that he and his brothers are the closest of kin to Cleonymus, then he and his opponents can be no closer than first cousins once removed, and they may be only second cousins or even more distantly related. Since Isaeus argues elsewhere (7.32) that the bonds of kinship are closer between brothers than first cousins, one may question how much the speaker's kinship with his opponents really mattered to him. He is clearly playing to a popular prejudice against litigation between kin (as discussed by Christ, 1998, 169), but the description of the speaker's opponents as 'kinsmen' (*sungeneis*) conflicts with his later statement that he and his brother had no relations apart from Cleonymus (see on 'For we had no children or other relatives', §45).

6 And I think, gentlemen: The address to the judges engages them with the speaker's argument, focusing their attention on a point that he considers important. Its repetition at §7 heightens the tone of indignation in the speaker's attack on his opponents for pursuing the litigation.

unjustly put at risk: In a *diadikasia*, where all parties were technically on an equal footing, Isaeus uses the language of adversarial litigation to depict his clients as innocent victims who have been forced to defend themselves against an unjust prosecution.

7 procured speakers: Isaeus's client complains that his opponents have enlisted the support of experienced political speakers (Gk. *rhētores*), presumably to assist them as supporting speakers. Such tactics (to the extent that they were acceptable at all) would have been more appropriate in adversarial litigation, especially public cases, than in a *diadikasia* between kinsmen. For the circumstances in which the use of a supporting speaker (Gk. *synēgoros*) was considered acceptable, see Rubinstein (2000, 126). The Greek verb *paraskeuazein*, here translated as 'procure' (lit. 'to prepare', 'to have ready') frequently has pejorative connotations in forensic oratory. Cf. 'concocted', §7, and for further primary references see Wyse (1904, 591).

to punish enemies: The speaker plays on the Athenians' ambivalent attitude towards litigation. Taking revenge on, or punishing, personal enemies was an acceptable motive for pursuing an adversarial case against them, provided the prosecution had a sound legal basis, but the prosecutor had to bear in mind that his action might be interpreted as disproportionately aggressive or undesirably contentious. (Cf. Christ, 1998, 161–63.) As the speaker has already pointed out at some length, such behaviour would not have been tolerated in a *diadikasia*, which was (formally, at least) non-adversarial and which normally involved the public exposure of quarrels between kin.

9–16. Cleonymus's will, his quarrel with Deinias, and relations with his nephews (narrative and testimony)

The main narrative, explaining the circumstances in which Cleonymus made his will and later tried to revoke it, is relatively short. Unlike speeches such as Isaeus 7 and 9, which describe family quarrels originating in an earlier generation, it covers only events within the speaker's own lifetime, starting with the death of his father while the speaker himself was still a child. The chronology is typically vague, and although the sequence of events is clear, there is no indication of the time lapse between them.

9 Our uncle Deinias, our father's brother: It is notable that the speaker does not name his father (cf. on 'Eponymus of Acharnae', 2.3), who is not mentioned again except in passing at §11.

guardian: If an Athenian died while his oldest son was a child, one or more guardians were appointed to manage the father's estate until the son came of age. The father could nominate a guardian for his children in his will, but if he did not do so it is likely that the duty of guardianship fell to the father's brother or closest male relative (cf. Harrison, 1968, 99–100).

when we were orphaned: The Greek word for 'orphan' (*orphanos*) refers to anyone whose father has died, whether or not the mother is still alive. We are not told how old the speaker and his brother were when their father died, so they may not have been small children, but *orphanos* is an emotive word which would have played to the sympathy of the judges.

gentlemen: The opening of the main narrative is conventionally marked by an address to the judges.

since they had previously been friends: As in the English phrase 'friends and relations', the Greek word for 'friends' (*philoi*) often refers to people who are on good terms with each other but not members of the same family. So these words might be taken to suggest that Deinias and Cleonymus were not brothers, but that is not conclusive: *philoi* could be used as an adjective meaning 'friendly'. (Cf. on 'on friendly terms', 6.3.) For a clearer indication that Deinias and Cleonymus were unrelated, cf. on 'not punishing Deinias, but injuring his closest relations', §20.

10 under the influence of this anger: On Cleonymus's hostility to Deinias, see on 'not because he blamed us', §3.

perform the customary rites for him until we grew up: On the 'customary rites' after an Athenian's death, see the introductory note to 4.18–26. It may be significant that the speaker does not mention who actually did conduct the burial and funeral rites for Cleonymus. The fact that he neither claims the credit for doing so himself, nor criticizes his opponents for not doing so, perhaps suggests that it was in fact the opponents who took on the responsibility.

The speaker's point, presumably, is that Cleonymus was afraid Deinias would neglect to perform the customary rites on his behalf if the duty fell to him as guardian of his nephews. It is plausible that a guardian's duties would have included the conduct of any commemorative rites for which his wards would become responsible as adults, but there is no other evidence for this.

11 when Deinias immediately asked him: Deinias, as his nephews' guardian, would have been protecting their interests by asking why Cleonymus had excluded them from his will. It is interesting that Deinias not only knew, at the time, that Cleonymus had made a will, but was also aware of its contents. There may have been a more aggressive confrontation than the speaker discloses.

anything against us or our father: Apart from the identification of Deinias as his father's brother (§9) this is the speaker's only reference to his father. That may be because he had no significant role in events, but it is possible that he was involved in a quarrel or disagreement with Cleonymus that is not mentioned in the speech. Isaeus's chronology is, as usual, conveniently vague, but even if the speaker did not remember his father well, and was too young at the time to understand what happened after his death, he could have been told about events by older family members.

in the presence of all the citizens: This implies that the confrontation between Deinias and Cleonymus took place in the Assembly, or at some other large public gathering. The wording may be intended to disguise the fact that the speaker has no witnesses to the confrontation.

thus testifying: The speaker treats Cleonymus himself as a 'witness' in the case, but even if Cleonymus said what the speaker claims he did, the inference drawn by the speaker may not be justifiable. On the idea that someone (normally an opponent) can 'testify' through his actions rather than a formal witness statement, see on 'my opponents themselves', 2.38.

while he was angry with Deinias and not thinking straight: Here, for the first time, the speaker infers from Cleonymus's anger towards Deinias that he was not in his right mind when he made the will. According to Arist. *Rhet.* 2.1.8, anger is one of the emotions that change people's judgments.

gentlemen: By addressing the judges directly, the speaker engages them in his argument, steering them towards the conclusion he wants them to reach.

12 strongest indication: The Greek word *tekmērion* (lit. 'sign', 'token' or 'proof'), also used at 4.1, 12. and 6.1, may refer to any fact or piece of evidence from which a speaker invites the judges to draw inferences in support of a proposition that he wants to prove. Arist. *Rhet.* 1.2 defines it as a 'necessary sign', in the sense that it forms the basis of a syllogism leading to a logically irrefutable conclusion. In practice, speechwriters often exaggerate the significance of a *tekmērion*, which may be no more than an indication that a particular conclusion is probable rather than necessary. (See Griffith-Williams (2013, 54) and cf. on 'evidence', §13 and 'some significant signs, §31.)

took us into his own house and brought us up: It appears that Cleonymus became his nephews' guardian after the death of Deinias. The speaker does not explicitly say so, but he may have omitted this information to give the impression that Cleonymus brought them up out of the kindness of his heart rather than as a legal duty.

rescued our property from creditors scheming to deprive us of it: It appears that Cleonymus rescued his nephews' property by paying off their creditors at his own expense – hence, presumably, the allegation at §2 that they were in debt to his estate. Since the nephews were minors at the time, it may be inferred that their father had left his financial affairs in disorder. This could well have been a source of contention between him and Cleonymus, especially if the speaker's father had in his lifetime borrowed money from Cleonymus which he had not repaid. Cleonymus's financial assistance to his nephews is mentioned again at §27.

13 A brief passage of argument forms a bridge between the opening part of the narrative, dealing with the circumstances in which Cleonymus made his will, and the next part, which focuses on the events immediately preceding Cleonymus's death. By marking the transition in this way Isaeus emphasizes the logical connection between the two parts of the narrative and deflects attention from the lapse of time between them.

You need to consider his intentions in the light of these actions rather than the will: The speaker does not deny the existence and authenticity of Cleonymus's will, but he argues that it did not represent Cleonymus's true intentions at the time of his death. The most effective way in which he could demonstrate this was by showing that the testator's actions were at variance with a wish to leave his estate to the beneficiaries named in his will. There is, however, more than one way of interpreting Cleonymus's actions: he may have given a home to his nephews, and taken responsibility for their debts, out of a sense of duty rather than any real affection for them.

evidence: For the meaning of *tekmēria*, here translated as 'evidence', see on 'strongest indication', §12. The speaker seeks to discredit Cleonymus's will by arguing that valid inferences can be drawn only from rational actions, not from those taken in the heat of anger. The argument presupposes that he is right in his contention that Cleonymus was motivated by anger against Deinias when he made his will; cf. on 'because he was angry', §3.

in which we all naturally make mistakes: The speaker solicits sympathy for Cleonymus by appealing to the personal experience of the judges. For the idea that anger distorts judgment, cf. on 'while he was angry with Deinias and not thinking straight', §11.

14 but when one of the archons arrived at the door he actually sent him away: The speaker does not explain why, if Poseidippus had refused to fetch one of the city's officials, one of them nevertheless arrived at Cleonymus's door and had to be turned away (an assertion he repeats at §15). No doubt the opponents had a different version of the story, perhaps claiming that the speaker himself had taken the initiative in summoning an official without Cleonymus's knowledge.

angry with him: Or possibly 'angry about this', since the Greek demonstrative pronoun could be either masculine or neuter. At this point, in any event, Cleonymus's anger is not directed against Deinias, but against Poseidippus because of his refusal to summon the official.

this time it was Diocles whom he told to summon the archons on the next day: This part of the speaker's story is not supported by witness testimony. It is possible that Diocles was another of the speaker's opponents, but perhaps more likely that after Poseidippus's refusal to cooperate, Cleonymus would have turned to a neutral acquaintance, such as a neighbour, to carry out his wishes.

15 witnesses: Isaeus groups together the witness statements on a number of key points in the speaker's story, perhaps with the intention of disguising their weakness. There are some significant omissions from the list of attested 'facts': there is no testimony on Polyarchus's wishes about the descent of the family's estate (§4), or the public confrontation between Cleonymus and Deinias (§11).

that Cleonymus did not make this will because of a grievance against us but because of his enmity towards Deinias: The speaker repeats, this time apparently with the support of witness testimony, his claim that Cleonymus's motive for making his will was hostility to Deinias, not ill feeling towards his nephews. There is no testimony on Cleonymus's later relations with the nephews.

next, that after Deinias's death he ... brought us up: The witnesses' testimony on Cleonymus's care of his nephews and management of their financial affairs was presumably limited to the basic facts, not necessarily supporting the conclusions drawn from them by the speaker at §§12 and 27.

and, in addition: The speaker links the testimony on events in his childhood with those immediately preceding Cleonymus's death, glossing over an interval of probably at least a few years and possibly as long as 20 years or more.

that he sent Poseidippus for the official ... even sent him away: Again, the testimony about events on the day before Cleonymus's death is apparently limited to the fact that Poseidippus refused to summon or admit the official. This may not in itself have been contentious, but the speaker's opponents would undoubtedly contest his interpretation of Cleonymus's motive for sending for an official. (Cf. on 'saying that Cleonymus...', §18.) Moreover, the testimony does not appear to cover Cleonymus's request to Diocles to summon an official on the following day (§14).

16 their friends, even including Cephisander: Cephisander, who is mentioned again at §28 as a relative of the speaker's opponents, is the only one of those who proposed the compromise to be identified by name. Isaeus presumably had a reason for this: perhaps Cephisander was a prominent member of the family, or a key witness for the speaker's opponents, or possibly a well-known public figure. It is clear from the wording that he was not himself one of the rival claimants.

thought it appropriate for us to share the estate: The language here is

Oration 1 51

too vague to justify any conclusions about the precise role of Cephisander and his associates in the dispute. Isaeus does not use the language of formal arbitration in this speech (cf. on 'we agreed to submit the dispute for arbitration', 2.29) and it is more likely that this was simply an informal attempt by members of the family to find a compromise solution to the dispute.

a third of all Cleonymus's property: A possible explanation of this offer is that there were two nephews of Cleonymus (the speaker and his brother) and four beneficiaries of the will, each of whom would receive a sixth of the estate.

Please call the witnesses: Until some time in the early fourth century, witnesses at Athenian trials gave their evidence orally, but following a change in the law their testimony had to be submitted to the court in the form of written statements, which were read out at the trial by the clerk. The formula 'please call the witnesses', which introduces the three items of witness testimony produced in this speech (cf. §32) continued in use after the transition from oral to written testimony, indicating that the witnesses were present in court and required to come forward to confirm their testimony. On the transition from oral to written testimony, and its implications for the dating of this speech, cf. Griffith-Williams (2013, 53–54).

17–29. Whose version of events is the more probable? (Argumentation)
After a narrative in which little more than an outline of the facts has been given, Isaeus relies chiefly on probability arguments to persuade the judges that his clients have a better claim to the estate than their opponents. In the first part of the argument the speaker focuses on the specific circumstances of the case, explaining why the version of events he has just given is more likely to be true than that of his opponents. His argumentation presupposes not only that he and his brother were Cleonymus's next of kin, but also that Cleonymus, at the time of his death, was more favourably disposed towards the speaker and his brother than towards their opponents. Neither of these points has been conclusively proved by the preceding narrative and testimony.

17 **Well now, gentlemen:** Here, and again at §33, The address to the judges marks the resumption of the speech after the reading of witness testimony.

as we can: All the speaker's argumentation rests on the premise that he and his brother were closer than their opponents to Cleonymus both in kinship and in affection. If the premise is accepted, then the conclusion

– that it is incredible that Cleonymus intended to disinherit his nephews – is entirely logical. But the factual basis of the argument has not been convincingly proved, and was no doubt strongly challenged by the opposing party.

in terms of both descent and affection: On 'affection' as a translation of *philia*, see on 'through his affection', §4. Despite the emphasis on his kinship with Cleonymus, the speaker is not arguing that 'kinship is the most important factor in inheritance cases' (Edwards, 2007, 16), but neither is *philia* 'elevated in this speech to a position equal to kinship as a basis for deciding on the disposition of Cleonymus' inheritance' (Konstan, 1996, 87). Rather, the speaker's point is that when a man's closest relations are also his closest friends, there is no reason for him to make a will in favour of anyone else. (Cf. on 'either in kinship or in affection', §38.)

any other argument is superfluous: Although his underlying point is sound, the speaker perhaps dismisses rather too lightly the need to prove that a will represented the testator's true wishes.

what does not belong to them: The accusation that a speaker's opponents are claiming 'what does not belong to them' or 'stealing other people's property', is a commonplace of Athenian speeches from inheritance disputes. Cf., e.g., Isae. 4.11, 29; 8.1, 4; 10.2, 22; Lys. 32.25; [Dem.] 44.28, 35.

concocted mendacious arguments: In this section the speaker backs up the general allegations he made against his opponents in the introductory sections by examining their argument and specifying the respects in which he claims they are lying. It is possible, however, that he is misrepresenting their case or suppressing or distorting relevant facts. On the Greek verb *paraskeuazein* (here translated as 'concocted') see on 'procured', §7.

18 rely: See on 'are relying', §3.

Saying that Cleonymus ... confirm his bequest to them: It now appears from the speaker's account that Cleonymus's wish to retrieve his will from the archon's office was uncontested, and that the parties differ only in their interpretation of his intentions. The speaker presents Cleonymus's options as a straight choice between confirming the existing terms of the will and revoking it completely, leaving Cleonymus's nephews as his intestate heirs. On that basis he has no difficulty in representing his opponents' case as absurd, but there may have been other possibilities which he ignores. Cleonymus may, for example, have wanted to exclude only one of several beneficiaries from his will (as his quarrel with Pherenicus, described at §§30–32, might suggest) or to redistribute his property among them.

Consider, though ... deprive us of his property: Rather than always presenting the argument from the speaker's point of view Isaeus sometimes invites the judges to consider the issues for themselves and draw their own conclusions. (Cf. on 'consider from which of them Cleonymus would inherit', §44.) But the alternatives presented to the judges for consideration are carefully slanted to lead them to the conclusion the speaker wants, presupposing that Cleonymus, before his final illness, had become friendly towards his nephews and hostile to the beneficiaries of his will.

having made it in anger: Cf. on 'because he was angry', **§3**.

his intention to deprive us of his property: The implication, that Cleonymus's intention in making his will was to deprive his nephews of his property, is highly tendentious. In other speeches from inheritance cases, the verb *aposterein* ('to deprive') is most often used as an accusation against the speaker's opponent. (See on 'rob Hagnon and Hagnotheus', 4.21.)

19 Others who have done wrong to their relatives in anger: The speaker now generalizes his argument about actions motivated by anger rather than reason. By claiming that repentance of such actions against one's relatives is a universal human characteristic, he seeks to convince the judges that Cleonymus must have repented of the 'wrong' he did to his nephews in making his will.

accusing him of utter insanity: The speaker, by subtly misrepresenting his opponents' argument, tries to put the idea into the minds of the judges that Cleonymus cannot have been in his right mind when he made the will. This implies (although the argument is not explicitly spelt out) that Cleonymus's 'anger' when he wrote his will amounted to a form of mental derangement that would have made it invalid under Solon's law. (The Greek word *paranoia*, 'insanity', alludes to the wording of the law, discussed in the General Introduction, p.3.)

20 what greater madness: Cf. 'accused him of such madness', §34. The judges would have recognized the Greek word *mania* ('madness') as another allusion to the Solonian law according to which a will was invalid if the testator was insane (*maniōn*, or *paranoōn*). Whether they would have accepted Cleonymus's (alleged) behaviour as an example of *mania* or *paranoia* is a matter of interpretation; cf. Harris (2013c, 195): 'Note how closely the [speaker] keeps to the wording of the law while at the same time expanding the meaning of madness (*mania*) to cover any senseless act.'

not punishing Deinias, but injuring his closest relations: This appears to confirm that Cleonymus's nephews were his sister's sons: if Deinias had been Cleonymus's brother, then he rather than the nephews would have been the next of kin.

his nephews: The speaker makes repeated claims to be Cleonymus's next of kin, but this is the only occurrence of the word 'nephews' in the speech and only the second time he has specified their relationship (cf. on 'Cleonymus's father and our grandfather', §4). This contrasts with the approach taken by Thrasyllus, the speaker of Isaeus 7, who mentions four times that he is Apollodorus's nephew as well as his adopted son (7.4, 35, 43, 45).

Who in his right mind, gentlemen...?: The speaker again implies that Cleonymus's will was invalid under Solon's law (cf. on 'accusing him of utter insanity', §19). Addresses to the judges also become more frequent in this passage of argumentation; the six addresses in §§20–29 have no resumptive or transitional function but are used to draw the judges into the speaker's argument and implicitly invite them to agree with him. (Cf. 'really, gentlemen' and 'everyone else, gentlemen', §24; 'For the only document he could revoke, gentlemen', §25; 'And yet, gentlemen,' §27; and 'All of that, gentlemen', §29.) On Isaeus's use of irony, especially in rhetorical questions, to ridicule his opponents' actions or arguments, see on 'they are now treating us so well', 2.33.

21 his closest kinsmen and most intimate associates: Again, the speaker's argument presupposes both that he and his brother were Cleonymus's next of kin and that, by the time of his death, Cleonymus was on terms of greater intimacy with them than with anyone else.

23 he was angry: Here, again, the object of Cleonymus's anger is Poseidippus rather than Deinias; cf. on 'angry with him', **§14.**

25 For the only document he could revoke, gentlemen: It appears, both from the speaker's language and argumentation in this passage and from Isaeus's account of Euctemon's revocation of his will (6.31–32) that the only way of revoking a will, as distinct from amending it, was by physically destroying it.

the one deposited in the archon's office: There was apparently no legal requirement for a will to be deposited in official custody, and there are no other extant cases in which this was done. There is no indication of Cleonymus's reasons for choosing this course of action, but he may have been exceptionally concerned for the safety of the document because he knew that there was dissension within the family. Perhaps a more common practice was to leave a will for safekeeping with a trusted kinsman, as Euctemon did in Isaeus 6 and as the speaker's opponents claim that Astyphilus did in Isaeus 9.

26 against the laws and justice and the dead man's intention: Cleonymyus expressed his intention through his will, but if the will is invalid then his intention is legally irrelevant: the estate will go to his next of kin as determined by the law.

Oration 1

27 those to whom, in his lifetime, he gave more help from his own means than to any of his other relatives: On Cleonymus's financial assistance to his nephews, cf. on 'rescued our property', §12. The speaker's reasoning here is questionable: if Cleonymus did give more money to the nephews than to any other family members, that may have been because they were in the greatest need, not because he held them in the greatest affection. It is possible, moreover, that he deliberately excluded them from his inheritance, thinking that they had already received enough from him during his lifetime.

30–32. Cleonymus's quarrel with Pherenicus (argumentation, narrative, and testimony)

In these sections the speaker examines Cleonymus's relationship with his various kinsmen, attempting to prove that he had quarrelled with his testamentary heirs and was therefore likely to have wanted to revoke his will. The story of Cleonymus's falling out with Pherenicus has been postponed from its chronological place in the narrative, presumably in order to give it greater emphasis and link it more firmly with the argumentation about kinship and friendship. As Usher (1999, 132) observes, this is 'a rather late point at which to introduce such an important piece of evidence'.

30 At that time, on the one hand, he happened to be in dispute with Deinias: In the first part of an extended antithesis, the speaker describes Cleonymus's relationships at the time when he made his will. Again it is Deinias, the speaker's guardian, and not the speaker himself, who is represented as having been Cleonymus's enemy.

not yet on friendly terms with us: Cleonymus was 'not yet' on friendly terms with the speaker and his brothers when he made his will. It is plausible that his attitude to them changed after he had taken them into his household, but the speaker's account is vague and he never explains why Cleonymus did not revoke his will at an earlier date.

Now, on the other hand...: In the second part of the antithesis, the speaker claims that by the time of his death Cleonymus had fallen out with 'some of' the beneficiaries of his will, and become closer to his nephews than anyone else. He provides no evidence, however, that Cleonymus had quarrelled with any of his beneficiaries apart from Pherenicus.

31 I don't need to explain: By leaving the cause of the quarrel unexplained, Isaeus is perhaps trying to give the impression that it was more serious than it really was.

some significant signs: According to Arist. *Rhet.* 1.2 16–18, a 'sign' (Gk. *sēmeion*, plural *sēmeia*) was a form of proof that fell short of complete certainty, whereas a *tekmērion* was logically irrefutable. Isaeus, in this speech, seems to use the two words interchangeably; cf. on 'strongest indication', §12, and 'evidence', §13.

to which I shall also be able to produce witnesses: The speaker seeks to add credibility to his story by signalling that he is about to adduce witness testimony in support of his account.

he did not invite Pherenicus: It is clear from this passage that Pherenicus was one of the speaker's opponents; in fact, he is the only one who can be identified with certainty from the speech. (Cf. on 'having sent Poseidippus', §3.)

As Parker (2005, 43) points out, the sharing of private sacrifices was 'an important index of intimacy' in classical Athens, with particular significance in inheritance disputes. Cf. Isae. 8.16, with Griffith-Williams (2013) *ad loc.*

shortly before his death: This imprecise chronological allusion is perhaps intended to give the impression that Cleonymus did not have time to become reconciled with Pherenicus before he died.

Panormus: Isaeus does not explain why Cleonymus and Simon were travelling to Panormus (a harbour town on the south-east coast of Attica) but his inclusion of this specific detail adds credibiity to his account.

with Simon: This is the only reference in the speech to Simon, whose identity is unclear. The author of the *hypothesis* ('argument') to the speech, written in late antiquity, includes him with Pherenicus and Poseidippus among the beneficiaries of the will, but this is probably an error since he appears to have been a friend rather than a relative of Cleonymus (as noted by Edwards, 2007, 211, n.2).

32 told him all about their enmity: Again, Isaeus passes over an opportunity to elaborate on the origin of Cleonymus's quarrel with Pherenicus, although he mentions that Cleonymus explained it to Simon.

Presumably Cleonymus intended to disinherit Pherenicus, but he might not have wanted to go so far as to revoke the entire will and leave his property to his nephews as intestate heirs.

Please call witnesses: See on 'Please call the witnesses', §16.

33–38. Kinship and friendship (argumentation)

The speaker builds on his discussion of family relationships to press home the point that Cleonymus would not have been likely to leave his property to those with whom he was on bad terms, ignoring those who were closest to him. The argument is still based on premises that have not been conclusively proved, and attributes arguments to the speaker's opponents which they would have been most unlikely to accept.

34 accused him of such madness: See on 'what greater madness', §20.

35 in practice willing to annul it and share the estate with us: Isaeus takes his argument from the proposed compromise a step further, suggesting that the opponents themselves are effectively prepared to annul Cleonymus's will by taking only a share of his estate.

rejected it as incorrect: The speaker's claim that Cleonymus himself 'rejected' the will as incorrect is an exaggeration; the Greek verb *apodokimazein*, with its 'decisive legal connotation' (Usher, 1999, 132) gives a spurious authority to his point.

against the law and justice, and the dead man's intention: The speaker repeats a phrase he used at §26, except that here he refers to the 'law' in the singular, implying a specific law which the will has contravened. But despite his repeated allusions to Solon's law on wills in §§19–20, he never refers to it explicitly, relying on the law on intestate succession to support his case. (See on 'our degree of kinship' §4.)

36 from our opponents themselves: The speaker's attribution of arguments to his opponents is highly tendentious.

somehow related to him by descent: The speaker continues to be evasive about his opponents' relationship to Cleonymus (cf. on 'next of kin', §4) while trying to play down their claim to the estate.

37 based on the degree of kinship: See on 'our degree of kinship', §4.

more closely related to him The speaker has repeatedly claimed that he and his brother are Cleonymus's next of kin, without providing any conclusive information.

everyone knows: Although the speaker has not proved that Cleonymus was on terms of greater friendship with him and his brother, he tries to convince the judges by presenting this as a matter of common knowledge. The topos, which was frequently used by Athenian speechwriters as a substitute for witness testimony or other hard evidence, plays on the judges' unwillingness to admit ignorance of something that was supposedly common knowledge. Cf. on 'everyone knows', 4.27, 'most of you know', 6.1, and see Arist. *Rhet.* 1408a32–36: 'But the hearers are also impressed in a certain way by a device used to excess by speechwriters: 'Who does not know?' 'Everybody knows'; for the hearer agrees, because he is ashamed to appear not to share what is a matter of common knowledge.'

but from our opponents themselves: Cf. on 'from our opponents themselves', §36.

38 in all other cases: There was no formal rule of precedent in Athenian law, but according to Lanni (2006, 118), litigants refer to decisions in previous cases in one fifth of the extant forensic speeches. The present instance (which is not included among Lanni's examples) resembles a modern appeal to precedent to the extent that the speaker is ostensibly appealing for consistency in decision making. In reality, he is making a special plea based on the circumstances of his own case, harking back to his claim that he and his brother were closer to Cleonymus in kinship *and* affection. (Cf. on 'in terms of both kinship and friendship', §17.)

whenever you were faced with the choice ... either kinship or affection: In previous inheritance cases involving a disputed will (according to the speaker's interpretation) the judges have voted either for the deceased's next of kin or for the beneficiary of the will, who was chosen by the testator because he was closer to him in affection. In the present case, however, they are not faced with a choice between kinship and affection, because he and his brother were closer to Cleonymus in both respects.

agreed by everyone: The speaker concludes this part of his argument with the unsubstantiated assertion that his superior claim on grounds of both kinship and affection is recognized by everyone (including, by implication, his opponents).

39–40. The obligations of kinship (argumentation)

Moving away from the specific circumstances of the case, the speaker now uses arguments based on the laws about 'heiress daughters' (*eplikēroi*) and on the care of the elderly to persuade the judges that he and his brother have a better claim to the estate than their opponents. His point (which would have had no legal force in an inheritance dispute but might have made an emotional impact on the judges) is that since these laws impose obligations on the next of kin, it would be unfair to deprive them of their right to inherit.

39 Polyarchus, Cleonymus's father and our grandfather: Cf. on 'and so did Polyarchus...', §4.

leaving daughters who were not provided for: Although it is not directly relevant to the circumstances of the case, the hypothetical scenario of daughters left 'unprovided for' would have appealed to the sentimental Athenian view of the 'heiress daughter' (Gk. *epiklēros*) as a figure deserving pity and in need of protection. (For the legal position of the daughter, see on '*epiklēros*', 6.46.)

Oration 1

our degree of kinship: Cf. on 'our degree of kinship', §4. Relationship within the *anchisteia* determined not only the order of intestate succession but other rights and obligations towards family members, including the duty of care in old age. (For discussion, see Leão and Rhodes (2016, 95–96.)

This is the third of four times that the speaker appeals to his superior position in the *anchisteia* of Cleonymus (cf. §§4, 37 and 47), but he never specifies the relationship between Cleonymus and his testamentary heirs, so it is impossible to know whether the claim is justified.

either to marry the daughters ourselves or give them to other husbands with dowries: This passing reference to the law on *epiklēroi* confirms that the deceased's next of kin were entitled to claim an *epiklēros* in marriage, but not obliged to do so provided they made suitable alternative arrangements.

Kinship: The Greek word here is *sungeneia* (denoting blood relationship or descent from common ancestors), a vaguer term than *anchisteia* (for which see on 'our degree of kinship, §4).

41–43. Kinship versus wills (argumentation)

The argument now turns to wills in general. The speaker (like the speaker of Isaeus 4) aims to persuade the judges that it is safer to vote in favour of consanguinity than a will, which may not be genuine. He does not go so far as to argue that the next of kin should always have preference over a testamentary heir, but he does, nevertheless, play on the Athenians' mistrust of written documents. Cf. Thompson (1981, 14) and Harris (2013c, 195).

41 So, gentlemen: Again, here and at §43, an address to the judges engages them in the speaker's argument and invites them to agree with his conclusion.

as you do: Cf. Harris (2013c, 195): '[The speaker] reminds the court how judges often decide in favour of the closest relatives against those who make their claim on the basis of a will. But he does not pretend that they do this on the grounds of equity, an unwritten principle that the nearest relative ought to inherit. The reasons why they vote this way are, first, that wills are often forged and, second, that testators do not make correct decisions.'

kinship: Again (cf. on 'kinship', §39) the Greek word is *sungeneia*.

it's impossible to lie about it to you: There is some force in the argument that it is easier to prove a relationship to the deceased than to establish the authenticity of a will; but the speaker is exaggerating in his claim that a relationship cannot be misrepresented, which may in fact be exactly what he is doing. He has repeatedly asserted that he and his brother are Cleonymus's next of kin, but he is vague about his own relationship to Cleonymus and says nothing at all about that of his opponents. (Cf. on 'next of kin', §4.) His evasiveness gives rise to a strong suspicion that he is indeed lying, or at least suppressing part of the truth.

Many people ... have produced false wills: The speaker plays on the Athenians' suspicion of written documents.

complete forgeries: The most obvious (but not necessarily the most frequent) reason for a will to be rejected as invalid is that it was not genuinely written by the supposed testator. The speakers of both Isaeus 4 and Isaeus 9 claim that the wills produced by their opponents are forgeries.

not in their right mind: Solon's law on wills (discussed in the General Introduction, p. 3) provided an alternative basis on which a will could be found to be invalid: that the testator was not in his right mind, and free from undue influence, when he wrote it.

42 And now you all understand: The speaker is really trying to persuade the judges of a 'fact' which he claims they already know.

our kinship: As at §§39 and 41, the Greek word here is *sungeneia*, not the more legally significant *anchisteia* (cf. on 'our degree of kinship' §4).

none of you knows: The speaker cannot prove definitively that the will was invalid, but it may be sufficient for him to cast doubt in the minds of the judges. A similar argument is used at 4.23.

maliciously pursuing: Cf. on 'we are not pursuing a malicious action', §50. As explained in the introduction to this speech (pp. 22–23), Isaeus uses the language of adversarial litigation to condemn the stance of the speaker's opponents. The verb *sykophantein*, translated here as 'maliciously pursue', is normally used as part of a defence strategy to present the prosecutor in an adversarial trial as a sykophant, 'a person who unfairly or dishonestly exploited the legal system' for his own benefit' (Johnstone, 1999, 57). The spelling 'sykophant' is used to distinguish the Greek term from its modern English derivative, 'sycophant', which has a different meaning. Parallels cited by Johnstone include Dem. 36.3, 12, 54, 60; Hyp. 1.1–2; Isoc. 16.1–2; and Lys. 25. 1–3. The terminology is not used in Isaeus's other *diadikasia* speeches, but it does occur in Isaeus 11, where the speaker is defending himself in an adversarial trial against an allegation of negligent guardianship (Isae. 11.4, 23).

acknowledged even by our opponents themselves: The speaker tries to give the impression that his claim that he and his brothers are Cleonymus's next of kin is not in dispute. But even if his opponents did not deny his relationship to Cleonymus, they did not necessarily accept that he was next of kin. Later, the speaker hints that his opponents may be claiming the estate on grounds of consanguinity as well as relying on the will. (Cf. on 'shamelessly talking about close affection and kinship', §47.)

43 in accordance with descent, which is agreed by both sides: The speaker maintains his pressure on the judges to vote on the basis of consanguinity, which is less open to doubt than the authenticity of the will.

when he revoked the will: This is a rhetorical exaggeration: even according to the speaker's account, Cleonymus did not actually carry out his intention of revoking the will. Cf. on 'left his property', §1.

angry and not thinking straight: In the closing sections of his argument the speaker reverts to the theme of Cleonymus's 'anger', again drawing an explicit inference about the validity of the will.

44–47. Kinship and friendship (argumentation)

In the concluding sections of argumentation the speaker contends that he and his brother have a better claim to the estate because Cleonymus would have inherited from them if they had died intestate in his lifetime. If, on the other hand, the opponents had died intestate, their property would have gone to their children and not to Cleonymus (whose relationship to them is still not specified).

The argument is tendentious (cf. on 'the same rights of kinship', 4.23): reciprocity was not a recognized principle of Athenian inheritance law; and, as Wyse, (1904, 225–26) points out, Isaeus relies on the purely accidental fact that the speaker's opponents had offspring who would inherit from them, whereas the speaker and his brother did not. Cleonymus could not, in any event, have become the intestate heir of his nephews unless they had all died, since the surviving brother would have been next of kin to each other.

44 you yourselves expect to inherit from those who are entitled to inherit from you: On the surface, the argument appears logical, but there must have been many Athenians who did not enjoy a reciprocal right of inheritance with their next of kin.

If ... our family or our opponents' had been left without heirs: The hypothesis is based on the premise that either the speaker's *oikos* or that of his opponents had become extinct, i.e. that they died leaving no direct descendants (lit. 'if our house [*oikos*] had been left empty'). On the 'empty *oikos* topos in Athenian inheritance speeches, see on 2.15.

consider from which of them Cleonymus would inherit: Once again (cf. on 'Consider, though', §18), the speaker ostensibly offers alternative options for the judges to consider, instead of simply telling them his own conclusions.

since it is right that the people who take his property should be the ones from whom he was entitled to inherit: Although there is no legal basis for the argument from reciprocity, it may have appealed to the Athenians' sense of fairness.

45 it would have been his sons, not Cleonymus, who took control of the property he left: The conclusion presupposes that the opponents' offspring had survived to take up their paternal inheritance, excluding Cleonymus as a collateral relation.

Cleonymus would have inherited all our property: This passage provides evidence that uncles were among the collateral relatives entitled to inherit from an Athenian who died leaving no direct descendants and without leaving a will. (There is no extant case in which an uncle actually inherited, or claimed, the estate of his nephew.) Their position in the order of succession cannot be established with certainty, because the text of the relevant law (Leão and Rhodes, 2016, fr. 50b) is defective, but it is most likely that paternal uncles came after brothers and sisters of the deceased and their descendants (Harrison, 1968, 144–46). In accordance with the principle of male precedence, all those related to the deceased on his father's side (within the *anchisteia*, i.e. up to children of cousins) had priority over those on his mother's side. So, if Cleonymus was the maternal uncle of the speaker and his brother (cf. on 'And so did Polyarchus, Cleonymus's father and our grandfather', §4), then they had no surviving relatives on their father's side by the time he died.

For we had no children or other kinsmen: What the speaker means is, presumably, 'no other kinsmen more closely related to us than Cleonymus'. Otherwise, it would be difficult to reconcile this statement with his description of his opponents as 'kinsmen' (cf. on 'although they are our kinsmen', §5).

47 So, Athenians: The direct address to the judges underlines the speaker's eagerness to persuade them of the validity of his argument. Modern editors have 'corrected' the ms. *Athēnaioi* ('Athenians'), which does not occur elsewhere in Isaeus's speeches, to *andres* ('gentlemen'), his preferred form of address (see on 'gentlemen', §1). There are, however, some arguments in favour of preserving the form used in the mss. First, there are parallels for the use of two different forms of address in the same speech: Isaeus introduces a different form of address, 'judges' (Gk. *dikastai*) towards the end of three of his speeches, apparently to emphasize their specifically judicial function (see on 'judges', 4.30). Secondly, the exceptional use of the ethnic address 'Athenians' would be consistent with Isaeus's use elsewhere in this speech of language more commonly found in adversarial litigation. (Cf. on 'unjustly put at risk', §6, 'maliciously pursuing', §42, and 'we are not sykophants', §50.) Unlike 'judges', which distances the speaker from his addressees, 'Athenians' draws them together, emphasizing their shared ethnicity and common values.

in both respects, giving and receiving: The speaker has already argued that he and his brother were closest to Cleonymus both in kinship and in friendship; he now contends that they are connected to him 'both in giving and in receiving'. The argument creates an impression of reciprocity between them which is clearly illusional, since only one party could in practice inherit from the other. Moreover, it would appear from indications elsewhere in the speech that the nephews were far more in Cleonymus's debt than he in theirs.

degrees of kinship: See on 'our degree of kinship', §§4 and 39. Here, the speaker seems to imply that his opponents claim to be Cleonymus's next of kin, so that they, rather than the speaker and his brother, are entitled to inherit the estate even if the will is invalid. Isaeus's evasiveness about the exact relationship between Cleonymus and the beneficiaries of his will (cf. on 'next of kin', §4 and 'our degree of kinship', §39) makes it impossible to know the true position, but may suggest that this was indeed the fatal weakness in his clients' case.

because they expect to receive something: The speaker slurs his opponents by imputing a materialistic motive to them. He has cleverly absolved himself and his brother from any counter-accusation along similar lines, by arguing that they would have been happy to leave their property to Cleonymus, whereas the opponents are eager to take his estate without offering anything in return. The speaker never mentions the value of Cleonymus's estate, but it may be inferred from the apparent fierceness of the contest for it that it was substantial.

48–51. Conclusion

The conclusion is short and, compared with the closing sections of some of Isaeus's other speeches, unemotive in tone. There is no supplication of the judges (as at 2.47, 8.45 and 9.37), no appeal for their help (as at 2.47, 8.45 and 9.35), and no injunction to them to vote in accordance with justice (as at 2.47, 7.45 and 8.46). The absence of these conventional features is in keeping with the tone of the speech as a whole, which, on the surface at least, is rational and logical.

48 a summary of what I have said: The speaker does not really summarize his own case in the concluding sections, but simply continues his attempt to discredit that of his opponents.

to which you should all pay attention: Rather than a supplication or a plea for help, the speaker makes an unemotional appeal for the attention of the judges.

49 either that they were more closely related than we were to Cleonymus, or that they were on more affectionate terms with him: Using the familiar contrast between kinship and affection, the speaker succinctly demolishes his opponents' case: they cannot prove that either they are legally entitled to receive Cleonymus's estate as his next of kin, or that he made a will in their favour because of his greater affection for them.

50 to convict Cleonymus himself of insanity: In a final allusion to Solon's law on wills, the speaker reminds the judges that they will 'convict' Cleonymus of insanity (Gk. *paranoia*) if they accept the opponents' story, because if Cleonymus really did intend to confirm the will in their favour, he must have been out of his mind. Cf. on 'accusing him of utter insanity', §19.

we are not pursuing a malicious action: The language here recalls that of §42, where the speaker accused his opponents of 'maliciously pursuing' him and his brother.

51 Finally, gentlemen: This concluding address to the judges focuses their attention on the speaker's final point.

while our opponents understand that it's right for us to receive part of the inheritance: Isaeus ends he speech with an apparently powerful argument: that it would be unfair if the court were to award the whole of the estate to his clients' opponents, when they themselves have offered to share it. The argument, which is reinforced by the attribution of the offer to compromise to the opponents themselves rather than merely to their supporters (cf. §§2, 16, 28) is unlikely to have had any legal validity, but it may have appealed to a sense of justice among the judges.

ISAEUS 2: ON THE ESTATE OF MENECLES

INTRODUCTION

After Menecles died, his brother submitted a formal claim to his estate as next of kin. The claim was opposed by Isaeus's client, the speaker, whose name is unknown but who identifies himself as a son of Eponymus of Acharnae. He says that he was adopted by Menecles, his former brother-in-law, 23 years before the latter's death. Exercising his right as a son adopted *inter vivos*, he attempted to block the brother's claim with a *diamartyria* in which a witness (his father-in-law, Philonides)[1] testified that the estate was 'not subject to adjudication'. Menecles's brother responded by prosecuting Philonides for false testimony, and the speech preserved as Isaeus 2 is the defence speech from the ensuing *dikē pseudomartyriōn*.[2] It was delivered by the adopted son himself, formally speaking as a *synēgoros* (supporting speaker) on behalf of his father-in-law,[3] but in effect setting out his own claim to inherit the estate; his narrative and argumentation would probably have been very much the same if the case had been tried by way of a *diadikasia*.

There was apparently no Athenian law explicitly covering adoption *inter vivos*, but it is abundantly clear from this speech (and from Isaeus 7, where the speaker also defends an adoption *inter vivos*) that Solon's 'law on wills'[4] was interpreted in the fourth century as permitting an Athenian with no natural legitimate sons to adopt a son and heir during his lifetime. Not only does the speaker cite this law in support of his own case; it is also clear from his argumentation that his opponent has relied on a clause in the same law which made an adoption invalid if the adoptive father was subjected to undue influence by a woman (in this case, the speaker's sister, who had been Menecles's second wife).

---

1 The late antique hypothesis to the speech identifies Philonides as the witness, and this is generally accepted by modern editors.
2 See General Introduction, p. 6, for an explanation of the procedure.
3 Rubinstein (2000, 28) notes that it 'seems to have been quite common that a witness who was attacked in a dikē pseudomartyriōn would receive synegorial support from the person on whose behalf he had testified.'
4 See General Introduction, p. 3, for details.

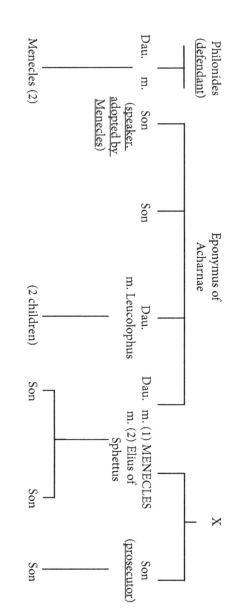

Figure 2.

We have no information from external sources about the families of Menecles or Eponymus, but an approximate date for the speech may be inferred from the speaker's reference (§6) to his military service on a campaign led by Iphicrates in Thrace. If, as most commentators believe, this was his campaign in support of prince Corys, around 383 BC, then (given the time that elapsed between Menecles's divorce and the adoption, and the subsequent 23 years before his death) the speech was probably delivered around the mid 350s. This makes it one of Isaeus's latest speeches.[5]

The speaker's story

According to the speaker his father, Eponymus, was a close friend of Menecles, and the friendship between the two families continued into the next generation after the death of Eponymus. When Menecles's first wife died, leaving him childless, he asked the speaker and his brother to give him their younger sister in marriage. (Their older sister was already married.) They were happy to comply, knowing that Eponymus would have approved of the match. After some years the marriage produced no offspring, and Menecles regretfully decided to divorce his wife so that she could bear children to another husband. She was, initially, reluctant to leave Menecles, but was eventually persuaded to consent to the divorce. Her brothers gave her in marriage to Elius of Sphettus, to whom Menecles transferred the dowry he had received with her, giving her all her personal clothing and jewellery.

Later, concerned by the prospect of a lonely old age, Menecles decided to adopt a son who would care for him while he lived and bury him after his death. He did not want to adopt his brother's son, because that would have left the brother without a male heir, and he had no other blood relations, so there was no-one closer to him than his two former brothers-in-law, the sons of his great friend Eponymus. So he asked them whether one of them would be willing to become his adopted son, and they agreed that it should be the speaker because his brother was frequently away from Athens.

Menecles duly completed the formalities of the adoption by introducing the speaker into his phratry (in the presence of his brother and nephew, who made no objection) and enrolling him in his deme. He then lived

---

5 Cf. Edwards (2007, 31–32).

for a further 23 years, during which he and the speaker enjoyed their relationship as father and son with no quarrels or regrets. Menecles found a wife for the speaker, and the couple earned the praise of the demesmen for their respectful care of Menecles, after whom they named their first son. The speaker earned credit for himself and Menecles by serving on military campaigns and acting as gymnasiarch in the deme. After Menecles died, the speaker conducted his funeral, carried out all the customary rites, and erected a monument to him.

At some time after the adoption, Menecles had needed to raise money to repay a loan which he owed to the estate of an orphan (Nicias's son). So he tried to sell a piece of land, but his brother objected to the sale, claiming part of the land in question for himself. Menecles sold the rest of the land for 70 minas, of which he paid 67 to the orphan, and then started a legal action against his brother. After much hostility the parties agreed to submit their dispute to arbitration. The arbitrators ruled in favour of Menecles's brother, and Menecles was forced to give the land to his brother as a gift. That left him with a very reduced estate.

This episode, according to the speaker, revealed the brother's true motive for disputing the adoption: he had no genuine legal case, but was acting out of spite. He had, all along, resented Menecles's decision to adopt a son from outside the family, because he wanted to get Menecles's property for himself and his son. Having acquired as much as he could while Menecles was still alive, he is now seeking to take over the rest of the property and leave Menecles 'childless' – that is, without an heir to continue his line of descent and carry out the annual commemorative rituals for him.

The story according to Menecles's brother

Although we do not know exactly what Menecles's brother had said in his prosecution speech, it is easy enough to reconstruct at least the main points of his case by reading 'between the lines' of Isaeus's response. An important feature of the speaker's story is that Menecles was left, after repaying the orphan and ceding part of his property to his brother, with a very reduced estate. The brother had presumably blamed the speaker himself for that, accusing him of seeking the adoption for his own financial benefit and then squandering the property while Menecles was alive. He probably said that Eponymus of Acharnae and his family were acquaintances of Menecles, but the close friendship between them was a fabrication invented by the speaker. Eponymus died leaving his family in straitened financial circumstances, and his sons, who had struggled to find a modest dowry for their older sister, could not afford a dowry at all for the younger one. So, when Menecles's first wife died, leaving him elderly and vulnerable, they seized the opportunity and persuaded him to accept their younger sister without a dowry. A further opportunity arose when Menecles divorced his wife and was once again left on his own. Menecles's brother had offered his own son to be adopted by Menecles, but the speaker and his brother enlisted the help of their sister (the former wife of Menecles) to persuade him to adopt the speaker instead. Their motive, ostensibly to support the old man in his loneliness, was in reality to get their hands on his property.

Menecles's brother needed a specific legal ground on which to contest the adoption. He could not deny that Menecles had completed the formalities of the adoption or that he was entitled to do so because he had no natural legitimate son, so he had to find another reason why the adoption was invalid. But even if there was some truth in his characterization of the speaker as a calculating fortune-hunter, that would not in itself have been sufficient to invalidate the adoption; there was nothing legally or morally wrong in arranging an adoption for the material advantage of either or both of the parties, provided no coercion or exploitation was involved.[6] But for an aggrieved family member such as Menecles's brother, the provisos in Solon's law about the adoptive father's state of mind offered a convenient reason (or pretext) to challenge an adoption, and in this case it is clear that Menecles's brother claimed that the adoption was invalid because Menecles had been influenced by a woman. So the role of the speaker's sister (Menecles's divorced wife) was crucial: far from the stereotypically dutiful wife in Isaeus's version of the story, she was almost certainly portrayed by Menecles's brother as a scheming seductress using her sexual charms even after the divorce to inveigle a confused and gullible old man, and colluding with her brother to get possession of Menecles's property.[7]

---

6 In Menander's *Samia* Moschion, whose natural father was apparently less wealthy, expresses his gratitude to his adoptive father Demeas for his affluent upbringing. Cf. Isae. 10.17 (trans. Edwards 2007) 'Others, when they are suffering from financial hardship, give up their own children for adoption into other families, to prevent them from sharing their father's loss of civic rights'
7 Thrasyllus, the speaker of Isaeus 7, is responding to a similar accusation, and

If this was indeed the case put forward by Menecles's brother, it raises an obvious question: why did he and his son not object to the adoption when Menecles introduced his adoptive son to their phratry and enrolled him in the deme? That question might have been answered in a number of ways. Perhaps Menecles's brother and nephew were away from Athens at the crucial time, and when they returned the adoption was a *fait accompli*; or perhaps they reluctantly decided it would be better not to cause a public scandal by opposing the adoption. In any event, once the formalities of the adoption were complete, there was nothing they could do in Menecles's lifetime to overturn it. Over the years (according to Menecles's brother) the speaker and his wife repaid Menecles's many kindnesses to them by manipulating him and squandering his property. Eventually, when he was unable to repay the debt he owed to the orphan, they persuaded him to try to sell some land (part of his father's estate) that belonged to his brother. The brother was forced to intervene, and won his land back when the dispute was submitted to arbitration. When Menecles died, he claimed the estate as next of kin in order to eject the shameless interloper from the family.

Evidence and argumentation

A story along these lines would have presented a challenge to Isaeus's skills as a speechwriter, regardless of whether Menecles's brother was telling the truth. While it was easy enough to find evidence that Menecles had carried out the formalities of the adoption, it was much harder to rebut the allegations about his state of mind. The provisos in the law were, presumably, designed to protect the vulnerable from exploitation and their relatives from being unfairly or irrationally disinherited. But they also created scope for abuse by unscrupulous family members, placing a heavy burden on an adopted son to rebut allegations of insanity or undue influence, and on the judges to decide which of the parties was telling the truth. The provision about female persuasion, in particular, played to male Athenians' suspicions about women, and a story about an unscrupulous woman manipulating a vulnerable man in pursuit of her own family's interests was likely to make a serious impression on a panel of Athenian judges.[8]

---

variations on the theme from the opposite point of view can be found in Isaeus 6 and 8.

8   Variations on this story can be found in several speeches of the Attic orators: Isaeus 6 (Alce persuades Euctemon to recognize one of her children as his legitimate

Oration 2

The speaker probably faced another difficulty, in persuading the judges that Menecles chose to adopt him even though they were not blood relations. Despite the freedom of choice allowed by Solon's law, most of the attested cases involve an adopter and adoptee who were already related by blood;[9] and the argumentation here, and elsewhere in Isaeus's speeches, suggests that an Athenian seeking to adopt a son would typically choose one to whom he was as closely related as possible. In Menecles's case the obvious candidate would have been his brother's son, and the judges might well have been predisposed to accept the brother's story that his offer to let Menecles adopt his own son had been thwarted by the machinations of the speaker and his sister.

It was important, then, for Isaeus to explain why Menecles did not choose to adopt his brother's son. Notably he does not attempt to argue that Menecles had fallen out with his brother and would not have wanted to leave his estate to the son of an enemy; the quarrel between Menecles and his brother, according to Isaeus's narrative, did not arise until after the adoption. He is left with the plausible but inconclusive point that Menecles thought it would be 'shameful' to adopt his brother's son because that would have left the brother without an heir of his own (§10). Apart from that, he focuses on the ties of friendship and marriage between Menecles and the speaker's family, as positive reasons for Menecles's adoption of the speaker.

Witness testimony

Isaeus adduces five items of witness testimony in the course of this speech, and it is worth considering the significance of this evidence to the speaker's case.

1. The first piece of testimony (from an unidentified witness or witnesses) confirms that Menecles received a dowry of 20 minas with the speaker's sister (§5). This has no direct bearing on the validity of

---

son, and colludes with Androcles and Antidorus to take control of his property); Isaeus 8 (Ciron's widow colludes with her notorious brother Diocles to keep Ciron's estate out of the hands of his family by his first wife); Dem 39 and [Dem.] 40 (Plangon tricks Mantias into recognizing her sons as legitimate).

9 See Rubinstein (1993, 117–25) for a catalogue of attested Athenian adoptions, including the relationship by blood between the adopter and adoptee.

the adoption, but the existence of a dowry was contested, so it does support the truth of the speaker's story. (On the significance of the dowry, see commentary on 'with a dowry of 20 minas', §3, and 'not without a dowry, as my opponent is always saying', §5.)
2. Phratry members, *orgeones* and demesmen testify that Menecles introduced the speaker to his phratry and religious association, and enrolled him in his deme (§16). These formalities were not contested by Menecles's brother, but evidence that they had been properly carried out would probably have been seen as an essential basis for proving a valid adoption.
3. The arbitrators who acted in the dispute between Menecles and his brother (or some of them) testify to their decision in favour of the speaker's opponents and the oaths sworn between the parties and the arbitrators (§34). This would have been useful evidence as to the basic facts of the dispute and its outcome, which, in any event, were probably not contested. But the speaker's interpretation of those facts is highly tendentious and no doubt differed substantially from his opponent's account.
4. Unidentified witnesses testify that the land that Menecles was forced to sell in order to repay the orphan raised 70 minas, of which the orphan received 67 minas (§34). Again, the fact (probably uncontested) supports the speaker's story that Menecles was left with limited resources after he was forced to relinquish some of his land to his brother and sell some more to settle his debt to the orphan; but the speaker's explanation of why this happened may or may not have been true.
5. 'Those who know the facts' testify that the speaker buried Menecles and performed the third day and ninth day ceremonies and all the other rituals associated with the burial. (§37). This, too, was probably uncontested, but the fact that the speaker had conducted Menecles's funeral would have had some evidential value in establishing his claim to have been Menecles's adopted son.[10]

All of this testimony, then, has some value in supporting the speaker's story, but none of it addresses the central issue in dispute: whether Menecles was of sound mind and free from the influence of his ex-wife when he adopted the speaker. Proving a negative is, of course, notoriously

---

10 On the 'customary rites' after a death, and their evidentiary value in disputed inheritance claims, see commentary on 4.18–26.

difficult, if not impossible, but it is striking that there is no testimony to support Isaeus's account of the private agreement between Menecles and the speaker, or Menecles's friendship with the speaker's father, Eponymus of Acharnae, which supposedly explained why Menecles wanted to adopt one of Eponymus's sons. It is also noticeable that, although some of Menecles's demesmen have testified to the formalities of the adoption, none of them is brought forward to support the claims that Menecles 'praised [the speaker and his wife] to all his fellow demesmen' (§18) or that the demesmen praised the speaker for his conduct of Menecles's funeral (§37).

Given the length of time that had elapsed since the adoption, it would not be surprising if some of the potential witnesses, especially to the earlier events, were no longer alive, but we have no way of knowing whether that was indeed the case. Both the speaker's brother and his sister's second husband, Elius of Sphettus, could have been important witnesses to the circumstances of the adoption (especially the brother, who was not only present but an active participant in the discussion with Menecles at §§11–12) but neither of them is mentioned again after the adoption.

These omissions. although significant, were not necessarily fatal to the speaker's case. An Athenian litigant would probably have found it difficult to win a case with no witness testimony at all, but testimony was not legally required, and the trial format, with each party presenting his case in a single speech, made it relatively easy to include unsubstantiated 'facts'. A skilled and experienced speechwriter knew how to influence the judges by shaping his client's story in conformity with their expectations,[11] and he could use a range of rhetorical or linguistic devices to compensate for the absence of solid evidence. If (as was often the case) it was impossible to prove the facts beyond doubt, he would use argumentation from probability to persuade the judges that his client's version was more likely to be true than the opponent's.

Stylistic devices

Isaeus uses a range of stylistic devices in this speech to enhance the plausibiity of the speaker's case, including repetition (hammering home

---

11 Cf. Griffith-Williams (2020b, 55–56).

the message that Menecles was 'not insane or persuaded by a woman' when he adopted the speaker, §§1, 19, 20, 25, 38). Irony, especially in the form of ironic rhetorical questions, is deployed in particular to ridicule the actions and motivation of the speaker's opponent (§§21, 23, 26, 33).[12] Both repetition and questions are characteristic features of Isaeus's style, but the ironic tone of the questions in Isaeus 2, verging at times on bitter sarcasm, is especially striking. Finally direct speech, which is extremely rare in Isaeus's surviving speeches, is used to good effect to 'dramatize' Menecles's proposal to adopt one of the two brothers (§§11–12) – and, no doubt, this device was deliberately used by Isaeus to compensate for the lack of witness testimony.

Conclusion

Isaeus's aim in writing this speech was to convince the judges that Menecles made a sane and rational decision to adopt his ex-wife's brother, free of any pressure or undue influence from her. We may think that the idealized narrative – with Menecles, the speaker, and his siblings all firmly in occupation of the moral high ground – seems too good to be true. It invites comparison with Menander's *Samia*, where the relationship between Demeas (adoptive father) and Moschion (adopted son) is portrayed in in less glowing and perhaps – allowing for the element of comic exaggeration – more realistic terms.[13] But we need to remember that Isaeus 2 was the case for the defence in an adversarial trial, delivered after a prosecution speech that had, in all likelihood, made a powerful and positive impression on the judges. In reality, there was probably some truth in both litigants' versions of events, but each of them had to present a black and white case to the court, with no room for shades of grey. Perhaps the strongest point in the speaker's favour was simply the length of time that had elapsed since the adoption, making it more than usually difficult to establish the true facts. Even if some of the judges had suspicions about the speaker's story they may have been reluctant, after 23 years, to annul an adoption indisputably carried out in compliance with the procedural formalities, and willing to give him the benefit of the doubt.

---

12   Cf. Hatzilambrou (2018a, 39).
13   See commentary on §§15, 18, and 42.

ISAEUS 2: ON THE ESTATE OF MENECLES

ἡγούμην μέν, ὦ ἄνδρες, εἴ τις καὶ ἄλλος ἐποιήθη ὑπό τινος κατὰ τοὺς νόμους καὶ ἐγὼ ποιηθῆναι, καὶ οὐκ ἄν ποτε εἰπεῖν οὐδένα τολμῆσαι ὡς ἐποιήσατό με Μενεκλῆς παρανοῶν ἢ γυναικὶ πειθόμενος· ἐπειδὴ δὲ ὁ θεῖος οὐκ ὀρθῶς βουλευόμενος, ὡς ἐγώ φημι, πειρᾶται ἐξ ἅπαντος τρόπου τὸν ἀδελφὸν τὸν αὑτοῦ ἄπαιδα τεθνεῶτα καταστῆσαι, οὔτε τοὺς θεοὺς τοὺς πατρῴους οὔθ᾽ ὑμῶν αἰσχυνόμενος οὐδένα, ἐμοὶ ἀνάγκη ἐστὶ πολλὴ βοηθεῖν τῷ τε πατρὶ τῷ ποιησαμένῳ με καὶ ἐμαυτῷ. [2] διδάξω οὖν ὑμᾶς ἐξ ἀρχῆς ὡς προσηκόντως τε καὶ κατὰ τοὺς νόμους ἐγένετο ἡ ποίησις, καὶ οὐκ ἔστιν ἐπίδικος ὁ κλῆρος ὁ Μενεκλέους ὄντος ἐμοῦ υἱοῦ ἐκείνου, ἀλλ᾽ ὁ μάρτυς διεμαρτύρησε τἀληθῆ. δέομαι δ᾽ ὑμῶν ἁπάντων καὶ ἀντιβολῶ καὶ ἱκετεύω μετ᾽ εὐνοίας ἀποδέχεσθαί μου τοὺς λόγους. [3] Ἐπώνυμος γὰρ ὁ Ἀχαρνεύς, ὁ πατὴρ ὁ ἡμέτερος, ὦ ἄνδρες, φίλος ἦν καὶ ἐπιτήδειος Μενεκλεῖ, καὶ ἐχρῆτο οἰκείως· ἦμεν δὲ αὐτῷ παῖδες τέτταρες ἡμεῖς, δύο μὲν υἱεῖς, δύο δὲ θυγατέρες. τελευτήσαντος δὲ τοῦ πατρὸς ἐκδίδομεν ἡμεῖς τὴν πρεσβυτέραν ἀδελφήν, ἐπειδὴ εἶχεν ὥραν, Λευκολόφῳ, προῖκα ἐπιδόντες εἴκοσι μνᾶς. [4] καὶ ἀπ᾽ ἐκείνου τοῦ χρόνου τετάρτῳ ἔτει ἢ πέμπτῳ ὕστερον ἥ τε ἀδελφὴ ἡμῖν ἡ νεωτέρα σχεδὸν ἡλικίαν εἶχεν ἀνδρὶ συνοικεῖν, καὶ τῷ Μενεκλεῖ ἡ γυνὴ τελευτᾷ ἣν εἶχε πρότερον. ἐπειδὴ οὖν ἐκείνη τὰ νομιζόμενα ἐποίησεν ὁ Μενεκλῆς, ᾔτει τὴν ἀδελφὴν ἡμᾶς, ὑπομιμνῄσκων τήν τε φιλίαν τὴν τοῦ πατρὸς καὶ ἑαυτοῦ, καὶ ὡς πρὸς ἡμᾶς αὐτοὺς ἦν διακείμενος· [5] καὶ ἡμεῖς εἰδότες ὅτι καὶ ὁ πατὴρ οὐδενὶ ἂν ἔδωκεν ἥδιον ἢ ἐκείνῳ, δίδομεν αὐτῷ, οὐκ ἄπροικον, ὡς οὗτος λέγει ἑκάστοτε, ἀλλὰ τὴν ἴσην προῖκα ἐπιδόντες ἥνπερ καὶ τῇ πρεσβυτέρᾳ ἀδελφῇ ἐπέδομεν· καὶ ἐκ τοῦ τρόπου τούτου, πρότερον ὄντες αὐτοῦ φίλοι, κατέστημεν οἰκεῖοι. καὶ ὡς ἔλαβεν εἴκοσι μνᾶς ὁ Μενεκλῆς ἐπὶ τῇ ἀδελφῇ προῖκα, τὴν μαρτυρίαν ταύτην πρῶτον βούλομαι παρασχέσθαι.

ΜΑΡΤΥΡΙΑ

[6] ἐκδόντες τοίνυν τὰς ἀδελφάς, ὦ ἄνδρες, καὶ ὄντες αὐτοὶ ἐν ἡλικίᾳ ἐπὶ τὸ στρατεύεσθαι ἐτραπόμεθα, καὶ ἀπεδημήσαμεν μετὰ Ἰφικράτους εἰς Θρᾴκην· ἐκεῖ δὲ δόξαντές του εἶναι ἄξιοι περιποιησάμενοί τι κατεπλεύσαμεν δεῦρο, καὶ καταλαμβάνομεν τῇ πρεσβυτέρᾳ ἀδελφῇ ὄντα δύο παιδία, τὴν δὲ νεωτέραν, ἣν εἶχε Μενεκλῆς, ἄπαιδα. [7] καὶ ἐκεῖνος δευτέρῳ μηνὶ ἢ τρίτῳ, πολλὰ ἐπαινέσας τὴν ἀδελφήν,

I should think, gentlemen, that if anyone was ever adopted by someone in accordance with the laws, I was, and no-one would ever dare to say that Menecles was insane or persuaded by a woman when he adopted me. And since my uncle is trying in every possible way – mistakenly, as I argue – to make his deceased brother childless, showing no respect for the ancestral gods or any of you, I am obliged to come to the assistance of both my adoptive father and myself. (2) So I shall explain to you from the beginning that the adoption was carried out in an appropriate and legal way, and that the estate of Menecles is not subject to adjudication because I am his son, and the witness in the *diamartyria* was telling the truth. And I beg, entreat and beseech you all to receive my speech with good will.

(3) Our father, gentlemen, Eponymus of Acharnae, was a friend and associate of Menecles, and was on intimate terms with him. We were his four children: two sons and two daughters. And after our father died my brother and I gave our older sister to Leucolophus, when she reached the appropriate age, with a dowry of 20 minas. (4) And four or five years later, when our younger sister was almost old enough to marry, Menecles's first wife died. After he had performed the customary rites for her, Menecles asked us for our sister in marriage, reminding us of the friendship between him and our father and his feelings towards us. (5) And we, knowing that our father would have married her to no-one else with greater pleasure, gave her to him, not without a dowry as my opponent is always saying, but with the same dowry as we gave to our older sister. And so it was that, having previously been his friends, we became his relatives. First, I want to produce testimony that Menecles received a dowry of 20 minas with my sister.

WITNESS TESTIMONY

(6) So we arranged marriages for our sisters, gentlemen, and since we ourselves were of the right age, we turned to soldiering and went abroad with Iphicrates to Thrace. We proved our worth there, and saved a little money before sailing back to Athens, where we found that our older sister had two children but the younger one, Menecles's wife, was childless. (7) And after a month or two Menecles spoke to us, praising our sister highly but saying that he was worried about his own advancing age and

λόγους ἐποιεῖτο πρὸς ἡμᾶς, καὶ ἔφη τήν τε ἡλικίαν ὑφορᾶσθαι τὴν ἑαυτοῦ καὶ τὴν ἀπαιδίαν· οὔκουν ἔφη δεῖν ἐκείνην τῆς χρηστότητος τῆς ἑαυτῆς τοῦτο ἀπολαῦσαι, ἄπαιδα καταστῆναι συγκαταγηράσασαν αὐτῷ· ἱκανὸς γὰρ ἔφη αὐτὸς ἀτυχῶν εἶναι. [8] ἐδεῖτο οὖν ἡμῶν δοῦναι χάριν ταύτην αὐτῷ, ἐκδοῦναι ἄλλῳ αὐτὴν μετὰ τῆς γνώμης τῆς ἑαυτοῦ. καὶ ἡμεῖς ἐκελεύομεν αὐτὸν πείθειν αὐτὴν περὶ τούτων· ὅ τι γὰρ <ἂν> ἐκείνη πεισθῇ, τοῦτ᾽ ἔφαμεν ποιήσειν. [9] κἀκείνη τὸ μὲν πρῶτον οὐδ᾽ ἠνέσχετ᾽ αὐτοῦ λέγοντος, προϊόντος δὲ τοῦ χρόνου μόλις ἐπείσθη· καὶ οὕτως ἐκδίδομεν αὐτὴν Ἠλείῳ Σφηττίῳ, καὶ ὁ Μενεκλῆς τήν τε προῖκα ἐπιδίδωσιν αὐτῷ, μετασχὼν τοῦ οἴκου τῆς μισθώσεως τῶν παίδων τῶν Νικίου, καὶ τὰ ἱμάτια, ἃ ἦλθεν ἔχουσα παρ᾽ ἐκεῖνον, καὶ τὰ χρυσίδια, ἃ ἦν, δίδωσιν αὐτῇ. [10] μετὰ δὲ ταῦτα χρόνου διαγενομένου ἐσκόπει ὁ Μενεκλῆς ὅπως μὴ ἔσοιτο ἄπαις, ἀλλ᾽ ἔσοιτο αὐτῷ ὅς τις ζῶντά γηροτροφήσοι καὶ τελευτήσαντα θάψοι αὐτὸν καὶ εἰς τὸν ἔπειτα χρόνον τὰ νομιζόμενα αὐτῷ ποιήσοι. τούτῳ μὲν οὖν ἑώρα ἕνα μόνον ὑὸν ὄντα, ὥστε ἐδόκει αὐτῷ αἰσχρὸν εἶναι ἄπαιδα τοῦτον καθιστάντα ἀρρένων παίδων αὐτῷ κελεύειν δοῦναι τοῦτον εἰσποιήσασθαι. [11] εὕρισκεν οὖν οὐδένα ἄλλον οἰκειότερον ὄνθ᾽ ἡμῶν ἑαυτῷ. λόγους οὖν πρὸς ἡμᾶς ἐποιεῖτο, καὶ ἔφη δοκεῖν αὐτῷ καλῶς ἔχειν, ἐπειδὴ οὕτως αὐτῷ ἡ τύχη συνέβη ὥστε ἐκ τῆς ἀδελφῆς τῆς ἡμετέρας παῖδας αὐτῷ μὴ γενέσθαι, ἐκ ταύτης τῆς οἰκίας ὑὸν αὐτῷ ποιήσασθαι, ὅθεν καὶ φύσει παῖδας ἐβουλήθη ἂν αὐτῷ γενέσθαι· "ὑμῶν οὖν" ἔφη "βούλομαι τὸν ἕτερον ποιήσασθαι, ὁποτέρῳ ὑμῶν καλῶς ἔχει." [12] καὶ ὁ ἀδελφὸς ἀκούσας ταῦτα [ἐπειδὴ προετίμησεν αὐτοὺς πάντων], ἐπῄνεσέ τε τοὺς λόγους αὐτοῦ, καὶ εἶπεν ὅτι δέοιτο ἥ τε ἡλικία καὶ ἡ παροῦσα ἐρημία ἐκείνου τοῦ θεραπεύσοντος αὐτὸν καὶ ἐπιδημήσοντος· "ἐμοὶ μὲν οὖν" ἔφη "συμβαίνει ἀποδημία, ὡς σὺ οἶσθα· ὁ δὲ ἀδελφὸς οὑτοσί" ἐμὲ λέγων "τῶν τε σῶν ἐπιμελήσεται καὶ τῶν ἐμῶν, ἐὰν βούλῃ τοῦτον ποιήσασθαι." καὶ ὁ Μενεκλῆς καλῶς ἔφη αὐτὸν λέγειν, καὶ ἐκ τοῦ τρόπου τούτου ποιεῖταί με. [13] ὡς οὖν κατὰ τοὺς νόμους ἐγένετο ἡ ποίησις, τοῦτο ὑμᾶς βούλομαι διδάξαι. καί μοι τὸν νόμον ἀνάγνωθι, ὃς κελεύει τὰ ἑαυτοῦ ἐξεῖναι διαθέσθαι ὅπως ἂν ἐθέλῃ, ἐὰν μὴ παῖδες ἄρρενες ὦσι γνήσιοι. ὁ γὰρ νομοθέτης, ὦ ἄνδρες, διὰ τοῦτο τὸν νόμον ἔθηκεν οὕτως, ὁρῶν μόνην ταύτην καταφυγὴν οὖσαν τῆς ἐρημίας καὶ παραψυχὴν τοῦ βίου τοῖς ἄπαισι τῶν ἀνθρώπων, τὸ ἐξεῖναι ποιήσασθαι ὅν τινα ἂν βούλωνται. [14] διδόντων οὖν τῶν νόμων αὐτῷ ποιεῖσθαι διὰ τὸ εἶναι ἄπαιδα, ἐμὲ ποιεῖται, οὐκ ἐν διαθήκαις, ὦ ἄνδρες, γράψας,

childlessness: she must not be rewarded for her goodness by growing old alongside him without children – his own misfortune was enough. (8) So he begged us to do him the favour of giving her to another husband, with his blessing. And we told him to persuade her about this; we would do whatever she agreed. (9) She, at first, resisted his suggestion, but with the passage of time she was with difficulty persuaded. And so we gave her in marriage to Elius of Sphettus, and Menecles handed over the dowry to him, having acquired a share in the lease of the estate of Nicias's children, and gave her the clothing she had brought with her to his house and her jewellery. (10) Some time after this, Menecles began to consider how he could stop being childless and have someone who would look after him in old age and bury him after his death, and then continue to carry out the customary rites for him. He saw that my opponent had only one son, so he thought it would be shameful to leave him without male children by asking him for his son for adoption. (11) And so he found no-one more closely related to him than we were. He spoke to us, saying he thought it would be a good thing, since fate had denied him children by our sister, if he could adopt a son from the same family from which he would have wished to have natural children. 'I want to adopt one of you,' he said, 'whichever of you is willing.' (12) And when my brother heard this, he approved of Menecles's proposal, saying that both his age and his loneliness needed someone to look after him and stay at home. 'As you know,' he said, 'I am often away from home, but my brother here' (meaning me) 'will look after your affairs as well as mine, if you want to adopt him.' Menecles agreed with what he said, and that is how he adopted me.

(13) I want to explain to you how the adoption was carried out in accordance with the law. Please read for me the law that allows a man to dispose of his property as he wishes, provided he has no legitimate sons. The legislator, gentlemen, made the law in this form because he saw that for people without children, the possibility of adopting whoever they wished was the only refuge from their solitude and their only comfort in life. (14) So, since the law allowed him to adopt because he was childless, he adopted me – not, gentlemen, by writing a will in

μέλλων ἀποθνήσκειν, ὥσπερ ἄλλοι τινὲς τῶν πολιτῶν, οὐδ' ἀσθενῶν· ἀλλ' ὑγιαίνων, εὖ φρονῶν, εὖ νοῶν, ποιησάμενος εἰσάγει με εἰς τοὺς φράτορας παρόντων τούτων, καὶ εἰς τοὺς δημότας με ἐγγράφει καὶ εἰς τοὺς ὀργεῶνας. [15] καὶ τότε μὲν οὐδὲν ἀντέλεγον αὐτῷ οὗτοι ὡς <οὐκ> εὖ φρονοῦντι· καίτοι πολὺ κάλλιον ἦν ζῶντα πείθειν ἐκεῖνον, εἴ τι βούλοιντο, μᾶλλον ἢ τελευτήσαντα ὑβρίζειν καὶ ἐξερημοῦν αὐτοῦ τὸν οἶκον. ἐπεβίω γὰρ ἐκεῖνος μετὰ τὴν ποίησιν οὐκ ἐνιαυτὸν ἕνα ἢ δύο, ἀλλὰ τρία καὶ εἴκοσιν ἔτη· καὶ ἐν τούτῳ τῷ χρόνῳ, τοσούτῳ ὄντι, οὐδὲν ἐκεῖνος μετέγνω τῶν πεπραγμένων ἑαυτῷ, διὰ τὸ παρὰ πάντων ὁμολογεῖσθαι ὅτι ἦν ὀρθῶς βεβουλευμένος.

[16] καὶ ὡς ἀληθῆ λέγω ταῦτα, τῆς μὲν ποιήσεως ὑμῖν τοὺς φράτορας καὶ τοὺς ὀργεῶνας καὶ τοὺς δημότας παρέξομαι μάρτυρας, ὡς δ' ἐξῆν ποιήσασθαι, τὸν νόμον αὐτὸν ὑμῖν ἀναγνώσεται, καθ' ὃν ἡ ποίησις ἐγένετο. καί μοι τὰς μαρτυρίας ἀνάγνωθι ταύτας καὶ τὸν νόμον.

ΜΑΡΤΥΡΙΑΙ. ΝΟΜΟΣ

[17] ὡς μὲν τοίνυν ἐξῆν τῷ Μενεκλεῖ ποιήσασθαι υὸν αὐτῷ ὅν τινα ἐβούλετο, ὁ νόμος αὐτὸς δηλοῖ· ὡς δὲ ἐποιήσατο, οἵ τε φράτορες καὶ οἱ δημόται καὶ οἱ ὀργεῶνες ὑμῖν μεμαρτυρήκασιν· ὥστε περιφανῶς ἀποδέδεικται ἡμῖν, ὦ ἄνδρες, ὁ μάρτυς τἀληθῆ διαμεμαρτυρηκώς, καὶ οὗτοι πρός γε τὴν ποίησιν αὐτὴν λόγον οὐδ' ὁντινοῦν δύναιντ' ἂν ἀντειπεῖν. 18] πραχθέντων δὲ τούτων ἐσκόπει ὁ Μενεκλῆς γυναῖκά μοι, καὶ ἔφη με χρῆναι γῆμαι· καὶ ἐγὼ λαμβάνω τὴν τοῦ Φιλωνίδου θυγατέρα. κἀκεῖνός τε τὴν πρόνοιαν εἶχεν ὥσπερ εἰκός ἐστι πατέρα περὶ υέος ἔχειν, καὶ ἐγὼ τὸν αὐτὸν τρόπον ὥσπερ γόνῳ ὄντα πατέρα ἐμαυτοῦ ἐθεράπευόν τε καὶ ᾐσχυνόμην, καὶ ἐγὼ καὶ ἡ γυνὴ ἡ ἐμή, ὥστε ἐκεῖνον πρὸς τοὺς δημότας ἐπαινεῖν ἅπαντας. [19] ὅτι δὲ οὐ παρανοῶν οὐδὲ γυναικὶ πειθόμενος ὁ Μενεκλῆς ἐποιήσατο, ἀλλ' εὖ φρονῶν, ἐνθένδε ἐστὶν ὑμῖν ῥᾴδιον ἐπιγνῶναι. πρῶτον μὲν γὰρ ἡ ἀδελφή, περὶ ἧς οὗτος τὸν πλεῖστον τοῦ λόγου πεποίηται, ὡς ἐκείνῃ πεισθεὶς ἐμὲ ἐποιήσατο, πολλῷ πρότερον ἦν ἐκδεδομένη ἢ τὴν ποίησιν γενέσθαι, ὥστ' εἴ γ' ἐκείνῃ πεισθεὶς τὸν υὸν ἐποιεῖτο, τῶν ἐκείνης παίδων τὸν ἕτερον ἐποιήσατ' ἄν· δύο γάρ εἰσιν αὐτῇ.[20] ἀλλ', ὦ ἄνδρες, οὐχ ὑπ' ἐκείνης πεισθεὶς ἐμὲ ἐποιήσατο υόν, ἀλλὰ μάλιστα μὲν ὑπὸ τῆς

anticipation of his death, as some other citizens do, and not while he was ill. He adopted me while he was in good health, of sound mind, and firm in his intention; he introduced me to his phratry in the presence of my opponents, and enrolled me with his demesmen and *orgeones*. (15) At the time, my opponents made no suggestion that he was not in his right mind, although if they had any objection it would have been much better to try to persuade him while he was alive than to insult him now that he is dead and try to leave his family without heirs. For Menecles did not live just a year or two after the adoption, but 23 years. And during that time, long as it was, he never regretted what he had done because it was generally agreed that he had been well advised. (16) And to prove to you that I am telling the truth about these matters I will produce phratry members, *orgeones* and demesmen as witnesses to the adoption, and the clerk will read you the law itself, in accordance with which the adoption took place. Please read these witness statements and the law.

WITNESS STATEMENTS. LAW

(17) The law itself makes clear that it was permissible for Menecles to adopt anyone he chose as his son, and the phratry members, demesmen and *orgeones* have testified to you that he did adopt. So it has been clearly demonstrated to you, gentlemen, that the witness who submitted the *diamartyria* was telling the truth, and my opponents cannot deny the fact of the adoption.

(18) After these events Menecles started to think about a wife for me, saying that I ought to marry, and I married the daughter of Philonides. So Menecles showed the appropriate fatherly forethought for me, and I cared for and respected him as if he had been my natural father. My wife did the same, and he praised us to all his fellow demesmen.

(19) From the following facts it will be easy for you to judge that Menecles was not insane or persuaded by a woman when he adopted me, but in his right mind. First of all, my opponent has devoted most of his speech to the allegation that Menecles was under the influence of my sister when he adopted me, but she had been married long before the adoption, so if he had been influenced by her he would have adopted one of her sons, since she had two. (20) But, gentlemen, he did not adopt me under her influence, but most of all because of his loneliness, secondly for

ἐρημίας [ἐπείσθη], δεύτερον δὲ διὰ τὰς προειρημένας αἰτίας καὶ διὰ τὴν εὔνοιαν τὴν ὑπάρχουσαν πρὸς τὸν πατέρα τὸν ἐμόν, τρίτον δὲ διὰ τὸ μὴ εἶναι συγγενῆ μηδέν· ἄλλον αὐτῷ, ὁπόθεν ἂν ἐποιήσατο ὑόν. ταῦτα τηνικαῦτα ἐνῆγεν ἐμὲ ποιήσασθαι· ὥστε οὐ παραφρονῶν φαίνεται οὐδὲ τῇ γυναικὶ πεισθείς, εἰ μὴ ἄρα τὴν ἐρημίαν αὐτοῦ καὶ τὴν ἀπαιδίαν οὗτος βούλεται τὸ ὄνομα τοῦτο προσαγορεύειν. [21] ἡδέως δ' ἄν μοι δοκῶ τούτου πυθέσθαι τοῦ φάσκοντος εὖ φρονεῖν, τίνα ποιήσασθαι ἐχρῆν [ἀπὸ] τῶν συγγενῶν; πότερα τὸν ὑὸν τὸν τούτου; ἀλλ' οὐκ ἂν αὐτῷ ἔδωκεν, ἄπαιδα αὐτὸν καθιστάς· οὐχ οὕτως οὗτός ἐστι φιλοχρήματος. ἀλλὰ τὸν τῆς ἀδελφῆς ἢ τὸν τῆς ἀνεψιᾶς ἢ τὸν τοῦ ἀνεψιοῦ; ἀλλὰ τὴν ἀρχὴν οὐκ ἐγένετο αὐτῷ οὐδεὶς τούτων τῶν συγγενῶν. [22] οὐκοῦν ἐξ ἀνάγκης ἦν αὐτῷ ἄλλον τινὰ ποιήσασθαι μᾶλλον ἢ ἄπαιδα καταγηρᾶν, ὥσπερ οὗτος ἀξιοῖ νυνὶ αὐτόν. ἐγὼ τοίνυν πάντας [ἀνθρώπους] ἂν οἶμαι ὁμολογῆσαι ὑμᾶς ὡς οὐκ ἂν ποιησάμενος ἄλλον οἰκειότερον ἐμοῦ ἐποιήσατ' ἄν. δειξάτω γὰρ οὗτος ὑμῖν. ἀλλ' οὐκ ἄν ποτε δύναιτο· ἦν γὰρ οὐδεὶς ἄλλος συγγενὴς αὐτῷ πλὴν τούτων. [23] ἀλλὰ νῦν οὗτος ἐπιτιμῶν αὐτῷ φαίνεται οὐχ ὅτι τὸν ὑὸν οὐκ ἐποιήσατο τὸν αὐτοῦ, ἀλλ' ὅτι τὸ παράπαν ἐποιήσατο καὶ οὐκ ἐτελεύτησεν ἄπαις. τοῦτ' ἔστιν ὃ ἐπιτιμᾷ, ἐπίφθονον πρᾶγμα καὶ οὐ δίκαιον ποιῶν· ὄντων γὰρ αὐτῷ παίδων ἐκείνῳ ὄντι ἄπαιδι καὶ ἀτυχοῦντι φαίνεται ἐπιτιμῶν. [24] καὶ τοῖς μὲν ἄλλοις ἅπασιν ἀνθρώποις καὶ Ἕλλησι καὶ βαρβάροις δοκεῖ καλῶς οὗτος ὁ νόμος κεῖσθαι, ὁ περὶ τῆς ποιήσεως, καὶ διὰ τοῦτο χρῶνται πάντες αὐτῷ· ὁ δὲ θεῖος οὑτοσὶ οὐκ αἰσχύνεται τὸν αὐτοῦ ἀδελφὸν ταύτης τῆς ἐξουσίας ἀποστερῶν νῦν, τοῦ ποιήσασθαι, ἧς οὐδὲ τοῖς οὐ γένει προσήκουσιν οὐδεὶς πώποτε ἐφθόνησεν. [25] οἶμαι δὲ κἂν τοῦτον, εἴ τις ἐρωτήσειεν αὐτὸν τί δή ποτ' ἂν ἐποίησεν εἰς τὴν αὐτὴν τύχην ἐκείνῳ καταστάς, οὐκ ἄλλ' οὐδὲν εἰπεῖν ἢ ὅτι ἐποιήσατ' ἂν ὅς τις αὐτὸν ἔμελλε ζῶντα θεραπεύσειν καὶ τελευτήσαντα θάψειν· καὶ δῆλον ὅτι κατὰ τὸν αὐτὸν τοῦτον νόμον ἡ ποίησις ἐγένετ' ἄν, καθ' ὅν περ ἡ ἐμή. εἶτα αὐτὸς μὲν εἰ ἦν ἄπαις, ἐποιήσατ' ἄν· τὸν δὲ Μενεκλέα ποιήσαντα ταὐτὰ τούτῳ παραφρονεῖν φησι καὶ γυναικὶ πειθόμενον ποιήσασθαι. [26] πῶς οὖν οὐ σχέτλια λέγων φαίνεται; ἐγὼ γὰρ οἶμαι πολλῷ μᾶλλον τοῦτον παραφρονεῖν τῷ τε λόγῳ τούτῳ ᾧ νυνὶ λέγει, καὶ οἷς ποιεῖ. τοῖς τε γὰρ νόμοις καὶ <τοῖς> δικαίοις καὶ οἷς αὐτὸς ἐποίησεν ἂν τἀναντία λέγων φαίνεται, καὶ οὐκ αἰσχύνεται μὲν αὐτῷ τὸν νόμον τὸν περὶ τῆς ποιήσεως ποιῶν κύριον, τῷ δὲ ἀδελφῷ τὸν

the reasons I have mentioned including his goodwill towards my father, and thirdly because he had no other blood relation from whose family he could have adopted a son. These were his reasons for adopting me at the time, so it is clear that he was not insane or persuaded by a woman, unless indeed that is how my opponent wants to describe his loneliness and childlessness. (21) I should like to know from my opponent, who claims to be of sound mind, which of his blood relations Menecles ought to have adopted. My opponent's son, perhaps? But he is not so fond of money that he would have given his son to Menecles and made himself childless. Or the son of his sister or his male or female cousin? But he had never had any such relation. (22) So of necessity he had to adopt someone else rather than grow old without a son, as my opponent thinks he should have done. Well now, I think all of you agree that he could not have adopted anyone more closely related to him than I was. Let my opponent suggest such a person to you. He would not be able to, for Menecles had no other blood relations but these.

(23) But now my opponent is obviously blaming Menecles, not because he didn't adopt his son but because he adopted a son at all, and did not die childless. That is what he blames him for, making it a matter of spite and not justice; although he has children of his own, he is obviously blaming Menecles for being childless and unfortunate. (24) All other men, Greeks and foreigners, approve of this law about adoption, and so they all make use of it. But this uncle of mine is not ashamed, now, to deprive his own brother of the freedom to adopt, which no-one has ever begrudged even to those who are not blood relations. (25) I think that even he, if anyone asked him what he would have done if he been in in the same situation as Menecles, would have to say that he would have adopted a son, if anyone was willing to care for him in his lifetime and bury him after his death. And it's clear that the adoption would have happened in accordance with the same law as mine. He, then, would himself have adopted if he had been childless, but he says that Menecles, who did the same, was insane and persuaded by a woman when he adopted me. (26) Isn't it clear, then, that he is speaking cruelly? In my opinion he is the one who is insane in what he is now saying and doing. For what he is now saying is clearly the opposite of the laws and justice, and of what he himself would have done, and he is not ashamed to acknowledge the validity of the law about adoption for himself, while trying to invalidate it for his brother.

αὐτὸν τοῦτον ζητῶν ἄκυρον ποιῆσαι. [27] εἶτα νῦν διὰ τί διαφερόμενος ζητεῖ οὗτος τὸν ἀδελφὸν τὸν ἑαυτοῦ ἄπαιδα καταστῆσαι, ἄξιόν ἐστιν, ὦ ἄνδρες, ἀκοῦσαι. εἰ μὲν γὰρ περὶ τοῦ ὀνόματός μοι διαφέρεται καὶ ἀναίνεται, εἰ ἐγὼ ἔσομαι ὑὸς Μενεκλέους, πῶς οὐ φθονερός ἐστιν; εἰ δὲ περὶ χρημάτων ἐστὶν ὁ λόγος αὐτῷ, ἐπιδειξάτω ὑμῖν ὁποῖον χωρίον ἢ συνοικίαν ἢ οἰκίαν κατέλιπεν ἐκεῖνος, ἃ ἐγὼ ἔχω νυνί. εἰ δὲ μηδὲν τούτων κατέλιπεν, ἃ δ᾽ ἦν αὐτῷ ὑπόλοιπα, ἐπειδὴ τῷ ὀρφανῷ τὸ ἀργύριον ἀπέδωκεν, οὗτος ἔλαβε ζῶντος ἐκείνου ἔτι, πῶς οὐ περιφανῶς ἐξελέγχεται ἀναιδὴς ὤν; [28] ὡς δὲ ἔχει, ἐγὼ ἐπιδείξω. ἐπειδὴ γὰρ ἔδει τῷ ὀρφανῷ τὰ χρήματα ἀποδιδόναι, ὁ δ᾽ οὐκ εἶχεν ὁπόθεν ἀποδῷ, τόκοι δὲ πολλοῦ χρόνου συνερρυηκότες ἦσαν αὐτῷ τὸ χωρίον ἐπώλει· καὶ οὗτος καιροῦ λαβόμενος καὶ βουλόμενος αὐτῷ ἐπηρεάζειν, ὅτι ἐμὲ ἐποιήσατο, διεκώλυε τὸ χωρίον πραθῆναι, ἵνα κατοκώχιμον γένηται καὶ ἀναγκασθῇ τῷ ὀρφανῷ ἀποστῆναι. ἠμφισβήτει οὖν αὐτῷ μέρους τινὸς τοῦ χωρίου, πρότερον οὐδὲ πώποτε ἀμφισβητήσας, καὶ ἀπηγόρευε τοῖς ὠνουμένοις μὴ ὠνεῖσθαι. [29] κἀκεῖνος ἠγανάκτει, οἶμαι, καὶ ἠναγκάζετο ὑπολείπεσθαι οὗ ἠμφισβήτησεν οὗτος. τὸ δὲ ἄλλο ἀποδίδοται Φιλίππῳ τῷ Πιθεῖ ἑβδομήκοντα μνῶν, καὶ οὕτω διαλύει τὸν ὀρφανόν, ἑπτὰ μνᾶς καὶ τάλαντον ἀποδοὺς ἀπὸ τῆς τιμῆς τοῦ χωρίου· τούτῳ δὲ λαγχάνει δίκην τῆς ἀπορρήσεως. λόγων δὲ πολλῶν γενομένων καὶ ἔχθρας πολλῆς ἔδοξεν ἡμῖν χρῆναι, ἵνα μή ποτε εἴπῃ τις ἐμὲ φιλοχρηματεῖν καὶ ἐχθροὺς ἀδελφοὺς ὄντας αὐτοὺς καθιστάναι, ἐπιτρέψαι τῷ τε κηδεστῇ τῷ τούτου καὶ τοῖς φίλοις διαιτῆσαι. [30] ἐκεῖνοι δ᾽ εἶπον ἡμῖν, εἰ μὲν ἐπιτρέποιμεν αὐτοῖς ὥστε τὰ δίκαια διαγνῶναι, οὐκ ἂν ἔφασαν διαιτῆσαι· οὐδὲν γὰρ δεῖσθαι ἀπέχθεσθαι οὐδετέροις ἡμῶν· εἰ δ᾽ ἐάσομεν αὐτοὺς γνῶναι τὰ συμφέροντα πᾶσιν, ἔφασαν διαιτήσειν. καὶ ἡμεῖς, ἵνα δὴ πραγμάτων ἀπαλλαγῶμεν, ὥς γε δὴ ᾠόμεθα, [31] καὶ ἐκεῖνοι ὀμόσαντες ἡμῖν πρὸς τῷ βωμῷ τῷ τῆς Ἀφροδίτης τῆς Κεφαλῆσι τὰ συμφέροντα γνώσεσθαι, διῄτησαν ἡμᾶς ἀποστῆναι ὧν οὗτος ἠμφισβήτησε καὶ δοῦναι δωρεάν· οὐ γὰρ ἔφασαν εἶναι ἄλλην ἀπαλλαγὴν οὐδεμίαν, εἰ μὴ μεταλήψονται οὗτοι τῶν ἐκείνου. [32] ἐκ δὲ τοῦ λοιποῦ χρόνου ἔγνωσαν ἡμᾶς εὖ ποιεῖν ἀλλήλους καὶ λόγῳ καὶ ἔργῳ, καὶ ταῦτα ὀμόσαι ἠνάγκασαν

(27) Next, gentlemen, it is right for you to hear why my opponent quarrelled with his brother and is now trying to make him childless. For if he now disagrees with me about my name, and rejects my claim to be the son of Menecles, surely he is a spiteful person? But if it's a question of money for him, let him explain to you what land or apartment building or house Menecles left that is now in my possession. If, on the other hand, he left no such property, but my opponent took from him during his lifetime all that remained to him after he had repaid the money to the orphan, is he not clearly exposed as being shameless? (28) I will tell you what happened. When the money was due to be paid back to the orphan, but Menecles did not have the resources available, and interest had been accumulating over a long period, he tried to sell the land. My opponent, seizing the opportunity and wanting to take it out on him for having adopted me, tried to prevent the land from being sold, so that it would become subject to seizure and Menecles would be forced to relinquish it to the orphan. So my opponent disputed a part of the land with Menecles, although he had never disputed it before, and tried to prevent the purchasers from buying it. (29) Menecles was, understandably, annoyed, and he was forced to keep back the piece of land that my opponent claimed. The rest he sold to Philippus of Pithus for 70 minas, and in that way he repaid the orphan, giving him a talent and seven minas from the price of the land. He brought a legal action against his brother for restraint of sale. After long discussion and a great deal of hostility, we agreed to submit the dispute for arbitration to my opponent's brother-in-law and our friends, so that no-one could ever say I was covetous and stirring up enmity between two men who were brothers. (30) They told us that if we referred the matter to them for a legal decision, they would decline to act as arbitrators, because they did not want to quarrel with either us or our opponents; but if we allowed them to decide what was most expedient for everyone, they would accept. So, in order to dispose of the matter, as we thought, we entrusted it to them on those terms. (31) After swearing an oath to us at the altar of Aphrodite at Cephale to decide what was expedient, they ruled that we should relinquish what my opponent claimed and give it to him as a gift. For they said there was no other way of settling the matter than for my opponents to receive a share of Menecles's property. (32) And for the future they decreed that we must treat one another well in both word and deed, and they made us

ἡμᾶς ἀμφοτέρους πρὸς τῷ βωμῷ ἦ μὴν ποιήσειν. καὶ ἡμεῖς ὠμόσαμεν εὖ ποιεῖν ἀλλήλους ἐκ τοῦ ἐπιλοίπου χρόνου, κατὰ δύναμιν εἶναι, καὶ λόγῳ καὶ ἔργῳ. [33] καὶ ὡς ὅ τε ὅρκος ἐγένετο, καὶ ἔχουσιν οὗτοι ἃ ἐγνώσθη αὐτοῖς ὑπὸ τῶν οἰκείων τῶν τούτου, εἶτα νυνὶ ταυτὶ τὰ ἀγαθὰ ποιοῦσιν ἡμᾶς, τὸν μὲν τεθνεῶτα ἄπαιδα βουλόμενοι καταστῆσαι, ἐμὲ δ᾽ ἐκβάλλειν ὑβρίσαντες ἐκ τοῦ οἴκου, τοὺς γνόντας αὐτοὺς ὑμῖν παρέξομαι μάρτυρας, ἐὰν ἐθέλωσιν ἀναβαίνειν (εἰσὶ γὰρ τούτων οἰκεῖοι), , εἰ δὲ μή, τοὺς παραγενομένους. [34] καί μοι τὰς μαρτυρίας ἀνάγνωθι ταυτασί· σὺ δ᾽ ἐπίλαβε τὸ ὕδωρ.

ΜΑΡΤΥΡΙΑΙ

λαβὲ δή μοι τὰς μαρτυρίας ἐκείνας, ὡς τό τε χωρίον ἑβδομήκοντα μνῶν ἐπράθη, καὶ ὡς ἀπέλαβεν ὁ ὀρφανὸς ἑπτὰ καὶ ἑξήκοντα μνᾶς πραθέντος τοῦ χωρίου.

ΜΑΡΤΥΡΙΑΙ

[35] ὁ θεῖος τοίνυν οὑτοσί, ὦ ἄνδρες, κεκληρονομηκὼς τῶν ἐκείνου ἔργῳ καὶ οὐ λόγῳ ὥσπερ ἐγώ, καὶ ἔχων ἐμοῦ πολλῷ πλείονα· ἐγὼ γὰρ τὰς τριακοσίας δραχμὰς ἔλαβον τὰς περιλειφθείσας ἀπὸ τῆς τιμῆς τοῦ χωρίου, καὶ οἰκίδιον ὅ ἐστιν οὐκ ἄξιον τριῶν μνῶν· οὗτος δὲ πλεῖον ἢ δέκα μνῶν χωρίον ἔχων, εἶτα προσέτι νῦν ἥκει τὸν οἶκον αὐτοῦ ἐξερημώσων. [36] καὶ ἐγὼ μὲν ὁ ποιητὸς ἐκεῖνόν τε ζῶντα ἐθεράπευον, καὶ αὐτὸς καὶ ἐμὴ γυνή, θυγάτηρ οὖσα τουτουὶ Φιλωνίδου, καὶ τῷ ἐμῷ παιδίῳ ἐθέμην τὸ ὄνομα τὸ ἐκείνου, ἵνα μὴ ἀνώνυμος ὁ οἶκος αὐτοῦ γένηται, καὶ τελευτήσαντα ἔθαψα ἀξίως ἐκείνου τε καὶ ἐμαυτοῦ, καὶ ἐπίθημα καλὸν ἐπέθηκα, καὶ τὰ ἔνατα καὶ τἆλλα πάντα ἐποίησα τὰ περὶ τὴν ταφὴν ὡς οἷόν τε κάλλιστα, ὥστε τοὺς δημότας ἐπαινεῖν ἅπαντας· [37] οὗτος δὲ ὁ συγγενής, ὁ ἐπιτιμῶν αὐτῷ ὅτι ὑὸν ἐποιήσατο, ζῶντος μὲν τὸ χωρίον τὸ περιλειφθὲν αὐτῷ περιείλετο, τελευτήσαντα δ᾽ αὐτὸν ἄπαιδα καὶ ἀνώνυμον βούλεται καταστῆσαι. τοιοῦτός ἐστιν οὗτος. καὶ ὡς ἔθαψά τ᾽ ἐγὼ αὐτὸν καὶ τὰ τρίτα καὶ τὰ ἔνατα ἐποίησα καὶ τἆλλα τὰ περὶ τὴν ταφήν, τὰς μαρτυρίας ὑμῖν τῶν εἰδότων ἀναγνώσεται.

swear at the altar that we would do so. So we swore to treat one another well in future, as far as we were able, in both word and deed. (33) I will produce for you as witnesses, if they are willing to come forward (for they are my opponent's friends) the men who made the decision: they will testify that the oath was sworn, that my opponents are now in possession of what was adjudged to them by those friends, and that they are now treating us so well that they want to make the deceased childless and throw me ignominiously out of his house. If they are not willing, I will produce those who were present. (34) Please read these depositions, and stop the water.

WITNESS STATEMENTS

Now please take these depositions that the land was sold for 70 minas and that the orphan received 67 minas after the land was sold.

WITNESS STATEMENTS

(35) Well then, gentlemen, my uncle here has inherited Menecles's property in reality, not just nominally as I have, and his share is much larger than mine. For I have received the 300 drachmas remaining from the price of the land and a small house worth less than three minas, whereas he has land worth more than ten minas and has, moreover, now come to court with the intention of leaving Menecles's family without heirs. (36) I, as his adopted son, cared for him during his lifetime, along with my wife the daughter of Philonides here, and gave his name to my little boy so that his family would not lose the name; and after his death I buried him in an appropriate style for both him and myself, and I set up a fine monument to him, and I performed the ninth day ceremony and all the other customary rites at the tomb so well t hat all the demesmen praised me. (37) But my opponent, his kinsman, who blames him for adopting a son, not only took away his remaining land while he was alive but, now that he is dead, wants to leave him childless and without a name. That's the kind of man he is. The clerk will read you the testimony of those who know the facts: that I buried Menecles and performed the third day and ninth day ceremonies and all the other rituals associated with the burial.

ΜΑΡΤΥΡΙΑΙ

[38] ὅτι τοίνυν ὁ Μενεκλῆς, ὦ ἄνδρες, ἐποιήσατό με οὐ παρανοῶν οὐδὲ γυναικὶ πειθόμενος, βούλομαι ὑμῖν καὶ αὐτοὺς τούτους μάρτυρας παρασχέσθαι, [καὶ] ἐμοὶ μαρτυροῦντας ἔργῳ καὶ οὐ λόγῳ, ἐξ ὧν ἔπραξαν αὐτοί, ὅτι ἐγὼ τἀληθῆ λέγω. τὰς γὰρ διαλύσεις φαίνονται πρὸς ἐμὲ ποιησάμενοι ἀμφότεροι οὗτοι, καὶ οὐ πρὸς τὸν Μενεκλέα, καὶ ὀμόσαντες ὅρκους <ἐμοὶ> καὶ ἐγὼ τούτοις. [39] καίτοι εἴ γε μὴ κατὰ τοὺς νόμους ἐγεγένητο ἡ ποίησις, μηδὲ κληρονόμος ἦν ἐγὼ τῶν Μενεκλέους ὑπ' αὐτῶν τούτων δεδοκιμασμένος, τί ἔδει αὐτοὺς ὀμνύναι ἐμοὶ ἢ παρ' ἐμοῦ λαμβάνειν ὅρκους; οὐδὲν δήπου. οὐκοῦν ὁπότε ἐποίησαν ταῦτα, φαίνονται αὐτοὶ οὗτοι ἐμοὶ μαρτυροῦντες ὅτι κατὰ τοὺς νόμους ἐποιήθην καὶ δικαίως εἰμὶ κληρονόμος τῶν Μενεκλέους. [40] ἐγὼ δ' οἶμαι καταφανὲς ὑμῖν ἅπασι τοῦτ' εἶναι, ὡς καὶ παρὰ τούτων αὐτῶν ὁμολογούμενόν ἐστιν ὅτι Μενεκλῆς οὐ παρεφρόνει, ἀλλὰ πολὺ μᾶλλον οὗτος νυνί, ὅς γε ποιησάμενος τῆς ἔχθρας διάλυσιν πρὸς ἡμᾶς καὶ ὀμόσας ὅρκους πάλιν νῦν ἥκει τὰ ὁμολογηθέντα καὶ ὀμοθέντα παραβάς, καὶ ἀφελέσθαι με ἀξιοῖ ταυτὶ τὰ λοιπά, οὕτως ὄντα μικρά. [41] ἐγὼ δὲ εἰ μὴ πάνυ τὸ πρᾶγμα αἰσχρὸν εἶναι ἐνόμιζον καὶ ἐπονείδιστον, προδοῦναι τὸν πατέρα οὗ εἶναι ὠνομάσθην καὶ ὃς ἐποιήσατό με, ταχὺ ἂν ἀπέστην αὐτῷ τῶν ἐκείνου· ἔστι γὰρ ὑπόλοιπον οὐδὲ ἕν, ὡς καὶ ὑμᾶς οἴομαι αἰσθάνεσθαι. [42] νυνὶ δὲ δεινὸν τὸ πρᾶγμα καὶ αἰσχρὸν εἶναι τῇδε νομίζω, εἰ ἡνίκα μὲν ὁ Μενεκλῆς εἶχέ τι, τότε μὲν ἔδωκα ἐμαυτὸν ὑὸν αὐτῷ ποιήσασθαι, καὶ ἀπὸ τῆς οὐσίας τῆς ἐκείνου, πρὶν πραθῆναι τὸ χωρίον, ἐγυμνασιάρχουν ἐν τῷ δήμῳ καὶ ἐφιλοτιμήθην ὡς ὑὸς ὢν ἐκείνου, καὶ τὰς στρατείας, ὅσαι ἐγένοντο ἐν τῷ χρόνῳ τούτῳ, ἐστράτευμαι ἐν τῇ φυλῇ τῇ ἐκείνου καὶ ἐν τῷ δήμῳ· [43] ἐπειδὴ δὲ ἐκεῖνος ἐτελεύτησεν, εἰ προδώσω καὶ ἐξερημώσας αὐτοῦ τὸν οἶκον ἀπιὼν οἰχήσομαι, πῶς οὐκ ἂν δεινὸν τὸ πρᾶγμα εἶναι καὶ καταγέλαστον δοκοίη, καὶ τοῖς βουλομένοις περὶ ἐμοῦ βλασφημεῖν πολλὴν ἐξουσίαν παράσχοι; καὶ οὐ μόνον ταῦτ' ἐστὶ τὰ ποιοῦντά με ἀγωνίζεσθαι τὸν ἀγῶνα τοῦτον, ἀλλ' εἰ οὕτω φαῦλος ἄνθρωπος δοκῶ εἶναι καὶ μηδενὸς ἄξιος, ὥστε ὑπὸ μὲν εὖ φρονοῦντος μηδ' ὑφ' ἑνὸς ἂν ποιηθῆναι τῶν φίλων, ὑπὸ δὲ παραφρονοῦντος, ταῦτ' ἐστὶ τὰ λυποῦντά με. [44] ἐγὼ οὖν δέομαι ὑμῶν πάντων, ὦ ἄνδρες, καὶ ἀντιβολῶ καὶ ἱκετεύω ἐλεῆσαί με καὶ ἀποψηφίσασθαι τοῦ μάρτυρος τουτουί. ἀπέφηνα δ' ὑμῖν πρῶτον μὲν ποιηθέντα ἐμαυτὸν ὑπὸ τοῦ Μενεκλέους ὡς ἄν τις δικαιότατα

WITNESS STATEMENTS

(38) Next, gentlemen, I'd like to bring forward my opponents themselves to testify – not in word, but in deed, from what they themselves have done – that I am telling the truth in my claim that Menecles was not insane or persuaded by a woman when he adopted me. For both of them obviously conducted a reconciliation with me, not with Menecles, and they swore oaths to me as I did to them. (39) Yet if the adoption had not been carried out legally, and if I had not been approved as Menecles's heir by my opponents themselves, why would they have needed to swear to me and receive oaths from me? There would have been no need at all. So when they did this, they clearly testified for me that I was legally adopted and that I am Menecles's rightful heir. (40) I think it's clear to all of you that everyone, including my opponents themselves, agrees that it's not Menecles who was insane, but rather this man now, who after reconciling the enmity with us and swearing oaths, has now come to court in contravention of his agreements and oaths with the intention of depriving me of what little remains of Menecles's property. (41) For my part, if I didn't think it a thoroughly shameful and disgraceful thing to betray the father who adopted me and called me his son, I would readily have relinquished the estate to my opponent, since, as I think you know, there is nothing left of it. (42) I think it would be a terrible and shameful affair if I had agreed to be adopted as Menecles's son at a time when he had some property, and out of that property, before the land was sold, I served as gymnasiarch in his deme, seeking honour as his son, and served in all the campaigns that took place at that time with his tribe and deme, (43) but now betrayed him after his death by walking away and leaving his house without an heir – wouldn't that seem a strange and ridiculous business, giving my detractors a good opportunity to criticize me? But that's not my only motivation for contesting this case; what really grieves me is that I might be thought such a wretched and worthless fellow that I couldn't find a friend in his right mind who would adopt me, but only a madman.

(44) So I beg you all, gentlemen, and beseech and entreat you to have pity on me and acquit the witness here. I have shown you, first, that I was adopted by Menecles in the strictest accordance with the laws, and that

ποιηθείη, καὶ οὐ λόγῳ οὐδὲ διαθήκῃ τὴν ποίησιν γεγενημένην, ἀλλ᾽ ἔργῳ· καὶ τούτων ὑμῖν τούς τε φράτορας καὶ τοὺς δημότας καὶ τοὺς ὀργεῶνας παρεσχόμην μάρτυρας· [45] καὶ ἐκεῖνον ἐπέδειξα τρία καὶ εἴκοσιν ἐπιβιόντα ἔτη. εἶτα τοὺς νόμους ἐπέδειξα ὑμῖν τοῖς ἅπασι τῶν ἀνθρώπων ἐξουσίαν διδόντας ὑεῖς ποιεῖσθαι. καὶ ἔτι πρὸς τούτοις ζῶντα τε φαίνομαι θεραπεύων αὐτὸν καὶ τελευτήσαντα θάψας. [46] οὗτος δὲ νυνὶ ἄκληρον μὲν ἐμὲ ποιεῖν τοῦ κλήρου τοῦ πατρῴου, εἴτε μείζων ἐστὶν οὗτος εἴτε ἐλάττων, ἄπαιδα δὲ τὸν τελευτήσαντα καὶ ἀνώνυμον βούλεται καταστῆσαι, ἵνα μήτε τὰ ἱερὰ τὰ πατρῷα ὑπὲρ ἐκείνου μηδεὶς τιμᾷ μήτ᾽ ἐναγίζῃ αὐτῷ καθ᾽ ἕκαστον ἐνιαυτόν, ἀλλὰ ἀφαιρῆται τὰς τιμὰς τὰς ἐκείνου· ἃ προνοηθεὶς ὁ Μενεκλῆς, κύριος ὢν τῶν ἑαυτοῦ, ἐποιήσατο ὑὸν ἑαυτῷ, ἵνα τούτων ἁπάντων τυγχάνῃ. [47] μὴ οὖν, ὦ ἄνδρες, πεισθέντες ὑπὸ τούτων ἀφέλησθέ μου τὸ ὄνομα, τῆς κληρονομίας ὃ ἔτι μόνον λοιπόν ἐστιν, ἄκυρον δὲ τὴν ποίησιν αὐτοῦ καταστήσητε· ἀλλ᾽ ἐπειδὴ τὸ πρᾶγμα εἰς ὑμᾶς ἀφῖκται καὶ ὑμεῖς κύριοι γεγόνατε, βοηθήσατε καὶ ἡμῖν καὶ ἐκείνῳ τῷ ἐν Ἅιδου ὄντι, καὶ μὴ περιίδητε, πρὸς θεῶν καὶ δαιμόνων δέομαι ὑμῶν, προπηλακισθέντα αὐτὸν ὑπὸ τούτων, ἀλλὰ μεμνημένοι τοῦ νόμου καὶ τοῦ ὅρκου ὃν ὀμωμόκατε καὶ τῶν εἰρημένων ὑπὲρ τοῦ πράγματος, τὰ δίκαια καὶ τὰ εὔορκα κατὰ τοὺς νόμους ψηφίσασθε.

the adoption was not made just verbally or in a will, but actually carried out. And I have brought forward the phratry members, demesmen and *orgeones* as witnesses to these facts. (45) And I have shown that Menecles survived for 23 years. Then I have shown you the laws that permit men without sons to adopt sons. And in addition to that, I manifestly cared for him while he was alive and buried him after he died. (46) My opponent, on the other hand, now wants to disinherit me of my father's property, however large or small it might be, and to make the dead man childless and nameless, so that there will be no-one who will honour the ancestral cults on his behalf or perform the annual sacrifices for him, but he will be deprived of the honours due to him. Menecles made provision in advance for this, when he was in control of his own property, by adopting a son in order to secure all these things. (47) So, gentlemen, don't be persuaded by my opponents to annul his adoption and deprive me of my name, which is all that remains of my inheritance, but since the matter has come within your responsibility, help both me and the man who is in Hades and – I beg you by the gods and spirits – don't stand by and let Menecles be foully abused by my opponents but, mindful of the law and the oath that you swore and what has been said about the matter, vote justly and in accordance with the laws and your oath.

COMMENTARY

1–2. Introduction

This is the defence speech from an adversarial trial (a *dikē pseudomartyriōn*), so it was the second to be delivered in court, after the speech for the prosecution. The prosecutor was Menecles's brother, who claimed the estate as next of kin and accused the defendant, Philonides, of falsely testifying in a *diamartyria* that the estate of Menecles was not subject to adjudication because Menecles had left a legitimate son (Philonides's son-in-law). The speech was delivered on behalf of Philonides by his son-in-law, who claimed that Menecles adopted him *inter vivos*. In the opening two paragraphs he sets out very succinctly, though not without bias, the basis of his claim to Menecles's estate, the nature of his opponent's allegations, and the legal procedure under which the dispute was being heard by the court.

1 I should think, gentlemen: On addresses to the judges in general, and in particular at the beginning of a speech, see on 'gentlemen', 1.1. In this speech Isaeus uses only his preferred form, 'gentlemen' (*ō andres*), which occurs 12 times. An address introduces the main narrative (§3). and marks the transition to a new section of narrative (§27) or the resumption of the speech after the reading of witness testimony or other documentary evidence (§§6, 17, 35, 38). The remaining five addresses are used for emphasis or to engage the judges in the speaker's argument (§§13, 14, 20, 44, 47).

insane or persuaded by a woman: According to Solon's law (see on 'the law…', §13), an adoption was invalid if it was carried out while the adoptive father was insane or under the influence of a woman. It becomes clear in the course of the speech that the speaker's opponent has challenged the adoption on the grounds that Menecles was acting under the influence of his ex-wife, the speaker's sister. The phrase '(not) insane or persuaded by a woman' occurs five times in this speech (cf. §§ 19, 20, 25 and 38). Such repetition, designed to enhance the persuasiveness of the speaker's central argument, is characteristic of Isaeus's style. (Cf. Hatzilambrou (2018a, 39) on repetition as 'part of [Isaeus's] strategy regarding the structure and advancing of his argument'.)

my uncle: Following Menecles's adoption of the speaker, Menecles's brother became legally the speaker's uncle. So, by referring to his opponent in these terms, the speaker tacitly invites the judges to agree that the adoption was valid. Cf. on 'my uncle here', §35.

to make his deceased brother childless: The idea of childlessness, which becomes a major theme of this speech, is introduced at an early stage. Menecles decided to adopt a son because he was lonely and childless (§§7, 10, 14, 20); he did not want to make his brother childless by adopting his only son (§10); but now the brother is trying to make Menecles childless again by challenging the adoption (§§27, 33, 37, 46).

ancestral gods: Parker (2005, 21) describes *patrōoi theoi* as 'an untranslatable phrase', which he renders as 'ancestral gods'. He continues: 'Ancestral gods are gods whom one has inherited a relation to, gods whom one's father worshipped... The breadth of that group will vary greatly according to context. In a certain sense, the gods of Athens en masse are *patrōoi theoi* for every Athenian citizen... There coexisted, however, a narrower sense in which the ancestral gods were the gods of the restricted group into which one was born, above all it seems those of the household and the phratry, perhaps also those of the deme.'

In the present context the speaker is alluding to the household gods who will, as he asserts, be dishonoured if Menecles is deprived of a son to continue his family and perform the commemorative rituals for him. This speech, which begins and ends with evocations of the gods (cf. 'the ancestral cults', §46), is rich in the language of Athenian religion. There are repeated references to the 'customary rites' for the dead (§§3, 10, 36) and to an oath sworn at the temple of Aphrodite at Cephale (§§31, 38–40).

any of you: In contrast with the ancestral gods, whose sphere of influence was the private household, the judges, individually and collectively, are addressed as representatives of the city as a whole and its legal system.

both my adoptive father and myself: According to the speaker, Menecles's brother has wronged not only the speaker by trying to deprive him of the inheritance, but also Menecles himself by trying to deprive him of an heir and successor who will keep his family alive. This sets the tone for the rest of the speech, where the speaker is presented as someone whose motivation in pursuing the litigation is not mercenary or selfish (as his opponent has apparently alleged).

2 from the beginning: Telling one's story 'from the beginning' is a commonplace of Athenian forensic oratory, often conveying a willingness to tell 'the whole truth'. (Cf., e.g., Isae. 7.4; Andoc. 1.8; Dem. 34.5; 37.3; 40.5; 43.1; 45.2; 49.4; 54.2; Isoc. 17.3; 18.4; Lys. 1.5; 7.3; 12.3; 32.3.) Typically in an inheritance dispute, the story begins at an earlier stage of the family history – in this case, not with the adoption, but with its origins in the friendship between Menecles and the speaker's father.

***diamartyria*:** A formal declaration, used in inheritance cases to block a claim from a collateral relative of the deceased by asserting that the estate was 'not subject to adjudication' because the deceased had left a legitimate natural or adopted son. (Cf. General Introduction, p. 6.)

I beg, entreat and beseech you all to receive my speech with good will: A conventional *captatio benevolentiae*, or plea for the good will (Gk. *eunoia*) of the judges. The introductions to five of Isaeus's speeches include such pleas (cf. 6.2, 7.4, 8.5, 10.3). The verb *deomai* ('I beg') is typically used, and the strength of the plea is intensified by the addition of one or two more verbs of pleading or supplication.

3–9. Menecles's relations with the speaker's family: friendship, marriage, divorce (narrative and testimony)

Isaeus's account of the events leading up to the adoption, the adoption itself, and the speaker's subsequent relations with Menecles is highly idealized. The narrative appears carefully designed to rebut the opponent's claim that Menecles was influenced by his ex-wife, and to defend the speaker himself against allegations that he had exploited Menecles to his own financial advantage.

3 our father, gentlemen: The plural 'our' includes the speaker's siblings (a brother and two sisters) who will shortly be introduced.

Eponymus of Acharnae: Acharnae, located to the north of the city of Athens, on the Attic plain south of Mount Parnes, was one of 139 demes (local territorial districts) of Attica. Under the reforms instituted by the sixth-century politician Cleisthenes, the demes became the main unit of local administration in Attica. Acharnae was the largest deme (Thuc. 2.19), and in the fourth century it was represented by 22 members (more than any other deme) on the 500-strong Athenian Council (Boule). We cannot be sure whether Eponymus and his family actually lived in Acharnae, because deme membership was hereditary and Athenians always retained their affiliation to their family's original deme even if they moved elsewhere.

Every male Athenian citizen had to be a member of a deme, and a deme-name or 'demotic' was part of his formal identity, in addition to his given name and patronymic. Although demotics are regularly used in official contexts where an Athenian needed to be formally identified, for example as a litigant initiating court proceedings, they are mentioned relatively rarely in forensic speeches, where their use is usually 'deliberate and calculated' (Brock, 2000, 16). So the speaker here gives his father (and, by extension,

Oration 2

himself) a precise legal identity. (Cf. 'Philoctemon of Cephisia', 6.3.) It is possible that Acharnae was also Menecles's deme, since he was a friend of Eponymus, but his deme is not named in the speech. (Cf Whitehead, 1986, 224, n.6, and see on 'at the altar of Aphrodite at Cephale', §31.)

a friend and associate of Menecles: This paves the way for the speaker's account of his sister's marriage to Menecles and his own adoption by him. See on 'the friendship between him and our father', §4.

gave our older sister to Leucolophus: Giving an Athenian woman in marriage was the duty of her legal representative or *kyrios* (her father or, if he was no longer alive, her guardian or nearest adult male relative). It appears from Isaeus's narrative that both the speaker and his brother were older than their two sisters. No exact ages are mentioned, but the brothers (or perhaps just the older one) must have been at least 18 when the older sister was given in marriage.

appropriate age: The customary age at marriage for an Athenian girl was around 16.

with a dowry of 20 minas: Although it was not a legal requirement, there was a strong expectation that an Athenian woman would be married with a dowry (sometimes seen as her share of her father's estate, though unlikely to be equivalent in value to the property inherited by her brothers). On the function of the dowry as a contribution to the household economy, and as a means of protecting the woman's interests, see Foxhall (1989).

A dowry of 20 minas was relatively modest, perhaps indicating that Eponymus's family was not well off after his death (although it should be borne in mind that the speaker and his brother also gave a dowry of the same value to their other sister). Cf. on 'not without a dowry', §5.

almost old enough to marry: See on 'appropriate age' above. Menecles was probably in his 40s or 50s when he married the speaker's sister, but such a difference in ages would not have been remarkable in classical Athens, where men did not normally marry before the age of 30 and often remarried after the death or divorce of a previous wife.

customary rites: On the 'customary rites' after a death, see the introductory note to 4.18–26, and cf. §36 below, where the speaker describes how he commemorated Menecles after his death.

4 four or five years later: The main narrative is presented in straightforward chronological sequence, but the intervals between events are rarely precise. Later in the speech (and characteristically for Isaeus) most indications of elapsed time are equally vague or even vaguer: 'after a month or two' (§7), 'with the passage of time' (§9), 'when some time had passed' (§10), 'after these events' (§18). There is one striking exception: Menecles lived for 23 years after the adoption (§15).

the friendship between him and our father: In this context 'friendship' Greek *philia*) denotes an elective relationship between two people who are not related by blood, based on mutual affection and esteem or on common interests and involving mutual expectations and obligations expressed through appropriate actions. (Cf. Griffith-Williams, forthcoming a; and, on *philia* as a subjective emotion, see on 'through his affection', 1.4.) The friendship between Menecles and Eponymus and their families is offered as an explanation for both Menecles's marriage to Eponymus's daughter and his choice of the speaker as his adopted son, but Isaeus gives no details of relations between the two men and produces no witness testimony about their friendship. That would appear surprising if, as is likely, Menecles's brother had cast doubt on the supposedly close relationship between the families and portrayed the speaker as an opportunistic outsider. But Isaeus may have decided, as a matter of strategy, that it was better to pass over this part of the narrative quickly and focus the judges' attention on the strong points in his client's case, notably the long and happy relationship between Menecles and the speaker after the adoption.

and his feelings towards us: For the idea that *philia* could be transmitted between generations, cf. Isoc. 1.2: 'children should inherit their father's friendships, like his property' (cited by Blundell, 1989, 48).

5 knowing that our father would have married her to no-one else with greater pleasure: Cf. Just (1989, 81): 'It should perhaps be noted that the girl's feelings about being married to her father's friend are not mentioned.'

not without a dowry as my opponent is always saying: Cf. on 'with a dowry of 20 minas', §3. The alleged absence of a dowry might imply that there was no legal marriage, but it is more likely that, by claiming that the speaker's sister had been given to Menecles without a dowry, Menecles's brother was 'trying to suggest that the alleged failure to provide a dowry for his sister showed that the speaker was a man of no substance who had foisted himself on Menecles for mercenary reasons' (Harrison, 1968, 49).

we became his relatives: The speaker and his brother cannot claim to be blood relations (*syngeneis*) of Menecles; the term translated here as 'relatives' is *oikeioi*, the derivation of which implies membership of a household or family (*oikos*). The speaker's intention is to emphasize that after Menecles married their sister, he and his brother were no longer merely 'friends' (*philoi*) of Menecles; the marriage made them members of his family in a broader sense, thus giving Menecles a stronger reason to adopt one of them as his son. On the distincton between *syngeneis* (blood relations) and *oikeioi* (family members more generally) cf. on 'no other blood relation', §20.

I want to produce testimony: This is the first of five items of witness testimony produced in this speech (the others are at §§16, 34 (twice) and 37). Each of them is introduced with a formula referring to the written document ('testimony') rather than calling the witnesses in person. Cf. on 'Please call the witnesses', 1.16.

The speaker does not identify the witness(es) who testified on the question of the dowry, but presumably they were members of the family, or the wider community, who were present when his sister was betrothed to Menecles.

6 the right age: The wording is vague: *en hēlikiai* is the standard term for men of military age (18–60); cf., e.g., Dem. 1.28, 4.7, 13,4, 21.95. Those aged 18–21 served as ephebes, undergoing a period of garrison duty, military training, and civic education before they became eligible for active service abroad (*Ath. Pol.* 42.4–5).

From the context, it appears that the campaign in Thrace under Iphicrates (see following note) was the first experience of service abroad for the speaker and his brother, so they were probably in their early 20s. That would be consistent with the fact that the speaker was not yet married (cf. §18).

went abroad with Iphicrates to Thrace: The speaker and his brother apparently fought with a mercenary force led by the famous Athenian general, Iphicrates, in Thrace around 383 BC. Menecles's brother may have tried to use their mercenary status as a slur against the speaker, but he, in response, could justifiably claim credit for service under such a distinguished commander.

saved a little money: This passing reference to the speaker's savings was probably designed to rebut any suggestion from his opponent that he had persuaded Menecles to adopt him because of financial need.

two children: There was a strong expectation that an Athenian marriage would produce children, so the speaker and his brother would have been satisfied that their older sister and her husband had started a family. On the Greek word *paidion* ('child') see on 'his child by his mistress', 4.10.

childless: A childless marriage, on the other hand, would be a cause of concern not only to the husband and wife themselves but also to the wife's kinsmen, who retained some responsibility for her wellbeing. According to Arist. *NE* 8.12.7, children create a bond between their parents, and for that reason childless couples are more likely to divorce.

7 after a month or two: See on 'four or five years later', §4.

praising our sister highly ... his own misfortune was enough: By accepting his own responsibility for the childless marriage, Menecles was trying to ensure that no suspicion of infertility would attach to his wife and reduce her chances of remarriage. Cf. Golden (2015, 138): 'Menecles's portrayal as a kind of fourth-century sensitive male may strike us as too flattering to him and too favorable to the speaker's case to be true, but there was good reason for him to behave tactfully, at least in public.'

worried about his own advancing age and childlessness: The emotive language was no doubt intended to elicit the judges' sympathy for Menecles. His concern about a childless old age also provides a plausible motive for adoption, paving the way for his later decision to adopt the speaker. (Cf. on 'how he could end his childlessness', §10.)

his own misfortune was enough: These words are followed in the manuscripts by a sentence that was obviously added later (probably a marginal comment mistakenly incorporated into the text by a scribe): 'And it is clear from these words that he loved her when he divorced her, since no-one makes supplications on behalf of someone he hates'. Isaeus never explicitly says that Menecles loved his wife, and that may well have been a deliberate strategy to avoid any suggestion that the prosecutor's allegation of female influence could have been true. Cf. Edwards (2007, 30): 'Given … that the prosecution were claiming the undue influence of the wife in the adoption, there is also a businesslike and rational tone to the narrative: three marriages and an adoption are arranged with the minimum of fuss, and there is no mention of Menecles and his wife being in love.'

8 giving her to another husband, with his blessing: Divorce was readily available in classical Athens, with no inherent stigma, either by consent or at the instigation of husband or wife. It appears to have been quite frequent, but the number of cases may be overrepresented in the sources. (Cf. Todd, 1993, 214–15.)

Isaeus is careful to present a scenario in which neither party was at fault and Menecles, in particular, had behaved irreproachably. 'Voluntary dissolution of marriage might arise from agreement to separate between the husband and wife. Isaios' second speech contains a pretty picture of such an agreement…' (Harrison, 1968, 39). Cf. Kapparis (2021, 161): 'Menekles is presented as a caring husband who loves his wife and wants the best for her. That is why, on his own initiative, he proposes to her brothers that she should be given in marriage to another man with his blessing.'

we would do whatever she agreed: The speaker and his brother showed respect for their sister by insisting that Menecles must not divorce her without her agreement, but she has no more than a minor role in the narrative.

9 resisted his suggestion ... with difficulty persuaded: Although not entirely without a mind of her own, the woman comes across as largely passive: complying, however reluctantly, with her husband's wishes. Notably, she is presented here as the object of persuasion, not the agent as the speaker's opponent undoubtedly portrayed her. (On portrayals of women by the Attic orators as 'the dutiful wife and mother', see Kapparis, 2021, 157–64.)

It is noticeable that Isaeus never presents the narrative from the woman's point of view, or uses her as a source of information about the events he described. Although women were not allowed to testify formally as witnesses in the Athenian courts, they often had information of potential relevance to litigation, especially about household matters. In such a case a litigant could invite the woman's husband or other relative to testify about what she had told him (see, e.g., Isae. 9,19, where a witness is identified as 'the husband of Astyphilus's aunt') or the litigant himself could simply refer in his speech to information given to him by a woman. (On the use of information provided by women in Athenian litigation, cf. Just, 1989, 33–39.) In this case, the marginalization of the woman may have been a deliberate strategy to make the judges think that she would not have been assertive enough to persuade Menecles to adopt her brother against his will.

with the passage of time: See on 'four or five years later', §4.

And so we gave her in marriage: It seems clear from the context that 'we' refers to the speaker and his brother, not including Menecles, so it was the woman's brothers, not her first husband, who formally betrothed her to the second husband. But Kapparis (2021, 182–83) finds the passage unclear as to who actually conducted the betrothal, leaving open the question 'whether a husband, as the woman's current *kyrios*, had the right to give her in marriage to another man'. In any event, as Kapparis rightly points out, there is insufficient evidence of the husband's legal rights in Menecles's situation: who conducted the betrothal may have been a matter of choice within the family, and in this case it was important to demonstrate that Menecles and his brothers-in-law were acting in harmony.

Elius of Sphettus: Sphettus was a rural deme, south-east of the city of Athens, with five representatives on the Athenian Boule. Again (cf. on 'Eponymus of Acharnae', §3) the demotic confers a precise legal identity on the person in question; as Brock (2020, 17) points out, demotics are commonly specified by forensic speakers in the context of marriage. Cf. Isae. 5.5, 26; 7.18; 8.8; 10.4; Lys. 19.15–16; Dem. 27.56, 29.48 (all cited by Brock). Elius is not mentioned again in the speech, so it is impossible to know whether he would have been available to testify at the trial.

handed over the dowry to him: When an Athenian marriage ended in divorce, the husband was required by law to surrender the dowry he had received with his wife. Isaeus's account may be idealized, but cf. Todd (1993, 215 n.17): 'Cases [of divorce] like Isai. 2.9, where there is amicable agreement within the family, may have been more common in reality than in the sources; and one function of the dowry was to moderate the behaviour of the parties in circumstances which might lead to divorce.'

having acquired a share in the lease of the estate of Nicias's children: As discussed by Wyse (1904), *ad loc.*, this parenthetical clause is inserted to explain how Menecles was able to find the value of the dowry so quickly. It seems to have been common practice, although it was not compulsory, for an orphan's estate to be leased, either on the instructions of the father or at the discretion of the guardian. (On the appointment of guardians for orphaned children, see on 'Our uncle Deinias...' 1.9, and on the leasing of orphans' estates, see on 'asked the archon to lease the estates of the 'orphans', 6.36.) Modern scholars have often assumed that Menecles himself was the guardian of Nicias's orphaned children (Forster, 1927, 38; Harrison, 1968, 291; Edwards, 2007, 29; Cudjoe, 2010, 237), but that was not necessarily the case. In the absence of positive evidence either way, what seems more likely is that when the archon, at the request of the guardian(s), offered the lease of the estate at a public auction (see on 6.36 for the procedure) Menecles was one of the successful bidders. It appears that his share of the property was in cash (cf. §§28, 34, discussed by Schulthess, 1886, 140), so the arrangement was in effect a secured loan, repayable with interest (§28) rather than a lease on part of the orphans' landed property. Cf. Harris (2006a, 216).

the clothing she had brought with her to his house and her jewellery: A woman's personal possessions were not part of her dowry, and there was no legal obligation on the husband to return them to her if the marriage ended. The fact that Menecles did so is another indication that the divorce was amicable. Cf. Kamen (2000) *ad loc.*

10–18. The adoption (narrative and testimony)

The first stage of an Athenian adoption *inter vivos* was a private agreement between the parties (§§11–12). Next, the adoptive father would complete the legal formalities by introducing his new son to his phratry and enrolling him in his deme (§14), following the same procedures as for the recognition of a natural legitimate son. In this case, the fact that Menecles had carried out these formalities was not disputed; the issue was whether he was of sound mind and not acting under the influence of a woman (his ex-wife) when he did so. So Isaeus is careful to introduce the facts of the adoption by explaining why Menecles wanted to adopt a son, and why he chose the speaker in particular.

10 when some time had passed: See on 'four or five years later', §4.

how he could stop being childless: The theme of childlessness is resumed, now as an explicit motive for adoption. (Cf. on 'worried about his own advancing age and childlessness', §7.)

look after him in old age: A law of Solon (Leão and Rhodes, 2016, frr. 55a–57b) placed an obligation on Athenians to provide care and support for their elderly parents. Presumably this applied to a son adopted *inter vivos*, as well as to a natural legitimate son. In any event, irrespective of any legal obligation, the speaker clearly wants to emphasize his filial relationship with Menecles. Cf. Rubinstein (1993, 66): '…it is clear from the description given by Menekles' adopted son of his own adoption that ideally an adoption *inter vivos* should be a faithful imitation of a biological father-son relationship, even on an emotional level.'

Isaeus does not explicitly mention the need for help with his financial affairs as a reason for Menecles to adopt a son. Menecles's brother had probably accused the speaker of *mis*managing Menecles's affairs, so, rather than rebut the allegation directly, Isaeus may have preferred to deflect attention from it by concentrating on other factors.

bury him after his death: The conduct of his father's funeral was another duty normally expected of a legitimate son, although it was not a legal requirement. On the evidentiary significance of the burial in contested inheritance cases, see introductory note to 4.18–26.

customary rites: The 'customary rites' carried out by the speaker after Menecles's death are described in more detail at §36.

only one son: The speaker needs to explain why Menecles did not adopt his brother's son, who (as his closest relative through a male line) would have been the obvious choice. It was generally accepted that at least one son should be left behind to inherit his natural father's estate and continue his *oikos*. So, although there was nothing in the law to prevent the adoption of an only son, this is an argument that would have carried some weight with the judges.

leave him without male children: Lit. 'make him childless (*apais*) of male children'. This implies that Menecles's brother had a daughter, or daughters (cf. on 'children of his own', §23), in which case he could have allowed his only son to be adopted and ensured his own succession by adopting a daughter's son. So it is possible that he had in fact offered to let Menecles adopt his son, and that Menecles (or Isaeus on his behalf) claimed the moral high ground for declining the offer. Cf. Kamen (2000) *ad loc.*: 'The speaker seems to be implying, by comparison, that the prosecutor had no such qualms about making his brother *apais*; the two brothers' morals are contrasted.'

11 no-one more closely related to him than we were: While they were not blood relations, Menecles and the speaker had become 'family' when Menecles married the speaker's sister (see on 'we became his relatives' §5), and the speaker now aims to give the impression that he and his brother were still part of Menecles's family. (Cf. Roussel, 1926, 39, n.2.) Legally. their relationship no longer existed after the divorce, but the friendship between Menecles and the speaker's family had started before his marriage, and there is no reason why it could not have continued after his divorce.

He spoke to us: According to Isaeus's narrative it was Menecles himself (not his ex-wife or the speaker) who initiated the adoption process by opening a discussion with the sons of his friend Eponymus.

'I want to adopt one of you,' he said: This brief dialogue between Menecles and the speaker's brother is one of the rare examples of direct speech in Isaeus's work. (The others are 6. 23 and 8.24.) It is unlikely that the speaker remembered exactly what was said when Menecles asked to adopt one of the brothers, but the device adds vividness and plausibility to his narrative. (Cf. Denommé, 1974, 135: 'Présenté sur ce ton, l'argument acquiert une telle vivacité qu'il cause une large brèche dans la thèse du défendeur'.) As discussed in the introduction to this speech (p. 73) it is noticeable that the private agreement between Menecles and the speaker is not supported by witness testimony.

12 both his age and his loneliness: Despite the implication that Menecles was already an old man, it is not clear exactly how old he was when he adopted the speaker. Since he lived for another 23 years (§15), he was most probably in his 60s, although it is not impossible that he was over 70. (Cf. 6.18, where Euctemon is said to have lived for 96 years.)

someone to look after him: The verb translated as 'look after' (*therapeusontos*) implies personal care rather than household management. (Cf. on 'look after him in old age', §10.)

often away from home: The speaker does not explain his brother's frequent absences from home, but the most likely reasons are either military service or trade. We are not told whether the brother was older or younger than the speaker, or whether he was married, either at the time of the adoption or later.

your affairs as well as mine: It is implied that the speaker was already carrying out business on behalf of his brother while the latter was away from Athens, and would continue to do so after Menecles adopted him. Nothing more is said about the arrangement between the brothers, but Cox (1998, 151) cites this as an example of the continuing 'influence of the paternal *oikos* on an individual adopted out'.

that is how he adopted me: An adoption *inter vivos* was, for practical purposes, effective once the private agreement had been concluded, and the adoptee could take up residence in his new father's house and assume the duties of a son (cf. Isae. 7.15). It might then be several months before the adoptive father had the opportunity to complete the legal formalities of the adoption (see on 'introduced me to his phratry' and 'enrolled me with his demesmen', §14). Rubinstein (1993, 34) argues 'that it was the public phase, that is, the enrolment of the adoptee in the phratry and deme of his adoptive father, which constituted the actual procedure of the adoption'.

13 the law that allows a man to dispose of his property as he wishes, provided he has no legitimate sons: An allusion to the Solonian law on wills cited at [Dem.] 46.14 (Leão and Rhodes, 2016: fr. 49a), making it clear that this law was interpreted in the fourth century as the authority for adoption *inter vivos* as well as testamentary adoption.

The legislator, gentlemen … their only comfort in life: With a typically tendentious appeal to 'the intention of the legislator', the speaker seeks to add authority to his own interpretation of the law, and to associate the judges with it by addressing them directly. In fact, the wording of the law is vague, and its original scope and intention are unclear. But adoption *inter vivos* was probably a later development, and it is more likely that Solon was concerned with the provision of an heir to inherit a childless Athenian's estate than with the personal wellbeing of the adoptive father.

14 not, gentlemen, by writing a will in anticipation of his death: The wording seems to imply that an adoption *inter vivos* was in some way preferable or superior to testamentary adoption. The underlying point (made more explicitly at Isae. 7.1–2) is that the validity of a will was less easy to prove, and therefore more readily open to challenge, than that of an adoption completed by the adoptive father himself during his lifetime. The argument is of course tendentious, but it may have been the case that adoptions *inter vivos* were less frequently challenged than testamentary adoptions, because any objections should have come to light in the course of the formal proceedings in the phratry and deme.

introduced me to his phratry: Membership of a phratry, one of a number of Athenian kinship groups, was hereditary. After the reforms of Cleisthenes, under which deme membership became the essential qualification for Athenian citizenship, membership of a phratry was no longer compulsory; but in practice it seems to have remained more or less universal, and it was still used as evidence of legitimate birth or citizenship. A male Athenian was probably introduced to his father's phratry on two occasions: first in infancy or early childhood and then during adolescence. (Cf. on 'the sacrificial victim', 6.22, and, for discussion of the evidence, see Lambert, 1993, 161–62.) Since introduction into the adoptive father's phratry was one of the formalities of an adoption *inter vivos*, witness testimony would be essential in the event of a dispute about the adoption. (Cf. on 'I will produce phratry members...', §16.) An adoptive son was presumably introduced to his new father's phratry at the *koureion*, which was celebrated annually at the festival of Apaturia in the month of Pyanepsion (October/November). (Cf. on 'the sacrificial victim', 6.22.)

my opponents: Here and elsewhere in the speech (§§15, 17, 30, 31, 38, 39, 40), the plural indicates that the speaker identifies Menecles's nephew as well as his brother as an opponent.

enrolled me with his demesmen: Enrolment in the adoptive father's deme completed the legal procedure of an adoption. Individual demes may have had different arrangements, but it appears that new members were normally admitted at the annual meeting, probably at the beginning of the year, at which the deme officials were appointed. On the timing and regularity of deme assemblies, see Whitehead (1986, 90–92).

***orgeones*:** Members of a religious association to which Menecles belonged, probably a subdivision of his phratry. The etymology suggests that *orgeones* were celebrants of *orgia* (rites). Membership of such associations was neither compulsory nor universal, but it was hereditary, so it would have been natural for an adopted son to become a member of his adoptive father's association. Members who were present at the introduction could, in the event of a dispute, be used as witnesses alongside phratry members and demesmen (cf. §16.) For further details and discussion, see Parker (1996, 109–11).

15 made no suggestion that he was not in his right mind: When Menecles introduced his adopted son to his phratry, it would have been open to any of the members (including his brother and nephew) to object that the adoption was not compliant with the law. If that had happened, the sacrificial victims would have been withdrawn from the altar, and the introduction could not have proceeded unless the dispute was resolved. (Cf. 6.22.)

If the speaker's account of his introduction to Menecles's phratry was true, the fact that Menecles's brother and nephew did not object would be a significant point in his favour. It is possible, however, that the brother had offered a different account, perhaps saying that he and his son had had been away from Athens at the relevant time or that they had misgivings about the validity of the adoption but had reluctantly agreed to accept it. (Cf, 6.22–24 where, according to the speaker, Euctemon succeeded at the second attempt in introducing Alce's son to his phratry, after his son Philoctemon, who had initially objected, was persuaded by other family members to acquiesce.)

insult him: The verb translated as 'insult' (*hybrizein*) is a strong one, implying in some circumstances an aggravated physical assault but here a contemptuous attack on Menecles's honour. The precise scope of *hybris* in classical Greek has been much discussed by modern scholars, e.g. MacDowell (1976), Fisher (1990), Cairns (1996).

leave his family without heirs: Literally 'make his house (Greek *oikos*) empty'. If a man died leaving no male heir, his 'house' became 'empty' in the sense that his line of descent died out and his property went to his collateral relatives (next of kin), who, unlike direct descendants, would not necessarily feel obliged to conduct the commemorative rituals for their dead kinsman. The fear of 'leaving an empty house' is cited by speakers in some inheritance cases as a motive for adopting a son; cf Isae. 6.5 and, especially, 7.29 (with Griffith-Williams, 2013, *ad loc.*): 'All men who are about to die take precautions to avoid leaving their houses empty, and to ensure that there will be someone to perform the sacrifices and customary rituals for them. So even if they die childless, they at least adopt children and leave them behind.' In this case (§§15 and 35) the 'empty house' topos is not used as a motive for Menecles's decision to adopt a son (cf. §10) but as a reproach to the speaker's opponent for his challenge to the adoption. (Cf. Isoc. 19.3, where the speaker makes a similar accusation against his opponent.) This is likely to have had a strong emotional impact on the judges; for wider discussion, see Griffith-Williams (2012, 146–48).

23 years: In a speech where the passage of time is normally expressed in vague terms (see on 'four or five years later', §4) it is striking that Isaeus tells us precisely how long Menecles lived after the adoption. It was almost certainly exceptional for an Athenian to live as long as this after adopting a son *inter vivos*, as the speaker's presentation through negation implies ('not just a year or two [as one might have expected]'), but his claims about the success of the adoption, and public approval of it, would have been impossible to prove. Once the formalities of introduction to the phratry and enrolment in the deme were complete, there was no opportunity for a legal challenge to an adoption *inter vivos* until after the adoptive father's death.

never regretted what he had done: Since Menecles was not available to give his own account of his relationship with the speaker, we may question whether he would have agreed with this. In Menander's *Samia* the misunderstandings between Demeas and his adopted son, Moschion, are no doubt contrived and exaggerated for comic effect, but the underlying psychology, with the father's anger and disappointment and the son's feelings of guilt, may still be an accurate reflection of real life. Moreover, as Sommerstein (2013, 15) points out, an adopted son in Athens would normally be the father's only (legitimate) son, and thus his only hope of care in old age and commemoration after his death, with the result that the father would be 'more than usually reluctant to believe any serious ill of his son'. So, if Menecles did have any doubts or regrets about the adoption, he might have been unwilling to admit them.

16 I will produce phratry members, *orgeones* and demesmen as witnesses: The most credible witnesses to the formalities of an adoption would be members of the adoptive father's phratry and deme who were present when he introduced his adopted son. (For *orgeones*, see on '*orgeones*', §14.) On 'deme solidarity' and the role of demesmen as witnesses in litigation, see Brock (2020, 21). Elsewhere in the speech, witnesses are either not identified at all (§5) or identified only as 'those who were present' (§33) or 'those who know the facts' (§37).

the law itself: Athenian litigants sometimes give special emphasis to the laws they cite, implying that their evidential value is superior to that of other documentary evidence. (Cf. Isae. 8.30, 45 with Griffith-Williams, 2013, *ad loc.*, and Rubinstein, 2018, 175–76.) But in this case, where the issue was not whether Menecles was entitled to adopt a son but whether he did so under the influence of a woman, the speaker cannot support his claim by reference to the law.

Please read these witness statements: As at §§34 and 37, the formula used to introduce this testimony makes it clear that the witnesses' written statements were read out in court by the clerk. On the transition from oral to written testimony in the Athenian courts, see on 1.1.

17 the law itself: The speaker repeats his emphatic reference to the text of the law as the most authoritative evidence (cf. on 'the law itself', §16).

testified to you that he did adopt: Even though the formalities of the adoption were not contested, it was essential for the speaker to establish, as the basis of his legal claim, that Menecles had introduced him to his phratry

Oration 2 107

and enrolled him in his deme as his adopted son. So, naturally enough, he places great emphasis on the testimony he has produced from those who witnessed these formalities.

telling the truth: We do not know the precise wording of the *diamartyria* submitted by Philonides, but if it followed the standard formula it is unlikely to have included any details about the adoption. A plausible reconstruction would be: 'Philonides testifies that the estate of Menecles is not adjudicable to [Menecles's brother] because Menecles left a legitimate son'. (Cf. Griffith-Williams, 2018, 96.) So, with the claim that Philonides was 'telling the truth', Isaeus is trying to present the adoption as a *fait accompli*, prejudging the disputed issues which he addresses later (on which see the following note.)

cannot deny the facts of the adoption: It is clear that Menecles's brother did not deny the fact that Menecles had indeed introduced the speaker to his phratry and enrolled him in his deme as his adopted son; what was in dispute was whether Menecles was in his right mind and acting independently of his ex-wife when he carried out these formalities..

18   After these events: Another vague expression of time; see on 'four or five years later', §4.

started to think about a wife for me: Isaeus completes his idealized account of the adoption with a detail showing that the father-son relationship between Menecles and the speaker was mutual: not only did the speaker assume the normal duties of a legitimate son, but Menecles took on the role of a natural father in arranging a marriage for him. Athenian men did not normally marry before the age of 30, so the speaker was probably still in his 20s when Menecles adopted him, and middle-aged by the time of the latter's death.

the daughter of Philonides: For the Athenian conventions on identifying women in forensic speeches, see on 'the daughter of Meixiades of Cephisia', 6.10.

as if he had been my own father: A harmonious relationship between adoptive father and adopted son was 'Not an outcome to be taken for granted; rather, a success worth stressing' (Golden, 2015, 120). Demeas, while expressing his disappointment in Moschion, clearly did not expect the same standard of behavious as he would have wanted from a natural son (Men. *Sam.* 342–347). For other indications that Athenians did not always show the same affection and loyalty to an adoptive father as to a natural parent, see, e.g. [Dem.] 60.4, Lyc. 1.48.

he praised us to all his fellow demesmen: Cf. Whitehead (1986, 228):

'Self-evidently, it was advisable to cultivate the esteem and approval of one's fellow demesmen as a whole. Such approval is claimed, for instance, by the speaker in Isaeus 2, for his (and his wife's) solicitous care of his adoptive father Menekles both before (2.18) and after (2.36) the latter's death.' It is noticeable, however, that the speaker brings no witness testimony from any of the demesmen in support of this claim.

Before his adoption the speaker was a member of the deme Acharnae (§3); he does not specify the deme to which Menecles belonged, but see on 'Eponymus of Acharnae, §3 and 'at the altar of Aphrodite at Cephale', §31.

19–26. The validity of the adoption (argumentation)
In this part of the speech Isaeus uses arguments from probability to support his client's version of events. First, although he cannot prove that Menecles's former wife played no part in persuading him to adopt her brother, he tries to show how unlikely it is that she would have done so. In a passage notable for its use of irony and rhetorical questions (§§21–26), he then turns the argument against his client's opponent, Menecles's brother, concluding that it is unreasonable for the brother to challenge the adoption and that he is acting purely out of spite. This leads neatly into the following sections of narrative (§§27–34) about the quarrel between Menecles and his brother.

19 easy for you to judge: The speaker tries to gloss over the difficulty of establishing Menecles's state of mind at the time of the adoption. The weakness of his argumentation in §§19–20 is apparent to a modern reader who has time to reflect on it and check the printed text of the speech. It may, however, have been more persuasive to an audience who simply heard the speech once (and in any event it is impossible to prove a negative, so Isaeus's client was not necessarily in the wrong).

not insane or persuaded by a woman: Cf. on 'insane or persuaded by a woman', §1. Isaeus uses the negation (repeated at §§20 and 38) to rebut the allegation made by the speaker's opponent. (On Isaeus's use of 'presentation through negation', see Griffith-Williams, 2013, 59–60.)

married long before the adoption: Once again (cf. on 'four or five years later', §4) the chronology is imprecise, and even if the speaker's sister did have two sons by her second husband it must be open to question whether they had been married long enough to produce them before the adoption. (Cf. Wyse, 1904, 252.) As we learnt from §10, Menecles started to think about adoption 'when some time had passed' after his former wife's remarriage, but it seems unlikely that he would have waited long enough for her to

Oration 2 109

have had two children – probably at least two years, and much longer, if he wanted to adopt an adult (see following note).

since she had two: The reasoning may have appeared persuasive to the judges: Menecles's ex-wife had two sons by her second husband, so they (unlike Menecles's brother, who had only one son) could easily have let Menecles adopt one of them. But it is unclear how old these sons were at the time of the adoption, and if, as seems likely, they were still children, they would have been unable to give Menecles the same care and support that he would have expected from an adult son. (On the Athenians' apparent preference for adopting adults rather than children, see on 'his child by his mistress', 4.10.)

20   But, gentlemen ... most of all because of his loneliness: By repeating Menecles's positive reasons for adopting the speaker, Isaeus probably hoped to deflect the judges' attention from the weakness of the argument in §19. Cf. on 'both his age and his loneliness', §12. Loneliness was a plausible reason for someone in Menecles's circumstances to adopt a son, but it does not explain why he chose the speaker.

his goodwill towards my father: See on 'the friendship between him and our father', §4.

no other blood relation: The speaker said that he and his brother became Menecles's 'relatives' (Gk. *oikeioi*) when their sister married Menecles (see on 'we became his relatives', §5), but he has never claimed himself to be a blood relation (Gk. *suggenēs*) of Menecles. So this must mean 'no other ... apart from his brother'.

not insane or persuaded by a woman: The repetition emphasizes the speaker's rebuttal of his opponent's allegation (cf. §§19 and 38.)

unless indeed that is how my opponent wants to describe his loneliness and childlessness: The speaker seeks to ridicule his opponent with this ironic suggestion. For Isaeus's use of irony, cf. on 'they are now treating us so well', §33.

21   who claims to be of sound mind: Menecles's brother has claimed that Menecles was not of sound mind when he adopted the speaker. Now, the speaker insinuates that the brother himself cannot be in his right mind if he thinks that Menecles should have adopted someone more closely related to him.

My opponent's son, perhaps?: The ironic tone continues. The speaker has already explained (§10) that Menecles would have considered it 'shameful' to adopt his brother's only son. Now, with the first of two ironic rhetorical questions, he turns the argument against Menecles's brother: he was surely not so materialistic that he would have given up the benefits of having a son in order to take possession of Menecles's property.

made himself childless: 'Childless' (Gk. *apais*) needs to be understood in this context as 'without a son'. Cf. on 'leave him without male offspring', §10 and 'children of his own', §23.)

Or the son of his sister or his male or female cousin? Another rhetorical question gives further emphasis to the speaker's point that Menecles had no blood relations who could have given him a son for adoption.

22 as my opponent thinks he should have done: This is a highly tendentious presentation of the opponent's point of view. In fact, Menecles's brother had almost certainly said that he did *not* want Menecles to grow old without a son, and so had offered him his own son for adoption.

more closely related to him: See on 'no-one more closely related to him than we were', §11.

no other blood relations but these: That is, apart from his brother and nephew (cf. on 'no other blood relation', §20.)

23 a matter of spite: If it was true that the material value of Menecles's remaining estate was very small, it would not have been credible for the speaker to accuse his opponent of acting out of greed. (Cf. Wyse, 1904, 254.) Instead, the motivation he attributes to Menecles's brother is *phthonos*, often best translated as 'envy' but with a wider semantic range that also encompasses 'spite' or 'grudging'. Sanders (2014, 84) comments on Isae. 2. 23–27: 'This *phthonos* is very close to Aristotle's definition. The uncle [i.e. Menecles's brother] is not motivated by obtaining a desired good, as he might be with covetousness or greed, since the amount of money in question is (for him) negligible. His desire is solely to deprive the hated nephew, and a focus on depriving someone else rather than one's own gain is *phthonos*. By focusing so closely on this motivation, the speaker turns the argument from one about rightful or wrongful possession between two equal appellants, into a dispute where one party is motivated solely by base character. This should help to win over the jury to his, the supposedly better man's, side.' I would modify Sanders's analysis to the extent that I think the *phthonos* attributed to Menecles's brother was directed primarily against Menecles himself: the brother (allegedly) wanted to deprive Menecles of his adopted son, and consequently to deprive the adopted son of the inheritance.

children of his own: The plural gives another indication that Menecles's brother had at least one daughter, as well as a son. Cf. on 'leave him without male offspring', §10.

obviously blaming Menecles for being childless and unfortunate: On

Isaeus's use of irony to ridicule the speaker's opponent, see on 'they are now treating us so well' §33.

24 All other men, Greeks and foreigners, approve of this law about adoption: Cf. Isoc. 19.50, where the speaker makes a similar point. According to Carey (1996, 43): 'Although the laws of Athens carry great authority, it appears that they gain still more authority if they can be shown to be in agreement with laws elsewhere in Greece, and even beyond. This is the case, for instance, with Isaios' discussion of the laws of adoption at 2.24; the same law, allowing a man without children to adopt an heir, is according to Isaios observed not only throughout Greece but also among barbarians; i.e. this is a truly universal law.' Cf. Harris (2013b, 106): 'When orators refer to a general rule that most Greeks follow, this rule is always in accord with the laws of Athens.'

begrudged: The Greek verb is *ephthonēsen*, here more appropriately translated as 'begrudged' rather than 'envied'. (See on 'a matter of spite', §23.)

25 insane and persuaded by a woman: See on 'insane or persuaded by a woman', §1.

26 Isn't it clear, then, that he is speaking cruelly?: Isaeus deploys another rhetorical question to ridicule the opponent's argument.

he is the one who is insane: Cf. on 'who claims to be of sound mind', §21; the speaker now makes explicit his insinuation that it is Menecles's brother, not Menecles himself, who is not in his right mind. The allegation is repeated at §40 (see on 'but rather this man now').

27–37. The dispute between Menecles and his brother (narrative and testimony)

Isaeus moves away from the facts of the adoption and discussion about its legal validity to a new section of narrative describing how Menecles and his brother fell out over a property transaction at some unspecified time after Menecles's adoption of the speaker. Isaeus's account is inevitably one-sided and incomplete, and the details are not entirely clear, so it is not surprising that scholars have found this section of the speech unsatisfactory as a source of information on Athenian property law and arbitration procedure. For example, Cudjoe (2010, 230) finds §§28–29 'incoherent and confusing' on the issue of pledging land as security for a lease. It would, however, be a mistake to dismiss the passage as no more than an irrelevant interpolation into the narrative: if Menecles's brother had accused the speaker of seeking the adoption for his own gain and then squandering Menecles's property (as discussed in the introduction to this speech, pp. 68–70), then this part of Isaeus's speech makes perfect sense as a rebuttal of these allegations, as well as an attempt to undermine the prosecutor's case by suggesting that his real motivation in claiming the estate was malice or spite. The true significance of the passage, in other words, lies not in the 'facts' of the dispute between Menecles and his brother but in the evidence it provides of the brother's hostility towards Menecles and the speaker.

27 surely he is a spiteful person?: Literally 'how is he not spiteful ?'(Gk. *phthoneros*; cf. on 'a matter of spite', §23). An Athenian audience would have taken this as an allegation of bad character, not merely a claim that Menecles's brother had acted out of *phthonos* on one or more specific occasions. As Sanders (2014, 75) explains Aristotle's theory of *phthonos* and its relevance to Attic oratory: 'the fact that *phthonos* is not so much reified as a bad emotion (as is 'envy'), but rather reflects back on the character of the person feeling it, requires us to consider the motivations of an accusation of *phthonos*: unlike an accusation of 'envy', it will not merely be questioning the moral motivation of someone at a particular moment, but will be branding them as someone morally base at all times and in all aspects. It is a statement about their character, and it will be very important to bear this in mind when we consider accusations and denials in the oratorical corpus that an opponent is/was motivated by *phthonos*.'

is he not clearly exposed as being shameless?: The second of two rhetorical questions in this section directed at the opponent's character rather than his argument. By making his point in the form of a question rather than a direct statement, the speaker invites the judges to agree with his conclusion.

28 When the money was due to be paid back to the orphan: The 'orphan' was the oldest of the children of Nicias, first mentioned at §9, to whom his paternal estate had to be restored by his guardian(s) when he came of age.

Menecles did not have the resources available: Menecles's brother had probably claimed that this was due to the speaker's extravagance in using up his adoptive father's assets for his own purposes.

interest had been accumulating: As explained by Wyse (1904), *ad loc.*, this does not necessarily imply that Menecles had defaulted on interest payments. It is possible that he had leased the orphan's property on condition that the full amount would be repaid, together with the accumulated interest, when the lease expired.

over a long period: Once again, Isaeus is vague about chronology, so it is impossible to tell how much time had elapsed between Menecles's acquisition of the lease and its expiry. By implication, however, it must have been at least several years – possibly as long as 15 years if the orphan was very young at the time of Nicias's death.

tried to sell the land: In classical Athens public notice of an intended transfer of land had to be given in writing to a public official at least 60 days in advance, to ensure that the land was not wrongfully sold. (Harrison, 1968, 305-08).

tried to prevent the land from being sold: Menecles's brother would have been entitled to object to the sale if he had some legal interest in the property in question, but Isaeus, unsurprisingly, does not say what this was. Perhaps the land Menecles wanted to sell was part of the inheritance he and his brother had received from their father, but which they had not yet divided. Cf. Cudjoe (2010, 231): 'It is most probable that Menekles' brother prevented him from putting up the land for sale because it was their patrimony that they were holding in common. …Their joint-ownership of the land is confirmed by the statement that Menekles' brother claimed a part of the property from him, though he had never previously made any such claim.' Another possible scenario, more consistent with the speaker's version of events, is that they *had* divided their paternal estate, and the land Menecles wanted to sell was part of his own share, but his brother tried to prevent the sale because he wanted it for himself.

subject to seizure: Cf. Harris (2006a, 216): 'There is only one way to explain the statement that the land would be subject to seizure if the money was not paid to the orphans: the land had been pledged as security for the money Menecles had reeived from the orphans.'

29 Philippus of Pithus: Pithus was a rural deme north-east of Athens contributing two or three members to the Boule. According to Brock (2020, 17) demotics are commonly used in connection with financial or commercial transactions: 'one can surmise that the underlying agenda is to imply both the reality and the regularity of the contract, loan, sale, mortgage, or whatever'.

brought a legal action against his brother for restraint of sale: According to Harrison (1968, 141) 'It is probable that the procedure known as *aporrēsis* was available to a joint owner who wished to interdict the sale or hypothecation of joint property.' Harrison argues that such a rule is not definitively attested by Isae. 2.29, because it is not certain that Menecles and his brother were joint owners of the property in question, but it may be 'indirectly deduced from Plaut. *Merc.* 451ff. which undoubtedly gives Athenian law.'

giving him a talent and seven minas from the price of the land: Menecles had sold the land for 70 minas (i.e. a talent and ten minas), so he was left with only three minas after repaying the orphan.

we agreed to submit the dispute for arbitration: The Athenian legal system offered two forms of arbitration (public and private) which enabled litigants to settle their disputes without the expense and possible delay associated with a full trial. Some types of cases could be referred by the authorities to a public arbitrator, while litigants in any case could choose to appoint private arbitrators. MacDowell (1978, 203–11) gives a succinct account of both systems. Private arbitration, as in this case, was voluntary, but once the parties had agreed to submit their dispute to abitration, the decision of the arbitrator(s) was binding and the case could not proceed to court. All references to arbitration in the Attic orators have been collected and annotated by Roebuck (2001) chapters 10 and 11, but his analysis is superficial and unreliable.

my opponent's brother-in-law and our friends: As Brock (2020, 16) points out, 'those who act as arbitrators are often assigned a demotic' (e.g. Isoc. 18.10, [Dem.] 33.14. It is, therefore, striking that the arbitrators in this case are not identified by name at all, even though others with a more peripheral role in the narrative are given names and demotics (Elius of Sphettus, §9, Philippus of Pithus, §29). Perhaps Isaeus decided not to identify the arbitrators as part of a strategy to play down the significance of their decision, which did not go in favour of his client.

so that no-one could ever say I was covetous and stirring up enmity between two men who were brothers: This is perhaps the strongest indication that the speaker's opponent accused him of exploiting Menecles for his own financial benefit. The speaker would have had no legal standing in an action brought by Menecles against his brother, but would naturally be expected to support his adoptive father in the litigation.

30 because they did not want to quarrel with either us or our opponents: According to Harris (2018, 222): 'One of the advantages of private arbitration was that the parties could appoint arbitrators who already had some knowledge of the case, but on the other hand the arbitrators might be reluctant to impose a decision that would offend litigants who were their friends or relatives.' The plural 'us or our opponents' aligns Menecles and the speaker against Menecles's brother and nephew. (Cf. on 'my opponents', §14.)

what was most expedient for everyone: The opportunity for a compromise solution, which would not have been possible if the case had gone to court, was one of the advantages of private arbitration. Cf. Harris (2018, 216–18).

31 After swearing an oath to us: The first step in a private arbitration would normally be an attempt to reconcile the opposing litigants. If reconciliation was impossible, the arbitrators would then invite the litigants to swear to abide by their decision. The arbitrators, in turn, would swear an oath and make their decision. Cf. Harris (2018, 214, n.4): 'If the arbitrator did not swear the oath, the decision might not be regarded as valid.'

at the altar of Aphrodite at Cephale: Whitehead (1986, 224, n.6) suggests that this reference to Cephale, one of the Attic demes, is 'the best clue' to the identity of Menecles's deme. (Cf. on 'Eponymus of Acharnae', §3.) Whatever the reason for the choice of this particular location for the arbitrators' oath, this passage is among the evidence showing 'that the sacred space in which an oath was sworn was a significant aspect of the oath and was worth stressing' (Sommerstein and Torrance, 2014, 137).

32 that we must treat one another well in both word and deed: As discussed by Harris (2018, 218) one of the advantages of private arbitration was that the arbitrators' decision (unlike that of a court) aimed not only to resolve the dispute but also to promote good relations between the parties in the future. Cf. Dem. 36.15 (cited by Harris).

33 they are now treating us so well: This is the most striking example in this speech of Isaeus's use of irony to '[add] emphasis to arguments which expose contradictions ... in the behaviour and statements of the other party' (Hatzilambrou, 2018a, 39). Cf. Denommé (1974, 131): 'Isée, donnant libre cours à son aggressivité, excelle à ridiculer l'adversaire et à le diminuer dans l'opinion des juges ... Isée passe même avec aisance du ton ironique au sarcasme acerbe.' Cf. on 'obviously blaming Menecles for being childless and unfortunate', §23.

to make the deceased childless: See on '"to make his deceased brother childless', §1.

throw me ignominiously out of his house: The ambiguity of the Greek word *oikos* ('house') is at play in this variation of the 'empty *oikos*' topos: the speaker accuses his opponents of trying either (literally) to throw him out of Menecles's house, or (figuratively) to eject him from the family. For the topos, cf. on 'leave his family without heirs', §15. On the multiple, and sometimes overlapping, definitions of *oikos*, see MacDowell (1989, 10–11).

I will produce for you as witnesses ... those who were present: On the formulae used to introduce witness testimony in this speech, see on 'I want to produce testimony', §5; and on the identification of the witnesses, see on

'I will produce phratry members, *orgeones* and demesmen as witnesses', §16.

34 Please read these depositions: See on 'please read these witness statements', §16.

stop the water: A water-clock (Gk. *klepsydra*) was used to time the speeches in an Athenian trial, to ensure that speakers did not exceed the limits for a particular type of case. One of the judges was appointed by lot to operate the water-clock, which would be turned off while the clerk read out laws, testimony, and other documents, since these did not count towards the length of the speech. An instruction to 'stop the water' was occasionally added to the speaker's request to the clerk to read the documents; cf. Isae. 3.12, 76. On the time limits for speeches in the Athenian courts, see Harrison (1971, 161–62).

Now please take these depositions: See on 'please read these witness statements', §16.

35 my uncle here: See on 'my uncle', §1. The deictic pronoun *houtosi* ('this man here') indicates that the person referred to was present in court, either as one of the speaker's own supporters or on the opposing side. It was probably accompanied by a gesture towards the man in question.

leaving Menecles's family without heirs: See on 'leave his family without heirs', §15.

36 Philonides here: Again, the deictic pronoun *houtosi* indicates that the speaker's father-in-law, Philonides, was present in court – as one would expect, given that he was formally the defendant in the case.

gave his name to my little boy: According to Greek tradition, a first son was named after his paternal grandfather and the second after the maternal grandfather. On the meaning of *paidion* (in this context, 'little boy') see on 'his child by his mistress', 4.10.

so that his family would not lose the name: Having just accused his opponent of trying to leave Menecles's family without heirs (§35) the speaker now points out that he himself wants to ensure the continuity of the family.

I buried him in an appropriate style: The brief account of the funeral demonstrates that the speaker not only followed the conventions but also fulfilled Menecles's own expectations of an adopted son (cf. on 'bury him after his death', §10).

ninth day ceremony: The period of mourning continued after an Athenian funeral, with more offerings at the grave on the ninth day (*ta enata*, or 'the ninth day ceremony') and further rituals at the end of the mourning period.

all the demesmen praised me: The demesmen's approval would have been a strong point in the speaker's favour, but, again, his claim is apparently not supported by testimony. (Cf. on 'he praised us to all his fellow demesmen', §18, and see the discussion of witness testimony in the introduction to this speech, pp. 71–73.)

37 took away his remaining land: The speaker wants to give the impression that his motive for defending the adoption is not financial, because he has nothing to gain materially from Menecles's estate since most of it has already been taken by Menecles's brother.

wants to leave him childless and without a name: Cf. on 'so that his family would not lose the name', §36.

That's the kind of man he is: The speaker portrays Menecles's brother as a morally bad character, not merely someone who has acted wrongly on specific occasions; cf. on 'surely he is a spiteful person?', §27.

The clerk will read you the testimony: On the formula used to introduce this testimony, see on 'please read these witness statements', §16.

those who know the facts: The identification of Athenian witnesses as 'those who know [the facts]' (*hoi eidotes*) is a strong indication that their function was not merely to support the litigant for whom they testified (as some modern scholars have claimed) but to provide an impartial account of events. (Cf. Isae. 9,20, 29; and, for the scholarly debate, see Griffith-Williams, 2008.)

38–47. Summary and conclusion

In the concluding paragraphs the speaker first gives a tendentious account of his opponents' actions, characterizing Menecles's brother rather then Menecles himself as the one who is insane, then briefly summarizes his own case and makes a conventional appeal to the judges to vote in his favour. The speech ends, as it began, on a religious note (cf. on 'ancestral gods', §1).

38 my opponents themselves: Isaeus's clients sometimes try to enlist their opponents as additional 'witnesses', claiming that their actions have supported the speaker's case. (Cf. Isae. 7.18, 8.14). The argument is clearly tendentious, since the opponents would not have recognized the motivation that the speaker imputes to them.

not in word but in deed: The evidential value of deeds (*erga*) was supposedly greater than that of mere words (*logoi*), but the topos often covers up a lack of more solid evidence. For the use of the topos with reference to the opponent's behaviour, cf. Isae. 3.55 (with Hatzilambrou 2018a, *ad loc.*), 6.12, 7.18, 8.14.

not insane or persuaded by a woman: Again (cf. §§19 and 20) the repetition emphasizes the speaker's rebuttal of his opponent's allegation.

39 why would they have needed to swear to me and receive oaths from me?: The speaker's point is that, by swearing an oath of reconciliation with him, Menecles's brother and nephew have implicitly recognized him as Menecles's son.

40 but rather this man now: The speaker repeats the insinuation that it is Menecles's brother, not Menecles himself, who is insane. (Cf. on 'who claims to be of sound mind', §21, and 'who claims to be of sound mind', §26.)

41 nothing left of it: The speaker is exaggerating; he has already said that he received three minas from the sale of the land and a small house (§35).

42 served as gymnasiarch in his deme: A gymnasiarch was a superintendent of games or athletic contests at festivals. Performance of this function, at the gymnasiarch's personal expense, was one of the liturgies (public services) required of the richest Athenians as a form of taxation. The minimum financial requirement for the liturgical class is uncertain, but it appears to have been at least three talents for the performance of liturgies on behalf of the state and for deme liturgies it was probably still substantial. Cf. Whitehead (1986, 152): 'It may be assumed that only the wealthier demesmen were called on to be liturgists, though the expense entailed must have been considerably less than that of most liturgies for the state.' So by mentioning this, the speaker draws attention both to his own sense of public duty and to the extent of Menecles's wealth before he was 'robbed' of part of it by his brother. On the possible identity of Menecles's deme, see on 'Eponymus of Acharnae', §3 and 'at the altar of Aphrodite at Cephale', §31.

served in all the campaigns ... with his tribe and deme: Having served as a mercenary before he was adopted (§6), the speaker, as Menecles's son, later performed official military service on behalf of the *polis*. The tribe (Gk. *phylē*) was the largest tactical unit of the Athenian army. The words 'in the deme' have been questioned by some editors, as a repetition from earlier in the sentence, and Wyse (1904) *ad loc.* also points out that the deme was not a recognized military unit. Whitehead (1986, 225) provides a plausible defence of the text: 'The speaker is not saying that he had fought in any official subdivision of the Athenian army called (even *un*officially) a 'deme'. He is saying that the men who would verify, from a military standpoint, his wholehearted assumption of the role of adoptive son of Menecles would be those in whose company he had spent the campaign – his fellow tribesmen and his fellow demesmen.'

Like Moschion (Men. *Sam.* 8–19) the speaker aims to show that his conduct as a responsible citizen reflected credit on his adoptive father, whose wealth he used for the benefit of the community. (Moschion, similarly, mentions his performance of a liturgy – in his case as *chorēgos*, or producer at the dramatic festivals – and leadership of his *phylē*.)

43 but wouldn't that seem a strange and ridiculous business…?: By framing his argument in the form of a rhetorical question, the speaker invites the judges to agree with his point of view.

leaving his house without an heir: Cf. on 'leave his family without heirs', §15. Here, in another variation on the topos, the speaker suggests that it would be wrong for him to give up his claim to the estate because that would leave Menecles's house empty.

44 So I beg you all, gentlemen, and beseech and entreat you: Cf. on 'I beg, entreat and beseech…', §2. Here, the speaker heightens the emotional tone of his appeal to the good will of the judges with a direct address in the vocative and three verbs of supplication.

acquit the witness: Philonides, who had testified on the speaker's behalf as the witness in the *diamartyria*, was now the defendant in the *dikē psuedomartyriōn*.

not made just verbally or in a will: Cf. on 'not, gentlemen, by writing a will in anticipation of his death', §14.

45 the laws that permit men without sons to adopt sons: See on 'the law itself', §16.

46 my father's property: By referring to Menecles as his father, the speaker emphasizes his entitlement to the estate.

make the dead man childless and nameless: See on 'to make his deceased brother childless', §1, and 'so that his family would not lose the name', §36.

honour the ancestral cults: Cf. on 'ancestral gods', §1.

perform the annual sacrifices for him: Cf. on 'leave his family without heirs', §15.

47 So, gentlemen: The speaker again addresses the judges directly, to engage their attention to his final appeal for their support.

don't be persuaded: A politer way of saying 'don't be deceived'. Like any other litigant, the speaker himself is of course trying to persuade the judges to accept his version of events, but he sees persuasion as a dangerous weapon when it is used by his opponent.

help both me and the man who is in Hades: Again (cf. §2) the speaker appeals for the judges' help not only on his own behalf but also that of

Menecles. This reference to the deceased as 'the man who is in Hades' (i.e. in the underworld, or home of the dead) is unique in Isaeus's speeches and reinforces the religious tone of the speech.

by the gods and spirits: This addition to the speaker's conventional plea for the goodwill of the judges, which is not found elsewhere in Isaeus, again adds to the religious tone of this speech. According to Serafim (2020, 69) the combination of this invocation of the gods with the subsequent reminder to the judges about the dicastic oath 'arguably aims to instil a fear in the souls of the judges that the omnipresent and omniscient gods were inspecting them'.

vote justly, in accordance with the laws and your oath: At the end of an Athenian trial there was no deliberation or attempt to reach a consensus among the judges; each of whose vote was cast individually and kept secret from the others, and the result was determined by a simple majority. Voting was by means of ballots or 'pebbles' (Greek *psēphoi*, whence the verb *psēphizasthai*, meaning 'to vote') placed into urns. For a detailed account of the system, see Harrison (1971, 164–65).

The dicastic oath, sworn by Athenian judges at the beginning of their term of office, included a promise to judge cases 'in accordance with the laws'. Harrison (1971, 48) suggests a reconstruction of the full text of the oath. For further discussion see Todd (1993, 54–55).

Harris (2013b, 112) cites this passage in support of his contention that 'litigants use the terms law and justice as virtual synonyms and never view the two as in conflict.' Further, 'The message of the Judicial Oath is clear: it bound the judges to vote in accordance with the laws. It is therefore not surprising that when orators mention or allude to the oath, they also mention the laws' (Harris, 2013b, 114).

ISAEUS 4: ON THE ESTATE OF NICOSTRATUS

INTRODUCTION

The speaker of Isaeus 4 says that Nicostratus was a mercenary soldier who died abroad after 11 years away from Athens, leaving an estate worth two talents. He left no direct descendants, and when the news of his death reached Athens his cousins Hagnon and Hagnotheus (sons of his father's brother) claimed the estate as his next of kin, but the amount of money at stake attracted a number of false claimants. Most of these were exposed at an early stage, except for Chariades, a fellow-soldier of Nicostratus, who persisted with his claim that Nicostratus had adopted him in a will. The case eventually came to trial as a *diadikasia* between Hagnon and Hagnotheus on the one hand and Chariades on the other, and Isaeus 4 is a short 'epilogue' or supplementary speech, delivered by a supporting speaker (*synēgoros*) after the main speech by one of the brothers.

According to the *hypothesis* ('argument') to the speech, written in late antiquity and part of the manuscript tradition, Isaeus himself delivered the speech, as a relative of Hagnon and Hagnotheus. As most modern scholars have recognized, this is almost certainly a mistake, based on a misunderstanding of the opening sentence of the speech. If Isaeus was a metic (as discussed in the General Introduction, p. 2) he would not have been entitled to speak in court; and in any event, the visible intervention of a professional speechwriter (a despised occupation in classical Athens) would not have enhanced the claimants' chances of success.[1]

As to the dating of the case, most modern scholars have accepted a textual emendation which would suggest that Nicostratus died in Ace (Akko in modern Israel) in 374 BC. For reasons explained in the commentary (§7), I have followed Wevers (1969) and Edwards (2002

---

1 Cf., e.g., Edwards (2007, 66–67). An alternative view is offered by Avramović (1997, 108–12), who, while acknowledging these objections and accepting that it is impossible to be certain, argues that this was an exceptional case in which Isaeus might well have intervened as a supporting speaker.

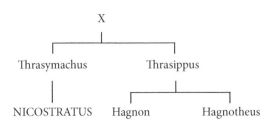

Figure 3.

and 2007) in rejecting the emendation, so there is no internal evidence for the date of the speech. Using his statistical method of dating, Wevers (1969, 25) proposes *c.* 350 BC.

The identity of Nicostratus

The main issue in dispute is the authenticity of Nicostratus's supposed will, but there was also disagreement about the identity of the man whose estate is contested: Chariades (initially, at least) claimed the estate of Nicostratus, son of Smicrus, while Hagnon and Hagnotheus assert their claim on the basis of their relationship to Nicostratus, son of Thrasymachus. Nicostratus was a very common name in ancient Greece,[2] so it is by no means impossible that there were in fact two men called Nicostratus, both mercenaries, who died around the same time: one the son of Thrasymachus and the other the son of Smicrus. According to Lentzsch (1932, 15–18) that could account for the discrepancies between the statements of the witnesses on opposing sides: both could have been telling the truth, if they referred to two different men. On the other hand, perhaps Chariades invented a different identity for Nicostratus as a diversionary tactic, or it may even have been simply a clerical error on his part. In any event, Isaeus exploits the discrepancy, accusing Chariades of using it as a distraction from the real issue in the case (§5).

---

2 *LGPN* records a total of 639 instances, including 222 in Attica.

Argumentation about kinship and wills

The antithesis between kinship and wills is a recurrent theme of the speech, and in a key section (§§11–17) the speaker argues in general terms that inheritance claims based on blood relationship are more credible than those based on wills. Like the argumentation in Isaeus 1 (discussed at pp. 20–21), this part of the speech has sometimes been taken as evidence of a general Athenian prejudice against wills and in favour of claims from the next of kin.

More specifically, Hunter (1993, 105) cites a number of passages from Isaeus (including 4.15–16 and 22) as evidence of 'a deeply ingrained negative attitude to adoption, which 'encouraged Athenians to challenge a deceased relative's choice of a son'. As I have argued elsewhere (Griffith-Williams, 2012, 149), such a prejudice appears to be incompatible with the importance attached in classical Athens to the continuity of the *oikos*, which, for an Athenian with no natural legitimate son, was best achieved by adoption. And even Athenian litigants who challenged wills expressed their respect for the principle of the law conferring freedom of testamentary disposition for those without natural heirs (e.g. Isae. 9.11, 10.22). Once again, then, these scholarly perceptions are not supported by a more nuanced and critical reading of the text.

As the commentary shows, the speaker makes some valid points about the ease with which a will can be forged and the difficulty of proving its authenticity, but the argument as a whole is tendentious and some aspects of it are at best indirectly relevant to the present case. The overall impression created by this section of the speech is that the speaker was not playing to an existing Athenian prejudice against wills and in favour of kinship, but straining to find persuasive reasons why the judges should reject Chariades's story. In the words of Thompson (1981, 24):

> If [Isae. 4.12] proves anything, it is not that Athenians were prejudiced "against devising property by will", but rather that they had reservations about the documents offered for probate. ...This does not rely on a prejudice which the jurors already have; instead, it seeks to inspire one in them. And, of course, it does not suggest that wills are a bad thing in themselves, merely that it is too easy to forge them.[3]

---

[3] For further discussion cf. Griffith-Williams (2012, 151).

The case for Chariades

How, then, would the judges have received Chariades's version of events? Given the Athenians' apparent preference for adoption within the family,[4] he may have met with some initial scepticism because he was not related to Nicostratus; but no doubt he produced a convincing narrative about the business and personal relationship between the two mercenaries which had led Nicostratus to adopt him as his heir. He probably pointed out that Nicostratus, having no son of his own, was anxious not to 'leave his *oikos* empty' (i.e. let his family die out), and in particular that he wanted to ensure that the annual commemorative rituals would be carried out on his behalf. The law, he might have argued, entitled Nicostratus to adopt anyone he chose, and in the circumstances – given that Nicostratus had no closer blood relations than cousins, with whom he had had no contact for many years – what better choice could he have made? There would have been nothing inherently implausible about such a narrative, and the 'empty *oikos*' topos was a powerful one, likely to make a strong emotional impact on the judges and perhaps even predispose them in favour of an adopted son and against the next of kin. The challenge for Isaeus, then, was to persuade the judges that his clients' version of events was more likely to be true than that of Chariades.

The case for Hagnon and Hagnotheus

We saw from Isaeus 1 and 2 that an Athenian will or adoption could be disputed on the grounds that it did not represent the testator's true wishes, or that the testator/adopter was not in his right mind, free from duress and undue influence, when he made it. In this case Hagnon and Hagnotheus simply deny that Nicostratus ever made a will, or adopted a son, at all; he would, they insist, have wanted his property to go to them as his next of kin, and the document produced in court by Chariades is a forgery. How could they prove this? Since the main speech in their case has not survived, we have no details of the story they told, but their supporting speaker tells us that they have challenged the credibilty of Chariades's witnesses, pointing out that if Nicostratus really had made a will, he would have summoned his own friends, not friends of Chariades,

---

4   As discussed in the Introduction to Isaeus 2, p. 71.

to witness it (§23). For their part, moreover, Hagnon and Hagnotheus have produced witness testimony to prove that they (not Chariades) buried Nicostratus, that they were never in dispute with him, and that Nicostratus and Chariades were not friends or business partners, as Chariades has claimed (§26). It might have helped their case if they had been in a position to say that they had a close and affectionate relationship with Nicostratus (like the speaker of Isaeus 1, who makes much of Cleonymus's affection for him and his brothers). It is hardly surprising, though, that they were unable to make such a claim: as cousins, they were relatively distant relations of Nicostratus, and in view of their youth (§26) they were probably still children when he left Athens 11 years previously. The most they can say is that they (unlike Chariades, who has a criminal record) have always been law-abiding citizens – so, if Nicostratus had really wanted to adopt a son, he would have been more likely to choose one of them than Chariades (§28). The significance of this 'character evidence' is discussed at pp. 127–28.

All the testimony mentioned by the supporting speaker was designed to suggest that Nicostratus would have been unlikely to adopt Chariades, but it is not conclusive, and it does not directly address the authenticity of the will at all. What further evidence could Hagnon and Hagnotheus have used? It would have been very difficult, if not impossible, for any Athenian litigant to prove conclusively that a will was forged. Apart from the alleged forger, the only person who knew the truth was the supposed testator, who obviously could not give evidence because he was dead,[5] and there were no scientific experts in classical Athens who could attest to the authenticity of a document. Even in modern litigation expert scientific evidence (if available) is not necessarily decisive; it is not uncommon to find a conflict of opinion between experts, leaving the judge or jury to decide which is most credible. So it is not surprising that, like many other litigants in the Athenian courts (not just in inheritance disputes) Hagnon and Hagnotheus, and their supporting speaker, relied heavily on argumentation from probability to persuade the judges that their version of the 'facts' was more likely to be true than that of their opponent.

In his attempt to cast doubt into the minds of the judges about the authenticity of the supposed will, the supporting speaker begins (§§7–10)

---

5 See commentary on 'since the man against whom they are testifying is dead', §12.

with a vivid, almost comic account of the competition for Nicostratus's two talents when the news of his death reached Athens. Some of the false claims were – as the speaker describes them – patently absurd, and he clearly wants the judges to discredit Chariades along with the other false claimants. This colourful narrative has fuelled theories propounded by some modern scholars about the inadequacy of the Athenian legal system to prevent fictitious claims to kinship, or to cope with a proliferation of forged wills. Karabélias (1992, 106) concludes a discussion of what he sees as the weaknesses of the Athenian system (notably its reliance on witness testimony) by evoking a 'malaise visible' in Athenian society, caused by 'la chasse aux héritages par le moyen de faux testaments'. Cohen (1995, 169), in a sceptical analysis of Isaeus 4, takes the case as a prime example of litigation as a form of social competition in which the legal issues are unimportant:

> Cases like that of the estate of Nicostratus, where no adult direct descendants were ready to defend their right to the patrimony, seem to have represented an open invitation to those ready to construct fictive genealogies or exaggerate the closeness of existing kin relations. ...Given the seemingly commonplace nature of such estate hunting, complete with false children, lying witnesses, fictive genealogies, forged wills, and fraudulent adoptions, Athenians seem to have regarded such inheritance litigation as an *agōn* much like a game of chance: you come forward with a perhaps unlikely or totally fraudulent case, but you rely upon the difficulty of clarifying such cases and the clout of your supporters, and hope that the wheel of fortune stops on your number.

A single, probably atypical case is not an adequate basis for conclusions about the nature of Athenian inheritance litigation in general, so assertions about the proliferation of fraudulent inheritance claims in classical Athens need to be treated with scepticism. In any event, a more nuanced reading of Isae. 4.7–10 would suggest that, at least in this particular case, the system had proved rather effective at filtering out weak or fraudulent claims before they came to court.

Character evidence

The argumentation about wills and kinship, which concludes the speaker's legal case on behalf of Hagnon and Hagnotheus, is followed by a comparison between the character of the two parties. On the one hand Hagnon and Hagnotheus have served in the official Athenian army, paid taxes, and generally behaved as law-abiding citizens, while their father Thrasippus also performed public services (liturgies) on behalf of the city. Chariades, on the other hand, is a criminal who has escaped justice, has never paid taxes, performed public services, or served in the official Athenian army.

Character evidence, defined by Adamidis (2017, 101–102) as 'proof or attestations about an individual's moral standing, his general nature, behavioural traits, and reputation in the general community', may be either positive or negative, evoking the good character of a litigant or portraying his opponent's character in a bad light. Its use in Athenian forensic oratory has been seen by some modern scholars as an attempt to influence the judges with 'irrelevant' evidence or arguments, inviting them to reach a decision on moral rather than legal grounds. According to Cohen (1995, 171–72), for example, the character evidence in Isaeus 4 provides an 'alternative ground' for the judges' decision, inviting them to forget all they have heard about the competing legal claims and award the estate to Hagnon and Hagnotheus because they are more deserving. It would be difficult, if not impossible, for the judges to decide who was telling the truth, so 'they might as well give the estate to those who are likely to use it to their (i.e., the judges'/*demos*') benefit.'[6]

The character evidence in this speech is not simply an invitation to the judges to award the estate to Hagnon and Hagnotheus because they are more deserving on moral grounds; in fact, it contributes to the speaker's argumentation from probability, supporting his contention that Nicostratus would have been happy for his estate to go to Hagnon and Hagnotheus, and would not have wanted to adopt Chariades (whose criminal record suggests that he would have been capable of forging a will). The positive record of Hagnon and Hagnotheus and their father (like that of Chaerestratus and Phanostratus in Isaeus 6) does, however,

---

6   Cf. Adamidis (2017, 79): Chariades 'had all the characteristics of a would-be forger', whereas Hagnon and Hagnotheus 'would be more worthy recipients of the estate'.

also convey the message that they are public-spirited citizens who would be likely to use the inheritance wisely for the benefit of the city as a whole. It is possible, then, that some of the judges may have been swayed by what they heard about the character of the rival claimants, especially if they found it difficult to decide which party was telling the truth about the facts, but the character evidence is only part of the speaker's case and does not amount to an alternative basis for the judges' decision. Indeed, the speech concludes with a reminder to them to vote in accordance with the dicastic oath, which required them to apply the relevant law.[7]

Conclusion

The argumentation in this speech, including the character evidence, has provided ample material for modern scholars interested in the nature of Athenian litigation and in Athenian attitudes to inheritance, especially the competing claims of kinship and adoption. As I have discussed in this introduction, and as the commentary explains in greater detail, some of their conclusions are, at best, questionable. Isaeus's aim in writing the speech was to undermine the case put forward by his clients' opponent, creating doubt in the minds of the judges about the authenticity of the document put forward by Chariades as Nicostratus's will. As in all his speeches, the arguments are chosen and shaped to meet the needs of the specific case, and should not be taken as representative of Athenian attitudes in general. It is worth remembering that if Isaeus had been hired by Chariades rather than Hagnon and Hagnotheus, the speech he produced would in all probability have emphasized the childless Nicostratus's desire for a son to continue his family line, urged the judges to respect the wishes of the deceased by confirming his will, and condemned the scheming of greedy and unscrupulous relatives who had shown no interest in Nicostratus while he was alive but were eager to get their hands on his property after his death.

---

7 Cf. Griffith-Williams (forthcoming b).

ISAEUS 4: ON THE ESTATE OF NICOSTRATUS

ἐπιτήδειοί μοι τυγχάνουσιν, ὦ ἄνδρες, ὄντες Ἅγνων τε οὑτοσὶ καὶ Ἁγνόθεος, καὶ ὁ πατὴρ αὐτῶν ἔτι πρότερον. εἰκὸς οὖν μοι δοκεῖ εἶναι, ὡς ἂν οἷός τε ὦ, συνειπεῖν αὐτοῖς. περὶ μὲν οὖν τῶν ἐν τῇ ὑπερορίᾳ πραχθέντων [ὡς] οὔτε μάρτυρας ἐξευρεῖν οἷόν τε, οὔτε τοὺς ἀντιδίκους, ἐάν τι ψεύδωνται, ἐλέγχειν ῥᾴδιον, διὰ τὸ μηδέτερον τούτων κεῖσε ἀφῖχθαι· τὰ δὲ ἐνθάδε [μοι] συμβεβηκότα δοκεῖ μοι ὑμῖν ἱκανὰ γενέσθαι ἂν τεκμήρια, ὅτι ἅπαντες οἱ κατὰ τὴν δόσιν τῶν Νικοστράτου ἀμφισβητοῦντες ἐξαπατῆσαι ὑμᾶς βούλονται. [2] πρῶτον μὲν οὖν, ὦ ἄνδρες, περὶ τῆς τῶν ὀνομάτων ἐπιγραφῆς ἄξιόν ἐστιν ἐξετάσαι, καὶ σκέψασθαι ὁπότεροι ἁπλούστερον καὶ κατὰ φύσιν μᾶλλον τὰς λήξεις ἐποιήσαντο. Ἅγνων μὲν γὰρ οὑτοσὶ καὶ Ἁγνόθεος Θρασυμάχου ἐπεγράψαντο τὸν Νικόστρατον, καὶ ἑαυτοὺς ἐκείνῳ ἀνεψιοὺς ἀποφαίνουσι, καὶ τούτων μάρτυρας παρέχονται· [3] Χαριάδης δὲ καὶ οἱ συνδικοῦντες αὐτῷ Σμίκρου μὲν πατρὸς εἶναί φασι τὸν Νικόστρατον, ἀμφισβητοῦσι δὲ τοῦ Θρασυμάχου υἱοῦ κλήρου. καὶ οἵδε μὲν οὐδὲν προσποιοῦνται ἐκείνου τοῦ ὀνόματος οὔτε γιγνώσκειν οὔτε προσήκειν αὐτοῖς· φασὶ μὲν οὖν εἶναι Θρασυμάχου Νικόστρατον, τούτου δὲ ὁμοίως τῆς οὐσίας ἀμφισβητοῦσι. [4] καὶ εἰ μὲν τὸ ὄνομα πατρόθεν τὸ αὐτὸ ὡμολόγουν εἶναι τοῦ Νικοστράτου, περὶ δὲ τοῦ κλήρου μόνου διεφέροντο, οὐδὲν ἂν ἔδει ὑμᾶς σκέψασθαι ἀλλ᾽ <ἢ> εἴ τι διέθετο ἐκεῖνος ὁ Νικόστρατος, ὃν ἀμφότεροι ὡμολόγουν· νῦν δὲ πῶς οἷόν τε τῷ ἀνδρὶ δύο πατέρας ἐπιγράψασθαι; τοῦτο γὰρ Χαριάδης πεποίηκεν· αὐτός τε γὰρ ἔλαχε <τῶν> τοῦ Σμίκρου Νικοστράτου, τούτοις τε <τῶν> τοῦ Θρασυμάχου λαχοῦσι παρακατέβαλεν ὡς τὸν αὐτὸν ὄντα. [5] ἔστι μὲν οὖν ἅπαντα ταῦτα ἐπήρεια καὶ παρασκευή. ἡγοῦνται γὰρ τούτους, ἁπλοῦ μὲν ὄντος τοῦ πράγματος καὶ μηδεμιᾶς αὐτοῖς ταραχῆς ἐγγιγνομένης, οὐ χαλεπῶς ἐπιδείξειν ὅτι οὐδὲν Νικόστρατος διέθετο· ἐὰν δὲ μὴ τὸν πατέρα τὸν αὐτὸν εἶναι φῶσι, τοῦ δὲ κλήρου μηδὲν ἧττον ἀμφισβητῶσιν, ἀκριβῶς ἴσασιν ὅτι πλείονι λόγῳ εἰπεῖν τουτουσὶ δεήσει ὡς Νικόστρατος Θρασυμάχου ἦν ἢ ὡς οὐδὲν διέθετο. [6] ἔτι δὲ καὶ ὁμολογοῦντες Θρασυμάχου μὲν εἶναι τὸν Νικόστρατον οὐκ ἂν εἶχον ἐξελέγξαι τούσδε ὡς οὐκ εἰσὶν ἐκείνῳ ἀνεψιοί· ἄλλον δὲ πατέρα τῷ τεθνεῶτι κατασκευάζοντες οὐ μόνον περὶ τῶν διαθηκῶν ἀλλὰ καὶ περὶ τοῦ γένους λόγον ἐμβεβλήκασιν. [7] οὐκ ἐκ τούτων δὲ μόνον γνοίητ᾽ ἂν ὅτι ἀλλότριοί τινες εἰσιν οἱ ταῦτα ἐπὶ τουτουσὶ ἐπάγοντες, ἀλλὰ καὶ ἐκ τῶν κατ᾽ ἀρχὰς

Hagnon here and Hagnotheus are friends of mine, gentlemen, like their father before them, so it seems natural for me to speak in their support as best I can. It's impossible to find witnesses of events in another state, and not easy to expose any lies our opponents might tell, since neither Hagnon nor Hagnotheus has been there, but I think that events here in Athens will be sufficient proof for you that all those who claim the estate of Nicostratus on the basis of a will are trying to deceive you. (2) First of all, gentlemen, you need to ask about the registration of the names, and consider which of the parties have submitted their claim in the more straightforward and natural way. For Hagnon here and Hagnotheos have entered Nicostratus as the son of Thrasymachus, and put themselves forward as his cousins, and they have produced witnesses to these facts. (3) Chariades and his supporters, on the one hand, say that Nicostratus was the son of Smicrus, and yet they are claiming the estate of the son of Thrasymachus. On the other hand, Hagnon and Hagnotheus do not pretend to recognize the name of Smicrus, and deny that it has anything to do with them; they say that Nicostratus was the son of Thrasymachus, and similarly it is his estate that they claim. (4) And if they agreed that Nicostratus' patronymic was the same, and were in dispute only about the estate, the only thing you would have to consider would be whether or not this Nicostratus, whose identity is agreed by both sides, left a will. Now, though, how is it possible to ascribe two fathers to one man? For that is what Chariades has done; he himself has claimed the estate of Nicostratus son of Smicrus, but he paid a deposit to contest the claim of Hagnon and Hagnotheus to the estate of Nicostratus son of Thrasymachus, as if he were the same man. (5) This is all an insult and a plot; they think that, unless they confuse the issue, it will be a simple matter for our side to prove that Nicostratus did not leave a will. And if they say that he had a different father, but claim his estate all the same, they know very well that Hagnon and Hagnotheus will need to devote more of their speech to proving that Nicostratus was the son of Thrasymachus than that he did not leave a will. (6) What's more, if they agreed that Nicostratus was the son of Thrasymachus, they would not be able to prove that Hagnon and Hagnotheus are not his cousins, but by inventing a different father for the dead man they have added an argument about kinship as well as about the will.

(7) You could know, not only from these matters but from everything that has happened since the beginning, that the men who are attacking

γεγενημένων. τίς γὰρ οὐκ ἀπεκείρατο, ἐπειδὴ τὼ δύο ταλάντω ἑξάκις εἰσηλθέτην; ἢ τίς οὐ μέλαν ἱμάτιον ἐφόρησεν, ὡς διὰ τὸ πένθος κληρονομήσων τῆς οὐσίας; ἢ πόσοι συγγενεῖς καὶ ὑεῖς κατὰ δόσιν προσεποιήσαντο τῶν Νικοστράτου; [8] Δημοσθένης μέν γε ἀδελφιδοῦς ἔφη αὐτῷ εἶναι, ἐπειδὴ δ᾽ ἐξηλέγχθη ὑπὸ τούτων, ἀπέστη· Τήλεφος δὲ δοῦναι αὐτῷ Νικόστρατον ἅπαντα τὰ ἑαυτοῦ. καὶ οὗτος οὐ πολλῷ ὕστερον ἐπαύσατο. Ἀμεινιάδης δὲ ὑὸν αὐτῷ πρὸς τὸν ἄρχοντα ἧκεν ἄγων οὐδὲ τριετῆ γεγονότα, καὶ ταῦτ᾽ οὐκ ἐπιδεδημηκότος τοῦ Νικοστράτου ἕνδεκα ἐτῶν Ἀθήνησι. [9] Πύρρος δὲ ὁ Λαμπτρεὺς τῇ μὲν Ἀθηνᾷ ἔφη τὰ χρήματα ὑπὸ Νικοστράτου καθιερῶσθαι, αὐτῷ δ᾽ ὑπ᾽ αὐτοῦ ἐκείνου δεδόσθαι. Κτησίας δ᾽ ὁ Βησαιεὺς καὶ Κραναὸς τὸ μὲν πρῶτον δίκην ἔφασαν τοῦ Νικοστράτου ταλάντου καταδεδικάσθαι, ἐπειδὴ δ᾽ οὐκ εἶχον τοῦτο ἀποδεῖξαι, ἀπελεύθερον αὐτὸν ἑαυτῶν προσεποιήσαντο εἶναι· καὶ οὐδ᾽ οὗτοι ἃ ἔλεγον ἀπέδειξαν. [10] καὶ οἱ μὲν εὐθὺς κατὰ τὰ πρῶτα ἐπὶ τὰ Νικοστράτου ἄξαντες οὗτοί εἰσι· Χαριάδης δὲ τότε μὲν οὐδαμοῦ ἠμφισβήτησεν, ὕστερον δὲ οὐ μόνον αὐτὸς ἀλλὰ καὶ τὸ ἐκ τῆς ἑταίρας παιδίον εἰσποιῶν ἦλθε. ταὐτὸ δ᾽ ἦν αὐτῷ ὡς ἢ τῶν χρημάτων κληρονομήσοντι ἢ τὸ παιδίον ἀστὸν ποιήσοντι. αἰσθόμενος δὲ καὶ οὗτος ὅτι περὶ τοῦ γένους ἐλεγχθήσοιτο, τὴν μὲν τοῦ παιδίου ἀμφισβήτησιν παρέλυσεν, ἑαυτῷ δὲ κατὰ δόσιν παρακατέβαλεν. [11] ἐχρῆν μὲν οὖν, ὦ ἄνδρες, ὅστις κατὰ δόσιν χρημάτων ἀμφισβητῶν ἡττηθείη, μὴ κατὰ τὸ τέλος ζημιοῦσθαι, ἀλλ᾽ ἐφ᾽ ὅσα περ ληψόμενος ᾔει, τοσαῦτα τῇ πόλει ἀποτίνειν· οὕτω γὰρ<ἂν> οὔθ᾽ οἱ νόμοι κατεφρονοῦντο οὔτε τὰ γένη ὑβρίζετο, πρὸ δὲ τούτων οὐδ᾽ ἂν τῶν τεθνεώτων οὐδεὶς κατεψεύδετο. ἐπειδὴ δὲ ἅπασι καὶ τῶν ἀλλοτρίων ἁπάντων, καθ᾽ ὅ τι ἂν τις βούληται, ἀμφισβητεῖν ἔξεστιν, ὑμᾶς χρὴ περὶ αὐτῶν ὡς οἷόν τ᾽ ἀκριβέστατα ἐξετάζειν καὶ μηδὲν εἰς ὅσον δύνασθε παραλείπειν. [12] ἐν μόναις δὲ ταῖς τῶν κλήρων εἰσαγωγαῖς δοκεῖ μοι προσήκειν τεκμηρίοις μᾶλλον ἢ μάρτυσι πιστεύειν. περὶ μὲν γὰρ τῶν ἄλλων συμβολαίων οὐ πάνυ χαλεπὸν τοὺς τὰ ψευδῆ μαρτυροῦντας ἐλέγχειν· ζῶντος γὰρ καὶ παρόντος τοῦ πράξαντος καταμαρτυροῦσι· περὶ δὲ τῶν διαθηκῶν πῶς ἄν τις γνοίη τοὺς μὴ τἀληθῆ λέγοντας, εἰ μὴ πάνυ μεγάλα τὰ διαφέροντα εἴη, αὐτοῦ μὲν καθ᾽ οὗ μαρτυροῦσι τεθνεῶτος, τῶν δὲ συγγενῶν μηδὲν τῶν πεπραγμένων εἰδότων, τοῦ δὲ ἐλέγχου μηδαμῶς ἀκριβοῦς

Hagnon and Hagnotheus in such a way are not members of the family. For who did not cut his hair when the two talents came into court six times? And who did not wear a black cloak, as if he would inherit the estate through mourning? And how many kinsmen and sons adopted by will laid claim to Nicostratus's property? (8) Demosthenes said he was his nephew, but then dropped his claim when he was exposed by Hagnon and Hagnotheus. Telephus claimed that Nicostratus had given him all his property, but he too gave up after a short time. Ameiniades came before the archon with a 'son' of Nicostratus who was not yet three years old, even though Nicostratus had not been in Athens for 11 years. (9) Pyrrhus of Lamptra said that the money had been dedicated by Nicostratus to Athena, and given to him by Nicostratus himself. Ctesias of Besa and Cranaus initially said that they had secured a judgment against Nicostratus for a talent, and when they failed to prove this they pretended that he was their freedman, but could not prove that either. (10) These, then, are the men who pounced on Nicostratus's estate at the beginning. Chariades made no claim at that stage, but later came forward trying to get not only himself but also his child by his mistress adopted. It was all the same to him whether he would inherit the property himself or have the child recognized as a citizen. But he too, realizing that he would be defeated on the issue of kinship, abandoned the child's claim and paid a deposit on his own behalf on the basis of the will.

(11) Anyone, gentlemen, who loses a claim to an estate on the basis of a will should not be fined at the usual rate but should pay the full value of the estate into the public purse, since in that way the laws would not be held in contempt and neither would blood relations be insulted; and, above all, no-one would tell lies against the dead. But since it is open to anyone who so wishes to claim anyone else's estate, you must scrutinize their claims as closely as you can, overlooking nothing. (12) And I think it's appropriate in inheritance disputes, as an exception, to place more reliance on circumstantial evidence than on witnesses. For in relation to other kinds of contracts it is not particularly difficult to expose those who give false testimony, since they are giving evidence against a party to the contract who is alive and present; but in relation to wills, how can anyone know who is not telling the truth (unless the discrepancy is very great) since the man against whom they are testifying is dead, his kinsmen know nothing about the facts, and there is no obvious way of

γιγνομένου; [13] ἔτι δέ, ὦ ἄνδρες, καὶ τῶν διατιθεμένων οἱ πολλοὶ οὐδὲ λέγουσι τοῖς παραγιγνομένοις ὅ τι διατίθενται, ἀλλ᾽ αὐτοῦ μόνου, τοῦ καταλιπεῖν διαθήκας, μάρτυρας παρίστανται, τοῦ δὲ συμβαίνοντός ἐστι καὶ γραμματεῖον ἀλλαγῆναι καὶ τἀναντία ταῖς τοῦ τεθνεῶτος διαθήκαις μεταγραφῆναι· οὐδὲν γὰρ μᾶλλον οἱ μάρτυρες εἴσονται, εἰ ἐφ᾽ αἷς ἐκλήθησαν διαθήκαις, αὗται ἀποφαίνονται. [14] ὁπότε δὲ καὶ τοὺς ὁμολογουμένως παραγενομένους οἷόν τ᾽ ἐστὶν ἐξαπατῆσαι, πῶς οὐκ ἂν ὑμᾶς γε τοὺς μηδὲν τοῦ πράγματος εἰδότας πολὺ [μᾶλλον] ἑτοιμότερόν τις παρακρούσασθαι ἐγχειρήσειεν; ἀλλὰ μὴν καὶ ὁ νόμος, ὦ ἄνδρες, οὐκ ἐάν τις διαθῆται μόνον, κυρίας εἶναι κελεύει τὰς διαθήκας, ἀλλὰ ἐὰν εὖ φρονῶν. σκεπτέον δὴ ὑμῖν πρῶτον μὲν εἰ ἐποιήσατο τὰς διαθήκας, ἔπειτα εἰ μὴ παρανοῶν διέθετο. [15] ἀντιλεγόντων δ᾽ ἡμῶν μηδὲ τὸ παράπαν γενέσθαι τὰς διαθήκας, ἐκ τίνος ἂν τρόπου, εἴ τις παρανοῶν διέθετο, γνοίητε, πρὶν περὶ αὐτοῦ τοῦ διαθέσθαι πιστεῦσαι; τοὺς μὲν οὖν κατὰ τὴν δόσιν ἀμφισβητοῦντας ὁρᾶτε ὅσον ἔργον ἐστὶν αἰσθέσθαι εἰ ἀληθῆ λέγουσι, τοὺς δὲ κατὰ τὸ γένος πρῶτον μὲν οὐδὲν δεῖ μάρτυρας παρασχέσθαι ὡς αὐτῶν ἐστιν ὁ κλῆρος (παρὰ πάντων γὰρ ὡμολόγηται τοῖς ἐγγυτάτω γένους τὰ τοῦ τελευτήσαντος γίγνεσθαι, [16] ἔπειτα οἱ νόμοι οὐ μόνον οἱ περὶ τῶν γενῶν ἀλλὰ καὶ οἱ περὶ τῶν δόσεων τοῖς συγγενέσι βοηθοῦσι. δοῦναι μὲν γὰρ ὁ νόμος οὐδενὶ ἐᾷ τὰ ἑαυτοῦ, ἐὰν ὑπὸ γήρως ἢ ὑπὸ νόσου ἢ ὑπὸ τῶν ἄλλων ἃ καὶ ὑμεῖς ἴστε παρανοήσῃ· κατὰ δὲ τὸ γένος καὶ τὰ τοῦ ὁπωσοῦν διακειμένου ὁ ἐγγύτατα γένους ἀναμφισβητήτως λαμβάνει. [17] χωρὶς δὲ τούτων ταῖς μὲν διαθήκαις διὰ μαρτύρων ὑμᾶς δεῖ πιστεῦσαι, ὑφ᾽ ὧν ἔνι καὶ ἐξαπατηθῆναι (οὐ γὰρ ἂν ἦσαν ψευδομαρτυρίων ἐπισκήψεις), τῇ δ᾽ ἀγχιστείᾳ δι᾽ ὑμῶν αὐτῶν· κατὰ γὰρ τοὺς νόμους οἱ συγγενεῖς ἀμφισβητοῦσιν, οὓς ὑμεῖς ἔθεσθε. [18] πρὸς δὲ τούτοις, ὦ ἄνδρες, εἰ μὲν οἱ κατὰ τὰς διαθήκας ἀμφισβητοῦντες ὁμολογουμένως Νικοστράτῳ ἐπιτήδειοι ὄντες ἐτύγχανον, τὸ μὲν ἀκριβὲς οὐδ᾽ ἂν οὕτως, ὅμως μέντοι μᾶλλον εἰκὸς ἦν ἀληθεῖς εἶναι δόξειν τὰς διαθήκας· ἤδη γάρ τινες οὐκ εὖ διακείμενοι τοῖς συγγενέσιν ὀθνείους φίλους τῶν πάνυ σφόδρα προσηκόντων περὶ πλείονος ἐποιήσαντο· νῦν δὲ οὔτε συσσίτους οὔτε φίλους οὔτ᾽ ἐν τάξει

refuting the evidence? (13) What's more, gentlemen, most people who make wills don't even disclose the content to those who are present, but simply invite them to testify that they have left a will, and it sometimes happens that a document is substituted or falsified contrary to the dead man's dispositions, for the witnesses will not know whether the will produced in court is the one they were called upon to attest. (14) So, since it is possible to deceive even those who are agreed to have been present, how much more readily could an attempt be made to mislead you, who know nothing about the matter?

And indeed, gentlemen, the law itself does not say that a will is valid just because someone has made it, but only if he was in his right mind. So you must consider first whether he made the will, and secondly whether he was not insane when he made it. (15) But since we deny that any will was made, how can you decide whether someone was insane when he made his will until you are confident that the will was actually made? So you see how difficult it is to understand whether those who claim an estate on the basis of a will are telling the truth, whereas those who claim on the basis of kinship first of all have no need to produce witnesses to testify that the estate is theirs (since everyone agrees that the property of a dead man goes to his next of kin), (16) and secondly the laws – not only those on kinship but also those about bequests – assist the kinsmen. For the law does not allow anyone to bequeath his property who is not in his right mind because of old age or illness or the other reasons that you know about, but the next of kin indisputably takes the property on the basis of kinship, whatever the state of mind of the deceased. (17) Apart from that, in order to have faith in a will you need to rely on witnesses, by whom you might be deceived (otherwise there would be no prosecutions for false testimony) but in relation to degrees of kinship you rely on yourselves, for kinsmen claim in accordance with the laws which you made. (18) In addition to this, gentlemen, if those who are claiming Nicostratus's estate on the basis of a will were recognized as close friends of his, although it would still not be certain, it would be more likely that the will was genuine, for some people who don't get on well with their kinsmen have preferred friends outside the family to their closest kin. But in this case Chariades and Nicostratus were neither messmates nor friends nor members of the same company […][1] and we have produced

---

1 There is a lacuna in the text at this point.

τῇ αὐτῇ < ... > τούτων δ᾽ ὑμῖν μάρτυρας ἁπάντων παρεσχήμεθα. [19] ὃ δὲ μέγιστον, καὶ μάλιστα τῆς Χαριάδου ἀναιδείας καταμαρτυρεῖ, τοῦτο σκέψασθε. ὅπου γὰρ τὸν αὐτὸν ποιησάμενον οὔτ᾽ ἀποθανόντα ἀνείλετο οὔτ᾽ ἔκαυσεν οὔτε ὠστολόγησεν, ἀλλὰ πάντα τοῖς μηδὲν προσήκουσι παρῆκε ποιῆσαι, πῶς οὐκ <ἂν> ἀνοσιώτατος εἴη, ὃς τῷ τεθνεῶτι μηδὲν τῶν νομιζομένων ποιήσας τῶν χρημάτων αὐτοῦ κληρονομεῖν ἀξιοῖ; [20] ἀλλὰ νὴ Δία ἐπειδὴ τούτων οὐδὲν ἐποίησε, τὴν οὐσίαν τοῦ Νικοστράτου διεχείρισεν; ἀλλὰ καὶ ταῦτα μεμαρτύρηται ὑμῖν, καὶ τὰ πλεῖστα οὐδ᾽ αὐτὸς ἀρνεῖται. προφάσεις δὲ οἴομαι ἀναγκαίας ἐφ᾽ ἑκάστας τῶν πράξεων εὑρῆσθαι· τί γὰρ ὑπολείπεται τῷ διαρρήδην ὁμολογοῦντι; [21] σαφῶς μὲν οὖν ἴστε, ὦ ἄνδρες, ὅτι οὗτοι οὐ δικαίως τῶν Νικοστράτου ἐφίενται, ἀλλὰ βούλονται μὲν ὑμᾶς ἐξαπατῆσαι, τουτουσὶ δὲ συγγενεῖς ὄντας ἐκείνου, ἃ οἱ νόμοι ἔδοσαν αὐτοῖς, ἀποστερῆσαι. οὐ μόνος δὲ Χαριάδης τοῦτο πεποίηκεν, ἀλλὰ καὶ ἄλλοι πολλοὶ ἤδη τῶν ἐν τῇ ὑπερορίᾳ ἀποθνησκόντων οὐδὲ γιγνώσκοντες ἐνίους τῆς οὐσίας ἠμφισβήτησαν· [22] ἐνθυμοῦνται γὰρ ὅτι κατορθώσασι μὲν <ἔσται> τὰ ἀλλότρια ἔχειν, διαμαρτοῦσι δὲ μικρὸς ὁ κίνδυνος· μαρτυρεῖν δὲ καὶ τὰ ψευδῆ τινες ἐθέλουσιν, οἱ δ᾽ ἔλεγχοι περὶ ἀφανῶν. συνελόντι πολὺ τὸ διαφέρον κατὰ γένος ἢ κατὰ δόσιν ἀμφισβητεῖν. ἀλλ᾽ ὑμᾶς χρή, ὦ ἄνδρες, πρῶτον μὲν τὰς διαθήκας σκοπεῖν, εἰ δοκοῦσι γενέσθαι· τοῦτο γὰρ οἵ τε νόμοι <ὑφ>ηγοῦνται καὶ δικαιότατόν ἐστι. [23] μὴ σαφῶς δὲ μήτ᾽ αὐτοὺς τὴν ἀλήθειαν εἰδότας, μήτε τῶν μαρτύρων τοῦ τελευτήσαντος ἐπιτηδείων ὄντων, ἀλλὰ Χαριάδου τοῦ τἀλλότρια βουλομένου λαβεῖν, τί ἂν εἴη δικαιότερον ἢ τοῖς συγγενέσι τὰ τοῦ συγγενοῦς ψηφίζεσθαι; καὶ γὰρ εἴ τι οἶδε ἔπαθον, οὐδενὶ ἂν ἄλλῳ ἢ Νικοστράτῳ τὰ τούτων ἐγένετο· κατὰ γὰρ τὸ αὐτὸ γένος ἂν ἠμφισβήτει, ἀνεψιὸς ὢν αὐτοῖς ἐκ πατραδέλφων. [24] μὰ Δί᾽ ἀλλ᾽ οὐκ ἔστιν ὁ Ἅγνων οὐδ᾽ ὁ Ἁγνόθεος τοῦ Νικοστράτου συγγενής, ὡς οἱ ἀντίδικοί φασιν, ἀλλ᾽ ἕτεροι. ἔπειτα τῷ μὲν κατὰ τὴν δόσιν τοῦ κλήρου λαχόντι μαρτυροῦσιν, αὐτοὶ δὲ κατὰ τὸ γένος οὐκ ἀμφισβητήσουσιν; οὐ γὰρ εἰς τοῦτό γε ἀνοίας ἥκουσιν ὥστε πιστεύσαντες ταῖς διαθήκαις οὕτω ῥᾳδίως τοσούτων χρημάτων ἀφίστανται. ἀλλὰ μὴν καὶ ἐξ ὧν αὐτοὶ οὗτοι λέγουσι, τούσδε τοῖς συγγενέσιν αὐτοῖς ἐπιδικάσασθαι συμφέρει τῶν Νικοστράτου μᾶλλον ἢ

witnesses to testify to you about all this. (19) And consider this, the most important point and the greatest testimony to Chariades's effrontery. Since he neither took away the body of his adoptive father for cremation, nor collected the bones, but left all this to be done by strangers, is he not to be considered most impious in claiming to inherit the property of the dead man, for whom he never performed any of the customary rites? (20) But, by Zeus, did he administer Nicostratus's property after neglecting these duties? But testimony on these facts, too, has been produced for you, and he himself has not denied most of them. I think the excuses that have been found for each of his actions are inadequate, but what else could he say when he directly admits the facts?

(21) Well now, gentlemen, you clearly know that these men are claiming Nicostratus's estate illegally and trying to deceive you and rob Hagnon and Hagnotheus, who are his kinsmen, of what the laws have given to them. Chariades is not alone in doing this, but many others have claimed the property of men who have died abroad, sometimes without even having known them. (22) For they think they will have someone else's property if they succeed, while they have nothing much to lose if they fail. Some are even willing to testify falsely, and there is no clear way of refuting them. In short, there is a big difference between claiming an estate on the basis of kinship and on the basis of a will. But you, gentlemen, must first consider the will and decide whether it is genuine, for that is what the laws instruct you to do and that is the most just procedure. (23) But since you personally have no certain knowledge of the truth, and since the witnesses are not close friends of the deceased but of Chariades, who is trying to get hold of someone else's property, what could be more just than to award the estate of a kinsman to his kinsmen? For indeed, if anything had happened to Hagnon and Hagnotheus, their property would have gone to no-one other than Nicostratus, for he would have claimed it by the same right of kinship, as their cousin, the son of their father's brother. (24) But, by Zeus, Nicostratus's kinsmen are not Hagnon and Hagnotheus, according to our opponents, but other people. Are they, then, testifying on behalf of the claimant under the will, instead of claiming for themselves through kinship? Surely they are not so insane as to put their trust so easily in the will and give up their own claim to so much money! But indeed, even from what they say themselves, it will benefit these kinsmen if the estate of Nicostratus is awarded to Hagnon

Χαριάδην.[25] εἰς γὰρ τὸν λοιπὸν χρόνον, εἰ μὲν οἴδε κατὰ τὸ γένος ἀμφισβητοῦντες λήψονται τὸν κλῆρον, ἐξέσται καὶ τούτοις, ὁπόταν βούλωνται, κατὰ τὸ γένος λαχοῦσιν ἐπιδεῖξαι ὑμῖν ὡς αὐτοὶ ἐγγυτέρω ἦσαν τοῦ Νικοστράτου, καὶ ὡς Σμίκρου ἦν καὶ οὐ Θρασυμάχου· ἐὰν δὲ Χαριάδης αὐτῶν κληρονομήσῃ, οὐκ ἔσται οὐδενὶ συγγενεῖ ἐπὶ τὰ Νικοστράτου ἐλθεῖν. καταδόσιν γὰρ ἔχοντος τοῦ ἐπιδεδικασμένου, τί φανοῦνται λέγοντες
οἱ κατὰ [τὸ] γένος λαγχάνοντες; [26] ὅπερ ἂν οὖν καὶ ὑμῶν ἕκαστος ἀξιώσειε, τοῦτο καὶ τουτοισὶ τοῖς νεανίσκοις βεβαιώσατε. παρέσχοντο δ᾽ ὑμῖν μάρτυρας πρῶτον μὲν ὡς ἀνεψιοί εἰσιν ἐκ πατραδέλφων Νικοστράτου, ἔπειτα δὲ ὡς οὐδεπώποτε ἐκείνῳ διάφοροι ἦσαν, ἔτι δὲ καὶ ὡς ἔθαψαν Νικόστρατον, πρὸς δὲ τούτοις ὡς Χαριάδης οὑτοσὶ οὐδαμῶς οὔτ᾽ ἐνθάδε οὔτ᾽ ἐπὶ στρατεύματι ἐχρῆτο Νικοστράτῳ, ἔτι δὲ καὶ τὴν κοινωνίαν, ᾗ μάλισθ᾽ οὗτος ἰσχυρίζεται, ψευδῆ οὖσαν. [27] καὶ ἄνευ τούτων ὦ ἄνδρες, ἄξιον ὑμῖν ἐξετάσαι ἑκατέρους αὐτῶν οἷοί εἰσι. Θράσιππος μὲν γὰρ ὁ Ἅγνωνος καὶ Ἁγνοθέου πατὴρ ἤδη τι καὶ ἐλητούργησεν ὑμῖν καὶ εἰσήνεγκε καὶ ἄλλως σπουδαῖος ἦν πολίτης· αὐτοὶ δὲ οὗτοι οὔτε ἀποδεδημήκασιν οὐδαμοῖ πώποτε, ὅποι ἂν μὴ ὑμεῖς προστάξητε, οὔτ᾽ ἐνθάδε μένοντες ἄχρηστοί εἰσι τῇ πόλει, ἀλλὰ καὶ στρατεύονται καὶ εἰσφέρουσι καὶ τἆλλα πάντα ποιοῦσι τὰ προσταττόμενα καὶ αὑτούς ὡς πάντες ἴσασι κοσμίους παρέχουσιν, [28] ὥστε πολὺ μᾶλλον τούτους προσήκει κατὰ δόσιν τῶν χρημάτων τῶν Νικοστράτου ἢ Χαριάδην ἀμφισβητεῖν. οὗτος γάρ, ὅτ᾽ ἐπεδήμει ἐνθάδε, πρῶτον μὲν εἰς τὸ δεσμωτήριον ὡς κλέπτης ὢν ἐπ᾽ αὐτοφώρῳ ἀπήχθη, τότε δὲ ἀφεθεὶς μεθ᾽ ἑτέρων τινῶν ὑπὸ τῶν ἕνδεκα, οὓς δημοσίᾳ ἅπαντας ὑμεῖς ἀπεκτείνατε, πάλιν ἀπογραφεὶς εἰς τὴν βουλὴν κακουργῶν, ὑποχωρῶν ᾤχετο καὶ οὐχ ὑπήκουσεν, [29] ἀλλ᾽ ἀπ᾽ ἐκείνου ἑπτακαίδεκα ἐτῶν Ἀθήναζε οὐκ ἀφίκετο, πλὴν ἐπειδὴ Νικόστρατος ἀπέθανε. καὶ ὑπὲρ μὲν ὑμῶν οὔτε στρατείαν οὐδεμίαν ἐστράτευται οὔτε εἰσφορὰν οὐδεμίαν εἰσενήνοχε, πλὴν εἴ τι ἄρα ἐξ ὅτου τῶν Νικοστράτου ἠμφισβήτησεν, οὔτ᾽ ἄλλ᾽ οὐδὲν ὑμῖν λελητούργηκεν. ἔπειτα τοιοῦτος ὢν οὐκ ἀγαπᾷ εἰ μὴ τῶν ἡμαρτημένων δίκην δώσει, ἀλλὰ καὶ τῶν ἀλλοτρίων ἀμφισβητεῖ. [30] εἰ μὲν οὖν οἴδε φιλοπράγμονες ἢ ἄλλοις ὅμοιοι πολίταις ἦσαν,

and Hagnotheus than to Chariades. (25) For if those who claim the estate on grounds of kinship are successful, then in future it will be open to them, whenever they like, to make their own claim on grounds of kinship and prove to you that they are more closely related to Nicostratus, and that he was the son of Smicrus and not Thrasymachus. If, on the other hand, Chariades inherits Nicostratus's estate, none of Nicostratus's kinsmen will be able to claim it. For when an estate has been the subject of a court judgment based on a will, what argument will those who claim through kinship be able to put forward? (26) So please confirm for these young men the result that each of you would expect for yourselves. They have produced witnesses to testify to you, in the first place, that they are Nicostratus's cousins, the sons of his father's brother; secondly, that they have never been in dispute with him; also that they buried Nicostratus; in addition, that Chariades here was never a friend of Nicostratus, either here in Athens or on campaign; and finally, that the business partnership, on which Chariades places so much reliance, is a fiction. (27) Leaving all that aside, gentlemen, it's appropriate for you to examine the characters of both sides. For Thrasippus, the father of Hagnon and Hagnotheus, has in the past performed public services on your behalf and paid contributions, and in general he was an excellent citizen. Hagnon and Hagnotheus themselves have never travelled anywhere abroad except on your orders, and while here in Athens they have not been useless citizens; they serve in the army, pay taxes, and carry out all their other civic duties, and, as everyone knows, behave as law-abiding citizens, (28) so that it would have been much more fitting for them than for Chariades to claim Nicostratus's estate under a will. For Chariades, when he was resident here in Athens, in the first place was dragged off to prison as a thief caught red-handed and then, after he and some associates were released by the Eleven, all of whom you publicly condemned to death, he was again indicted as a criminal before the Council, but he escaped trial (29) and for 17 years after that he never came to Athens, except when Nicostratus died. And he never served on any military campaign on behalf of the city or paid any tax, except perhaps after he claimed Nicostratus's estate, and neither has he performed any liturgies. And yet such is his character that he is not satisfied with evading justice for his misdeeds, but he is claiming property that belongs to others. (30) If Hagnon and Hagnotheus were meddlesome like some other citizens,

ἴσως ἂν οὐ περὶ τῶν Νικοστράτου χρημάτων ἠμφισβήτει, ἀλλ' ὑπὲρ τοῦ σώματος ἠγωνίζετο· νῦν δ', ὦ ἄνδρες δικασταί, τοῦτον μὲν ἄλλος, ἐάν τις βούληται, τιμωρήσεται, [31] τουτοισὶ δ' ὑμεῖς βοηθήσατε, καὶ μὴ περὶ πλείονος ποιήσησθε τοὺς ἀδίκως τἀλλότρια ἔχειν βουλομένους ἢ τοὺς γένει τῷ τεθνεῶτι προσήκοντας καὶ χωρὶς τούτων ἤδη τι ἐκεῖνον εὐεργετηκότας, ἀλλὰ καὶ τῶν νόμων ἀναμνησθέντες καὶ τῶν ὅρκων οὓς ὠμόσατε, πρὸς δὲ τούτοις καὶ τῶν μαρτυριῶν ἃς ἡμεῖς παρεσχήμεθα, τὰ δίκαια ψηφίσασθε.

perhaps he would not now be claiming Nicostratus's property but would be on trial for his life. As it is, judges, someone else will prosecute him, if anyone is willing. (31) But you must help Hagnon and Hagnotheus, and not give preference to those who unjustly seek to receive the property of others over those who are related by blood to the dead man and apart from that have before now been of service to him. Mindful both of the laws and of the oaths that you swore, and also of the testimony that we have put before you, vote in accordance with justice.

COMMENTARY

1. Introduction
The speaker of this short supplementary speech, whose identity is not known (see p. 121), establishes his credentials as a supporter of the claimants Hagnon and Hagnotheus, one of whom has already delivered the main speech. He adumbrates a major theme of this second speech: the contrast between inheritance claims based on kinship and those based on wills.

1 Hagnon here and Hagnotheus: When referring to the two brothers, the speaker always mentions Hagnon first. Although it is impossible to be certain, modern commentators have taken this to suggest that Hagnon may have been the older of the two brothers, and that it was he who delivered the main speech. (See, e.g., Edwards, 2007, 66.) On the deictic pronoun *houtosi* ('this man here'), see on 'my uncle here', 2.35; the phrase 'Hagnon here and Hagnotheu' recurs at §2.

gentlemen: On addresses to the judges in general, and in particular at the beginning of a speech, see on 'gentlemen', 1.1. After this, Isaeus uses his preferred form, 'gentlemen' (*ō andres*) 8 more times in this speech: to engage the judges in the speaker's argument (§§2, 13, 14, 21, 22) or to mark the transition from narrative to argumentation (§11) or to a new stage of the argument (§§18, 27). By way of variation, the occupational address 'judges' (*ō andres dikastai*) occurs once (§30).

their father: Identified at §27 as Thrasippus. Hagnon son of Thrasippus is named as the lessee of a silver mine in *c.* 338/7 (Davies, 1971, 257–58, cited by Edwards, 2007. 66, n.1.).

impossible to find witnesses of events in another state: Hagnon and Hagnotheus could not directly refute the evidence of Chariades's witnesses, who testified that Nicostratus made the will. They did, nevertheless, find witnesses to testify that Chariades had never been a friend or business partner of Nicostratus, either in Athens or abroad. Cf. §26, where the speaker summarizes the testimony brought on the brothers' behalf.

sufficient proof: For the meaning of *tekmēria*, here translated as 'proof', see on 'strongest indication', 1.12. The speaker foreshadows his more detailed argument (§§11–18) about the unreliability of witness testimony in disputes about wills, compared with 'circumstantial evidence' or inferences from signs.

all those who claim ... on the basis of a will: This includes not only

Chariades, the opponent of Hagnon and Hagnotheos in the *diadikasia*, but others who withdrew their claims before the dispute came to court (see §§7–10).

trying to deceive you: It is a commonplace of Athenian forensic oratory for a speaker to warn the judges against being 'deceived' by his opponent. Cf. Kremmydas (2013, 66–67): 'The wording used by the orator is cautious lest he alienate his audience; this topos portrays deception as an attempt, an intention, rather than a certainty... While its main rhetorical function is to undermine the opponent's *ethos*, it also implicitly aims at arousing hostile emotions towards him in the audience. At the same time, it predisposes the audience negatively towards the opponent.'

2–6. The identity of Nicostratus

The identity of the supposed testator in this case, Nicostratus, is disputed: according to Hagnon and Hagnotheus he was the son of Thrasymachus, while Chariades (initially, at least) identified him as the son of Smicrus. It appears that Chariades amended his claim before the case came to court, but Isaeus exploits the confusion as a means of discrediting him.

2   claim: A formal written claim (*lēxis*) was submitted to the court by anyone claiming a deceased Athenian's estate as his next of kin or as a son adopted by will. When there were two or more rival claimants, each of them had to submit his (or her) own *lēxis*. A claim could be submitted at any time of year except during the last month, Skirophorion, presumably to ensure that the case was handled throughout by the same archon (Harrison, 1968, 158–59). We do not have the text of a *lēxis*, but we may infer from this speech that it included, as a minimum, the name of the dead man, the claimant's own name, and the basis of his claim (i.e. blood relationship to the deceased or a will).

the son of Thrasymachus: A male Athenian's full name had three components: his given name, patronymic (father's name), and demotic (on which, see on 'Eponymus of Acharnae', 2.3). His father's name was thus a crucial part of an individual's identity, serving in various contexts to distinguish him from others with the same given name.

they have produced witnesses: No witness testimony is introduced in the course of this speech, but the speaker mentions testimony produced by Hagnon and Hagnotheus during the main speech. Here, and at §§18, 20, and 26, he refers to depositions about specific facts, while at §31 he refers in general terms to all the testimony produced on their behalf.

3 **supporters:** The Greek word is *syndikountes* (lit. 'co-litigants'), but this evidently refers to the witnesses who testified on Chariades's behalf that Nicostratus made the will. They are not named, but the speaker later tries to discredit them by saying that they were friends of Chariades, not of Nicostratus (§23).

yet they are claiming the estate of the son of Thrasymachus: It is not clear exactly what procedural manoeuvres took place before the case came to court, but presumably Chariades had amended his initial claim so that he was formally claiming the estate of Nicostratus the son of Thrasymachus. If he did not make the amendment voluntarily, it is likely that he would have been obliged to do so by a ruling of the archon at the preliminary hearing (*anakrisis*). Cf. Isae. 10.2, where the speaker complains that he was forced to change the basis of his claim at the *anakrisis*.

4 **deposit:** Litigants who claimed an inheritance in the Athenian courts were, at least in certain circumstances, required to pay a deposit of one tenth of the value of the disputed estate, which was forfeited to the state in the event of failure. In all the references in extant speeches, this deposit was paid by litigants who were either coming forward against an earlier claimant or challenging the occupant of an estate who had been successful in an earlier legal action. Wyse (1904, 374) reviews the primary evidence and concludes that it is not safe to infer that the first claimant to apply to the court was exempt from the deposit. Harrison (1971, 181–82) thinks it more plausible that the deposit was required only in specific situations, including when the claimant was trying to block a rival claim by means of a *diamartyria* (see on 6.12) or, as in this case, when he was asserting his right to succeed as an adopted son in the face of a *lēxis* submitted by the next of kin. For primary references and a fuller summary of the scholarly debate, see Griffith-Williams (2013, 101, n.36).

6 **an argument about kinship as well as about the will:** The antithesis between kinship and wills (or bequests) recurs throughout the speech. In general, the speaker's aim is to convince the judges that inheritance claims based on blood relationship to the deceased are more credible than those based on a will, but here his specific point is that by calling Nicostratus's identity into question (and thus also his relationship to Hagnon and Hagnotheus) Chariades has introduced a distraction from the real issue in this case: the authenticity of the supposed will.

7–10. The contest for Nicostratus's estate (narrative)
In this brief but colourful narrative Isaeus seeks to discredit Chariades by

suggesting that he was one of several fraudulent claimants to the estate, attracted by the size of Nicostratus's fortune. The use of personal names to identify all the unsuccessful claimants enhances both the vividness and the credibility of the narrative – and even its absurdity, given that at least two of the claimants, Ctesias of Besa and Cranaus, would have been known to the judges from the comic stage.

When a claimant to the estate of a deceased Athenian submitted his *lēxis* to the archon (see on 'claim', §2) it was publicized, initially, by being posted on the archon's noticeboard, then read out at the next full meeting of the Assembly, and finally through a proclamation by the herald (Harrison, 1968, 159). According to [Dem.] 43.5, the herald's proclamation asked whether anyone wanted to claim the estate on the basis of kinship or a will, or to pay a deposit as security for the costs of such a claim. If there was only one claimant, the estate was formally awarded to him (or her), but in the event of a contest the case proceeded to trial by means of a *diadikasia* after a preliminary hearing, the *anakrisis*, before the archon (on which see commentary on 6.12–16). In principle there was no limit to the number of claimants who could contest an estate in a *diadikasia*, but in practice it seems that there were rarely more than two.

Despite the lack of detail, these sections of the speech give some indication of the process by which a number of competing claims could be narrowed down to two before the case came to court, either by private negotiation between the claimants or with the intervention of the archon at a court hearing. According to Humphreys (2019, 250) it may have been the 'inordinate number of claims to the estate' that prompted Hagnon and Hagnotheus to seek the support of 'a respectable and disinterested advocate' as their supporting speaker.

7 For who did not cut his hair…?: A series of three ironic rhetorical questions evokes a somewhat absurd picture of fake mourning in Athens after the news of Nicostratus's death was received. Hall (2006, 389), while noting that humour is 'culturally and historically relative', includes this passage in a discussion of 'transparently obvious bids for jury laughter'.

came into court six times: Most modern editors and translators, including Wyse (1904), Roussel (1926), Forster (1827), and Cobetto Ghiggia (2012) have taken ἑξάκις ('six times') in the manuscripts as an error, and have accepted Valckenaer's emendation to ἐξ Ἀκῆς ('from Ace', i.e. Akko in modern Israel). The meaning would thus be 'when the two talents arrived from Ace', which has led to the hypothesis that Nicostratus died in 374 BC, when an army was assembled there for an invasion of Egypt by the Persian satrap Pharnabazus. Edwards (2002; 2007, 68) follows Wevers (1969, 21–23) in accepting 'six times', which is consistent with the multiple claims to the estate described at §§8–10. But the simple verb ἠλθέτην, meaning 'came' or 'arrived' (itself an emendation of the manuscript ἠλθέτον) then requires further emendation. Wevers's suggestion is ἠθληθήτην (literally 'were contested', as for a prize) but Edwards, whose emendation I have adopted, prefers εἰσηλθέτην (lit. 'entered' or 'came in', i.e. 'came into court').

how many kinsmen and sons adopted by will: Another example of the kinship/wills antithesis: some of the fraudulent claimants to Nicostratus's estate said they were related to him, others that he had left a will in their favour.

8 Demosthenes said he was his nephew: If Demosthenes really had been a nephew of Nicostratus, he would have had a better claim to the estate than Hagnon and Hagnotheus, who, as cousins, were more distantly related. Nothing more is known about this Demosthenes, who may or may not have had some connection with the famous orator. The name was a very common one; *LGPN* records 261 instances, including 73 in Attica.

exposed by Hagnon and Hagnotheus: Presumably Hagnon and Hagnotheus were able to persuade the archon that Demosthenes was an impostor.

Telephus: A relatively unusual name in Attica: only six out of a total of 65 instances in *LGPN*.

had given him all his property: This implies that Telephus claimed Nicostratus had left a will in his favour, but no detail is given.

Ameiniades: Nothing further is known of this alleged false claimant, but his name is uncommon: *LGPN* has only ten instances in total, of which nine were in Attica.

a 'son' of Nicostratus who was not yet three years old: Presumably Ameiniades put himself forward as the guardian of Nicostratus's supposed son. A similar accusation is made against Androcles and Antidorus in Isaeus 6; cf. on 'entering themselves as guardians', 6.36.

11 years: For the significance of a long absence from Athens, see on 'never travelled anywhere abroad except on your orders', §27.

9 Pyrrhus of Lamptra: The demotic gives Pyrrhus a specific legal identity (cf. on 'Eponymus of Acharnae', 2.3). Pyrrhus was a relatively common name (*LGPN* cites 61 instances in Attica, from a total of 296), so perhaps the reason for the use of the demotic was to distinguish him from others of the same name who might have been known to the judges.

dedicated by Nicostratus to Athena, and given to him by Nicostratus himself: Cf. Edwards (2007, 70, n.11): 'The speaker's brevity heightens the apparent absurdity. Pyrrhus may have claimed that Nicostratus left the money to him for the duration of his life, then it was to be dedicated to Athena; or that it was dedicated to the goddess on condition that payments were made to Pyrrhus during his lifetime.'

Ctesias of Besa: Papachrysostomou (2019, 233) identifies him with a character in fourth century comedy who was portrayed as an 'insatiable parasite' and 'satirized for his huge appetite' by Anaxilas (frr. 25, 29, 30 KA) and Philetaerus (fr. 3 KA). (Cf. Wyse, 1904, 378.) Again, the name is relatively common in Attica (48 instances, out of a total of 114 recorded by *LGPN*). A Ctesias of Besa was archon in the year 370/69 (cf. Cobetto Ghiggia, 2012, 157, n.11) but his connection with the comedic character, and with the person mentioned by Isaeus, is uncertain. Tartaglia (2019, 169) points out that the archon Ctesias of Besa seems too early for Anaxilas, who was active around the middle of the century, but the precise dates of his works are not known. The Ctesias of Isae. 4.9 and of Anaxilas's comedy, if both were written in the 350s, could have been a descendant of the archon. (On the dating of Isae. 4, see pp. 121–22 above.)

Cranaus: An associate (possibly son) of Ctesias of Besa, with whom he is portrayed in a comedy by Anaxilas (fr. 29 KA) in a competition for excessive eating (Wyse, 1904, 378; Papachrysostomou, 2019). Again, the identification of the comic character with the man mentioned at Isae. 4.9 remains conjectural, although the association of Ctesias and Cranaus in both Isae. 4 and fr. 28 KA is strongly suggestive of a link. (Cf. Tartaglia, 2019, 181.) The name Cranaus is uncommon; only seven instances are recorded by *LGPN*, of which three are in Attica.

their freedman: This passage implies that a freed slave's former owner(s) would have a claim on his property after his death, but it is not certain whether this was a general legal provision or simply a condition attached to manumission at the discretion of the former owner(s). Freed slaves in Athens, unlike Rome, did not automatically become citizens but acquired the status of metics (resident aliens). Cf. on 'He had a freedwoman', 6.19.

10 Chariades ... son: This sentence has caused problems for modern editors and translators; the text is probably corrupt, and the precise meaning is obscure. What is clear is that Chariades initially claimed the estate on behalf of his illegitimate son (as either a natural or adopted son of Nicostratus), but later dropped that claim and produced the 'will' in which he himself had supposedly been adopted by Nicostratus.

his child by his mistress: A child born to an Athenian man by a woman to whom he was not legally married was illegitimate, and ineligible either to inherit from his natural father or to be adopted into another family, so any attempt to 'legitimize' such a child by way of adoption would have been fraudulent. It is not clear what procedure Chariades followed: he could have claimed that Nicostratus had adopted the child *inter vivos*, or in a will, or perhaps this was an attempt at a posthumous adoption.

The Greek word translated here as 'child' is *paidion*, a diminutive of *pais* ('child', 'boy' or 'son'). As might be expected, the diminutive often refers to a baby or very young child, but that is not always the case; without qualification or contextual clues, *paidion* does not necessarily mean 'small child'. Cf. on 'my little boy', 2.36, and for discussion, see Golden (2015, 12).

In all the Athenian cases where we have any information about the age of the adopted son, he was an adult, perhaps (in the case of an adoption *inter vivos*) reflecting the need for someone mature enough to provide emotional and practical support for an elderly adoptive father (cf. on 'since she had two', 2.9). Another of Isaeus's clients makes the point (in a tendentious argument) that adopting a child would be risky, because it is impossible to predict how the child's character will develop (Isae. 7. 33, with Griffith-Williams (2013, 78-79). There was, in any event, no legal reason why a child could not be adopted, and the example of Moschion's adoption by Demeas (Men. *Sam.* 697) 'probably shows that adoption *inter vivos* of minors was not inconceivable to Menander's audience' (Rubinstein, 1993, 22).

recognized as a citizen: If the attempted adoption had been successful, the child would have been recognized not only as the legitimate son of Nicostratus but also as an Athenian citizen. The Greek word translated here as 'citizen' is *astos*, 'that is to say a legitimate son of an *astē* woman with all incumbent claims and rights' (Blok, 2017, 169). Only an adult male was a citizen in the fullest sense (*politēs*), entitled to participate actively in the public life of the city.

he too: Initially Chariades, like Demosthenes and Ameiniades, claimed the estate on the basis of blood relationship to Nicostratus.

on the issue of kinship ... the will: Chariades's claim on behalf of his illegitimate son was based on the child's alleged kinship with Nicostratus, but he abandoned this and instead claimed that he himself had been adopted in Nicostratus's will. It is not clear whether he had submitted a formal claim to the court on the child's behalf, or simply decided not to proceed with such a claim when he realized it would not succeed. (On the antithesis between kinship and wills, see on 'an argument about kinship as well as about the will', §6.)

paid a deposit: See on 'deposit', §4.

11–17. Wills and kinship (argumentation)
The speaker's argumentation reinforces the message conveyed by the narrative: it is all too easy for wills to be fabricated, and difficult to be sure that they are genuine, so the judges should err on the side of caution and vote for Hagnon and Hagnotheus as Nicostratus's next of kin. Initially he does not refer specifically to Nicostratus's supposed will, but seeks to create doubt about its validity by means of general arguments. He begins by proposing two changes to current practice that would tip the balance in favour of claims from the next of kin. The first is that unsuccessful claimants by will should face an increased financial penalty, and the second that in disputes about wills (unlike other litigation), greater weight should be placed on circumstantial evidence than on witness testimony. Caillemer (1879, 5) took these at face value as serious proposals by Isaeus for reform of a manifestly dysfunctional system. The speaker's argument is, however, tendentious, and it is worth remembering that, if Isaeus's clients had been claiming the estate under a will, he (like any competent advocate) would have found arguments in their favour and against the next of kin.

11 on the basis of will: Again, the argument is tendentious; the premise is that a claim to an estate based on a will is less likely to be genuine than one based on kinship.

the usual rate: A reference to the deposit of one tenth of the value of the estate (cf. on 'deposit', §4).

the full value of the estate: Even if an increased deposit might have deterred some fraudulent claimants, the speaker's proposal seems unduly punitive. Given the inherent uncertainty in any litigation, even some genuine claimants might have been put off by a requirement for unsuccessful claimants to forfeit the full value of the estate if they lost, which in some cases could have exceeded the claimant's own assets.

the laws would not be held in contempt: Using the rhetorical device known as a tricolon, the speaker justifies his proposal on three grounds, starting with the overarching objective of respect for the law.

neither would blood relations be insulted: On the force of 'insulted' (Greek *hybrizeto*), see on 'insult him', 2.15.

no-one would tell lies against the dead: This final element of the tricolon appeals to the Athenians' sense of respect for the dead, and may have been intended to remind the judges of Solon's law against speaking ill of the dead in public (*kakōs agoreuein*, Plut. *Solon* 21.1; Leão and Rhodes, 2016, fr. 32a).

anyone who so wishes: The wording is reminiscent of that used of a 'volunteer prosecutor' in public cases (cf. on 'if anyone is willing', §30). It was not open to absolutely anyone to initiate a private action, including a claim to an estate, but what the speaker means is that it was all too easy for anyone to fabricate a claim based on a will.

12 circumstantial evidence: The Greek word *tekmēria* could refer to any kind of evidence from which inferences may be drawn, including witness testimony (see on 'strongest indication', 1.12). Here a distinction is being made between the evidence (such as that of an eyewitness) that proves a fact directly, and 'indirect' or 'circumstantial' evidence, from which the existence of a fact may be inferred but not directly proved.

since the man against whom they are testifying is dead: Although the general line of argument is tendentious, this is a reasonable point; in fact, a similar observation was made by the English Court of Appeal in 2001: 'Probate proceedings peculiarly pose problems for the court because the protagonist, the testator, is dead and those who wish to challenge the will are often not able to give evidence of the circumstances of the will.' *Fuller v Strum* [2001] EWCA Civ 1879 (7 December 2001), cited by Griffith-Williams (2013, 15, n.51).

13 don't even disclose the content to those who are present: According to Rubinstein (1993, 34, n.5): 'We may infer from [Isae. 4.13 and [Dem.] 46.28] that it would seem at least plausible to the judges that a testator might wish to keep secret the contents of the will.' An Athenian would, nevertheless, consider it essential to make his will in the presence of witnesses, who might be required to testify in court in the event of a dispute.

14 only if he was in his right mind: This allusion to Solon's law on wills (see General Introduction, p. 3) introduces a line of argument which seems like an attempt to distract the judges from the real issue, given that (according to the speaker) Nicostratus did not make a will at all. But it could provide an alternative argument against the validity of the document produced by Chariades, in case any of the judges were inclined to accept it as genuine. (The speaker's later attack on the character of Chariades could be taken to imply – although he does not explicitly say this – that if Nicostratus really did make a will adopting such a villain, he cannot have been in his right mind.) In any event, the reference to other grounds on which a will might be found invalid could have created additional uncertainty in the minds of the judges.

15 on the basis of a will ... on the basis of kinship: Once again (cf. §§6, 7, 10), the argument is slanted towards those who claim an estate as next of kin, but this does not amount to 'a deeply ingrained negative attitude to adoption', which 'encouraged Athenians to challenge a deceased relative's choice of a son' (Hunter, 1993, 105). Athenian litigants who contested wills or adoptions are more likely to have been motivated by factors specific to their own case (greed, envy, malice, or perhaps a genuine sense of injustice) than by a general prejudice against testamentary disposition.

everyone agrees ... his next of kin: Another tendentious argument: if Isaeus had been writing a speech for Chariades, he might have said 'Everyone agrees that Nicostratus was entitled to make a will.'

16 those on kinship: Solon's law on intestate succession (discussed in the General Introduction, p. 4) set out the order in which a dead man's collateral relatives would inherit his estate if he died leaving no natural or adopted legitimate sons.

not in his right mind because of old age or illness: See on 'only if he was in his right mind', §14.

17 witnesses, by whom you might be deceived: Cf. on 'trying to deceive you', §1. In the absence of modern scientific evidence and reliable documentary records, witness testimony was the main form of evidence in the Athenian courts. The Athenians were, nevertheless, well aware that witnesses could be corrupt, and it was an obvious tactic for litigants to accuse their opponents' witnesses of lying.

prosecutions for false testimony: A witness in any trial (not just the deponent of a *diamartyria*, as in Isaeus 2 and 6) was liable to prosecution for false testimony in a *dikē pseudomartyriōn*, and a defeated litigant could effectively reopen the case by prosecuting his opponent's witness(es). The availability of this procedure could not, of course, prevent corrupt testimony, but it was an important safeguard, especially since the penalty on a third conviction was *atimia* (loss of citizen's rights).

degrees of kinship: For the legal significance of the Greek term *ankhisteia*, see on 'our degree of kinship', 1.4.

the laws which you made: The speaker follows the convention of addressing the judges in a particular case as representatives of the Athenian citizenry as a whole, past and present, in both their judicial and legislative capacities. The laws on intestate succession, to which the speaker here refers, were probably originated by the 6th century legislator, Solon.

18–26. Summary of the case for Hagnon and Hagnotheus (argumentation)
The speaker reverts seamlessly to the specifics of the dispute, summarizing the case for Hagnon and Hagnotheus and against Chariades. The brothers have brought witness testimony on five points: their blood relationship to Nicostratus, their good relations with him, their conduct of his funeral, the fact that Chariades and Nicostratus were not friends, and the absence of any business partnership between them.

In §19 the speaker places great emphasis on one particular piece of circumstantial evidence: the fact that Chariades did not remove Nicostratus's body for cremation, or collect the bones. This reflects the strong expectation in classical Athens that responsibility for a funeral and the associated arrangements would be assumed by the son and heir or other closest relation of the deceased. In a disputed case it was, therefore, in the interest of a claimant to show that he had conducted the funeral (or explain why he had been unable do so) and that his opponent had not, but there was no strictly legal connection between the conduct of a dead man's funeral and the right to inherit his estate. In sum, none of the speaker's arguments from probability conclusively prove that the will is not genuine, but their collective effect is to enhance the probability that Chariades's story is false.

18 In addition to this, gentlemen: The speaker now moves from general argumentation about kinship and wills to the specifics of the present case. It is difficult to understand why Hunter (1993, 105, n.1) cites Isae. 4.18 as indicative of 'a negative attitude to adoption': the speaker is not expressing a view about adoption in general, but arguing that the supposed adoption of Chariades by Nicostratus did not happen.

more likely that the will was genuine: While denying that Chariades was in fact a friend of Nicostratus, the speaker acknowledges that if they had been friends, the will would have been more likely to be genuine.

some people who don't get on well with their relatives have preferred friends outside the family to their closest kin: Family strife is cited as a reason for adoption at Isae. 1.10 and 7.29, and [Dem.] 44.63 (discussed by Rubinstein, 1993, 76–77). But (apart from Isaeus 2, where the speaker and his adoptive father were previously related by marriage but not by blood) Isaeus 4 is the only surviving speech from a case in which one of the parties claimed to have been adopted as a friend rather than a relative of the deceased.

messmates: The speaker denies that Nicostratus and Chariades were messmates, but he does not deny that a messmate would have been a suitable candidate for adoption; communal eating created a strong social bond in ancient Greece (Golden, 2015, 31).

we have produced witnesses: See on 'they have produced witnesses', §2.

19 And consider this: The speaker focuses the judges' attention on what he claims is a point of particular importance.

the greatest testimony to Chariades's effrontery: The speaker exaggerates the significance of Chariades's alleged failings. His emphasis on this point seems to suggest a lack of more compelling evidence.

neither took away the body of his adoptive father for cremation, nor collected the bones: When a soldier died away from Athens, his body would be cremated *in situ*, and the bones returned to Athens for burial. Hagnon and Hagnotheus were clearly not in a position to deal with the cremation, but they could still blame Chariades for failing to do so, and we learn at §26 that they did bury Nicostratus's remains when these were returned to Athens.

strangers: The speaker blames Chariades for allowing Nicostratus's body to be removed by 'strangers', but the reproach may or may not have been justified. Ideally, the duty would have been performed by the dead man's heir or next of kin, or at least his friends, but in a case of necessity it would have to be done by anyone who was available.

most impious: The speaker cannot claim that Chariades has acted illegally in failing to assume responsibility for Nicostratus's remains, but his use of the word 'impious' (Gk. *anosios*) underlines the religious nature of the funeral rites.

customary rites: The 'customary rites' (Gk. *ta nomizomena*) for an Athenian who had died comprised the funeral, 30 days of mourning, and annual commemorative rituals at the tomb.

20 But, by Zeus: According to Denommé (1974, 122–23), formulaic oaths (imprecations) are a feature of colloquial speech, the use of which conveys an impression of spontaneity; in Isaeus's speeches they are associated, in particular, with 'an intense effort to persuade'. Cf. Isae. 3.24, 25, 39, 49, 73; 4.24; 7.33; 11.35 ('By Zeus'); 6.61 ('By Zeus and Apollo'); 11.36 ('By the gods'); 6.58, 8.29 ('By the gods of Olympus'). Sommerstein and Torrance (2014, 234–35) identify the ironic use of 'by Zeus' by courtroom speakers to signal an imaginary objection put into the mouth of an opponent, which the speaker was setting up for a 'crushing refutation'.

did he administer Nicostratus's property…?: The rhetorical question is ironic, and evidently expects an answer in the negative. It apparently refers to Chariades's claim that he was a business associate of Nicostratus (cf. §26), but it is not clear what duties he has allegedly neglected to perform in relation to Nicostratus's property. For Isaeus's use of irony to ridicule his client's opponent, see on 'they are now treating us so well', 2.33.

testimony ... has been produced for you: See on 'they have produced witnesses', §2.

excuses: This is a loaded word (Gk. *prophaseis*), intended to discredit any explanation Chariades may have provided for his actions or failure to act.

when he directly admits the facts: Again, it is not clear precisely which 'facts' Chariades has admitted, apart from his failure to remove Nicostratus's body for cremation and collect the bones.

21 Well now, gentlemen: Once again (cf. on 'gentlemen', §11) the speaker uses a direct address to the judges to engage them in his argument.

trying to deceive you: Cf. on 'trying to deceive you', §1.

rob Hagnon and Hagnotheus: The Greek verb *aposterein* (lit. 'to deprive') is often used tendentiously in inheritance cases to imply robbery or fraud on the part of a speaker's opponent, pre-supposing that it is the speaker himself who is entitled to the property in dispute. Cf., e.g., Isae. 7.7, 25; 8.3, 27, 43, 45; 9.2, 23, 31; 10.6, 15, 17, 18, 28.

what the laws have given to them: On the Athenian law of intestate succession, see on 'those on kinship', §16.

many others: This is a vague statement, designed to create the impression that fraudulent claims to the estates of Athenians who died abroad were a common occurrence. Once again, the speaker is trying to cast doubt into the judges' minds about the reliability of wills, and we have no means of knowing the true extent of the problem.

22 nothing much to lose: A reference to the deposit paid by claimants in inheritance cases (see on 'deposit', §4 and 'the full value of the estate', §11).

But you, gentlemen: The speaker addresses the judges directly, ostensibly to remind them of their legal duty but actually in an attempt to steer them towards the conclusion he wants them to reach.

23 no certain knowledge of the truth: Cf. on 'none of you knows', 1.42.

not friends of the deceased but of Chariades: The speaker seeks to discredit Chariades's witnesses by pointing out that if Nicostratus had really made a will, he would have summoned his own friends to witness it, not those of Chariades.

the same right of kinship: Here, as in Isaeus 1, Isaeus is deploying a tendentious argument about reciprocal inheritance rights. In fact, if either Hagnon or Hagnotheus had died, the surviving brother would have inherited

Oration 4 155

his property as next of kin. Nicostratus, as their cousin, would have had no right to inherit until both of them were dead. (Cf. on 'you yourselves expect...', 1.44.)

24 by Zeus: See on 'But, by Zeus', §20.

Nicostratus's kinsmen ... other people: According to Chariades, Hagnon and Hagnotheus are not related to Nicostratus because he was the son of Smicrus, not Thrasymachus.

Surely they are not so insane...: The speaker ridicules Chariades's witnesses with the ironic argument that if they really were related to Nicostratus they would be claiming the estate for themselves, not testifying against their own interest on behalf of Chariades. For Isaeus's use of irony to ridicule his client's opponent, see on 'they are now treating us so well', 2.33.

25 in future ... that they are more closely related to Nicostratus: The Athenian system was not designed to establish who had the best claim to an estate in absolute terms, but rather to check the credentials of any claimants, and, in a contested case, decide which of the parties before the court had the best claim. Consequently, the winner in a *diadikasia* remained open to challenge from other claimants in the future (Harrison, 1968, 157). This lack of finality has sometimes been criticized because it could lead to seemingly unending litigation (as, especially, in the disputes about the estates of Dicaeogenes (Isaeus. 5) and Hagnias (Isaeus 11 and [Dem.] 43). There must, on the other hand, have been cases where the 'openness' of the procedure gave a legitimate claimant the means of securing justice, for example if a soldier was away from Athens for a long period and unaware of his kinsman's death, and found someone else in possession of the estate when he returned.

what argument will those who claim through kinship be able to put forward?: According to Wyse (1904) *ad loc.*, 'They might say that the will was forged or invalid', but perhaps the position was not quite so straightforward. As Wyse points out, the will of Dicaeogenes II was challenged more than 20 years after his death, but that was an exceptionally complex case of which we do not know the full details. There may well have been a perception that it was more difficult, even if it was not strictly impossible, to challenge a will once it had been validated by a court.

26 young men: The Greek word for 'young man' (*neaniskos*) does not refer to a specifically defined age group; on the inconsistency of classical usage, see Golden (2015, 11–12). Hagnon and Hagnotheus were old enough to have done military service away from Athens (cf. on 'never travelled anywhere abroad except on your orders', §27) so they were probably at least 21. Cf. on 'the right age', 2.6..

They have produced witnesses: See on 'they have produced witnesses', §2. The speaker now gives a brief summary of all the testimony produced on behalf of Hagnon and Hagnotheus.

that they have never been in dispute with him: The significance of this is that if Nicostratus had never quarrelled with Hagnon and Hagnotheus, he would have had no reason to disinherit them by adopting a son from outside the family. Since Nicostratus had been away from Athens for 11 years, and Hagnon and Hagnotheus were 'young men' at the time of his death, and probably still children when he left Athens, the opportunities for them to quarrel may in any event have been limited. (Cf. Lentzsch, 1932, 17.) So the argument would have carried some weight, but it falls short of positive evidence that the claimants had been on friendly or intimate terms with the deceased.

they buried Nicostratus: Hagnon and Hagnotheus have also produced witnesses to testify that they buried Nicostratus's remains after these were returned to Athens. For the evidentiary significance of this, see the introductory note to §§18–26.

Chariades here was never a friend of Nicostratus: The speaker has already conceded (§18) that Athenians do sometimes adopt friends outside the family, and that Nicostratus's will would have been more likely to be genuine if he and Chariades really had been friends. So this is a point of some importance, but there was clearly a conflict of evidence between the opposing parties, and it is impossible to know which side was telling the truth.

the business partnership ... is a fiction: Again, this is an important point, and it appears that Chariades has told a persuasive story about his business association with Nicostratus.

27–31. *The character of the rival claimants*
Isaeus concludes the speech by contrasting the good character of his clients, Hagnon and Hagnotheus (and their father, Thrasippus) with the criminal record of their opponent, Chariades. (Cf. the introduction to this speech, pp. 127–28.) Although this is not presented as part of the speaker's legal case, it does contribute to his argument from probability by suggesting both that Chariades would have been capable of forging a will, and that if Nicostratus had wanted to adopt a son, he would have been likely to choose Hagnon or Hagnotheus in view of their and their father's exemplary record of service to the state.

It is noteworthy that the speaker does not produce witness testimony in support of either his clients' or their opponent's character, and neither does he say that any such testimony was produced in the course of the main speech. The absence of supporting testimony might cast some doubt on the accuracy of his claims, but it is unlikely that they were completely invented (cf. Griffith-Williams, forthcoming b).

27 Leaving all that aside, gentlemen: These words mark the transition from legal argumentation to consideration of character.

performed public services: This indicates that Thrasippus was among the richest Athenians, who were required to perform services ('liturgies') as a contribution to the public purse. The minimum financial qualification for membership of the 'liturgical class' was probably at least three talents, and the range of services performed included acting as trierarch, gymnasiarch, or *chorēgos* (supervisor of dramatic festivals). Cf. on 'served as gymnasiarch in his deme', 2.42.

on your behalf: A more personalized way of saying 'on behalf of the city', emphasizing that the judges have all benefited individually from Thrasippus's services. (On the judges as representatives of the Athenian citizenry, see on 'the laws which you made', §17.)

paid contributions: A reference to the special war taxes (*eisphorai*) that were levied on the richest Athenians in times of need.

never travelled anywhere abroad except on your orders: Unlike Nicostratus and Chariades, who were mercenary soldiers, Hagnon and Hagnotheus did not leave Athens except on official military service for the city. There was no formal requirement for an Athenian citizen to live in Athens, but residence in (or absence from) the city could sometimes be taken as an indication of (lack of) patriotism or (dis)loyalty. (Cf., especially, Lys. 31.5–6.) In an unpublished conference paper, 'The citizen abroad', Chris Carey discusses this concept as part of a 'shifting set of expectations which form a penumbra of informal values around the harder core of formal responsibilities'. He suggests that 'The reasons for Isaios' remark [at 4.27] may be multiple but one aim may be to make the case, and [Hagnon and Hagnotheus's] case, matter to the judges. The arrival of the dead man's money in Athens led to a large number of claims and the whole business may have looked to some like a struggle between fortune hunters for the money of a man who never saw himself as part of the civic body.' (UCL/Jagiellonian University conference: 'Citizenship in classical antiquity: current perspectives and challenges', London, July 2019.)

not been useless citizens: Hagnon and Hagnotheus had clearly not performed liturgies themselves, perhaps because they were too young (cf. on 'young men', §26). In any event, each of them would have inherited no more than half of their father's estate (less, if there had been other brothers) so they may not have met the financial qualification. The speaker therefore mentions other ways in which they had been 'useful' to the state.

as everyone knows: On the 'common knowledge' topos as a substitute for hard evidence such as witness testimony, see on 'everyone knows', 1.27. In this context, it is likely that the specific services already mentioned by the speaker were genuinely known to the wider community.

28 more fitting for them ... under a will: The speaker is not inviting the judges to award the estate to Hagnon and Hagnotheus on the grounds that their exemplary behaviour makes them more deserving recipients than Chariades. His argument is that if Nicostratus *had* made a will (which the speaker denies) he would, in view of their behaviour, have been more likely to nominate them than Chariades as the beneficiaries.

For Chariades The speaker now turns from the good character of Hagnon and Hagntheus and their father to the criminal record of their opponent. This would have been taken by the judges as an indication that Chariades was capable of forging a will, even though his past wrongdoings do not involve inheritance fraud, so it supports the speaker's argument from probability. Cf. Lanni (2006, 60–61): 'The first justification for character evidence we find in the speeches [of the Attic orators] is that it assists the jury in finding facts through an argument from *eikos* or probability. The Athenians tended to view character as stable and unchanging.'

dragged off to prison: According to Isaeus's account, Chariades was arrested under the summary procedure known as *apagōgē* (lit. 'dragging away'). Certain categories of offenders, including thieves caught red-handed (see following note) could be summarily arrested by any citizen and taken before the appropriate authority (see on 'the Eleven', below). An offender who admitted his guilt was immediately executed, but those who denied the offence were put on trial. Hansen (1976) provides a full account of the procedure.

red-handed: The Greek term *ep' autophōrōi* is translated as 'in the act' by, e.g. Forster (1927), Edwards (2007), and Carey (2017) cf. 'en flagrant délit' (Roussel, 1926): and 'in flagrante' (Cobetto Ghiggia, 2012). Harris (2006b) has convincingly shown that it in fact has a broader meaning, applying not only to offenders who are caught *in flagrante delicto* but also to those whose guilt is clear or obvious because they are still in possession of incriminating evidence such as a stolen object ('red-handed'). The crucial feature that makes an offender subject to *apagōgē* (see previous note) is that there is direct evidence of guilt in the form of eyewitness testimony or possession of stolen property, not merely indirect or circumstantial evidence or an 'arguable case' against him. The victim of a theft which did not meet these criteria could prosecute the alleged offender in a private action, the *dikē klopēs*.

the Eleven: A board of public officials, selected annually by lot, who administered the state prison in Athens and supervised executions. Offenders arrested under the *apagōgē* procedure were normally brought before the Eleven. (See on 'dragged off to prison', above.) This passage implies that the officials who released Chariades and his associates were themselves executed for negligence, but nothing is known of such an incident, which Roussel (1926, 81, n.1) describes as 'peu vraisemblable'. Harris (2006b, 373) suggests that the story 'may be courtroom slander'.

condemned to death: Literally 'killed' (Gk. *apekteinate*). Cf. Gernet (1917, 112): 'Dans les termes qui représentent la pénalité, nous trouvons la désignation concrète et la conception comme personelle de la vengeance en acte... On ne dit même pas que l'on "condamne à la mort": on *tue*.' Cf. Dein. 1.23. Lyc. 1.122, Andoc. 1.97 (all cited by Gernet). In fact, the orators do sometimes speak of a death sentence in terms of 'condemning to death' (*thanaton katagignōskein*) rather than 'killing' (*apokteinein*); see, e.g., Lys. 1. 32, 13.96. The significant difference seems to be that *apokteinein* implies that the sentence was actually carried out, whereas *thanaton katagignoskein* could be used, e.g., of a death sentence passed *in absentia*.

criminal: On the specific meaning of the Greek term *kakourgos*, see Gagarin (2003).

for 17 years after that ... except when Nicostratus died: This implies that Chariades was unpatriotic, coming to Athens only to serve his own interests (in claiming the estate of Nicostratus) while neglecting the interest of the *polis* itself. Cf. on 'never travelled anywhere abroad except on your orders', §27.

property that belongs to others: See on 'what does not belong to them', 1.17.

30 meddlesome: An Athenian 'volunteer prosecutor' would want, ideally, to be seen as a concerned citizen acting in the interest of the city, but he could easily be characterized by his opponent as 'a meddler, who instead of minding his own business drags other people into court' (Kucharski, 2020, 179, with primary references; cf. Christ, 1998, 144–45).

prosecute: Lit. 'punish' or 'take vengeance on' (Gk. *timōrēsetai*). Cf. Dem. 22.29, where *timōroumetha* may be translated as 'we prosecute'; and Dem. 21.26, where the noun *timōria* (lit. 'punishment', 'vengeance') is used in the sense of 'prosecution'.

judges: Here, as in two of his other speeches (cf. Isae. 9.37 and 10.25) Isaeus chooses to remind his audience of their specifically judicial function at the end of the speech, by using the occupational form of address 'judges' (Greek *ō andres dikastai*) rather than his more usual 'gentlemen' (*ō andres*). (See on 'gentlemen', 1.1. for addresses to the judges in Isaeus's speeches more generally.)

if anyone is willing: An allusion to the role of the 'volunteer prosecutor' (Gk. *ho boulomenos*, lit. 'the one who is willing') in Athenian public actions.

31 been of service to him: That is, by conducting the burial (cf. §26).

the oaths that you swore: For the oath sworn by Athenian judges (the 'dicastic oath') see on 2.47.

the testimony that we have put before you: See on 'they have produced testimony', §2.

vote in accordance with justice: On the system of voting at Athenian trials, see on 2.47.

ISAEUS 6: ON THE ESTATE OF PHILOCTEMON

INTRODUCTION

Philoctemon, son of Euctemon of Cephisia, was killed on military service, leaving a will in which he adopted his sister's son, Chaerestratus, as his son and heir. Chaerestratus's claim to the estate was challenged by another family member, Androcles, who submitted a *diamartyria* in which he denied that Philoctemon left a valid will and claimed that Philoctemon's father, Euctemon, had two legitimate sons by a second wife. Chaerestratus prosecuted Androcles for false testimony, and Isaeus 6 is the prosecution speech from the *dikē pseudomartyriōn*, delivered by a supporting speaker (*synēgoros*).

This speech, in which narrative predominates strongly over argumentation, is, superficially at least, among the most accessible of Isaeus's speeches, and some modern readers, such as Roussel (1926, 106) and Avramovič (1997, 132) have even considered it his best. It tells a sensational story of family dysfunction, elder abuse, greed and corruption, attracting the attention of modern scholars in particular because of the details it provides about prostitution in fourth century Athens. It is also an important source of information on aspects of the Athenian legal system, notably the pre-trial hearing or *anakrisis*.

The obscurity of the historical circumstances and the complexity of the legal background to the case have, nevertheless, led to problems of interpretation and to scholarly misunderstandings. According to a consensus which has prevailed, from the 19th century onwards, the title given to the speech by the mediaeval copyist is misleading, and the disputed estate was really that of Euctemon, who survived his son Philoctemon by more than ten years.[1] Philoctemon, according to that view, possessed no property independently of his father, so it was more advantageous for Chaerestratus to remain in the *oikos* of his natural father, Phanostratus, than to claim Philoctemon's estate immediately after his death. Once Euctemon died, Chaerestratus, relying on his adoption by Philoctemon, claimed the estate as Euctemon's only surviving descendant through a male line; but he was

---

1 See, e.g., Wyse (1904, 483), Kamps (1938, 15), Harrison (1968, 139), Edwards (2007, 98), Humphreys (2019, 187).

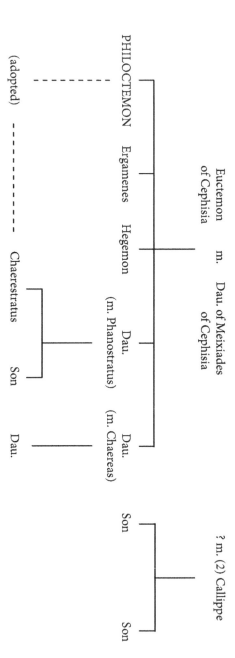

Figure 4.

not in a strong position because his claim to be Philoctemon's testamentary heir had not yet been recognized by the court.[2]

Both in the light of research on the historical background to the speech, and on the evidence of the text itself, that consensus needs to be challenged. Its longevity owes a great deal to the enduring influence exerted by the biased and hostile commentary of Wyse (1904). (Although Schweigert (1940), Labarbe (1953), and Thompson (1970) have all questioned the accepted chronology, their findings have, for the most part, been ignored or discredited.) If, for example, Isaeus gives no indication that ten years have elapsed since Philoctemon's death, then that, according to Wyse, is because Isaeus is a devious and unscrupulous speechwriter who wants to conceal the true facts from the judges (see commentary on §§3-9). In reality, despite the complexity of the narrative and the often confusing argumentation, a more open-minded reader would find sufficient evidence in the speech that the estate in dispute was indeed Philoctemon's, and that the interval between his death and Euctemon's cannot have been as long as ten years. The key factual and legal issues, which are addressed in detail in the commentary, are outlined in this introduction.

The story according to Isaeus

Euctemon of Cephisia was married to a daughter of Meixiades of the same deme. They had three sons (Philoctemon, Ergamenes, and Hegemon) and two daughters, one of whom was married to Phanostratus and the other to Chaereas. Euctemon lived to the age of 96. and all his sons predeceased him. Philoctemon, the last survivor of the three, was killed while commanding a trireme in a military action off Chios. He had no natural legitimate children, but left a will in which he adopted his nephew Chaerestratus (older son of his sister, the wife of Phanostratus)

---

2 See, e.g., Harrison (1968, 139): 'Chairestratos is the claimant in the case, alleging that he had been adopted by Philoktemon in his will; he did not put in his claim, however, immediately after the death of Philoktemon, but only on the death several years later of Philoktemon's father, Euktemon, and then his claim was to inherit not only Philoktemon's, but also Euktemon's estate. His failure to assert his rights under Philoktemon's will immediately must have been very damaging to his case...'. Cf. Edwards (2007, 98): 'But the potential weaknesses of the case are evident: it was Euctemon's estate that was in dispute, not Philoctemon's... and Chaerestratus had never been legally recognized as Philoktemon's adopted son.'

as his son and heir. Chaerestratus submitted a formal claim to the court, which was challenged by a collateral relative, Androcles, who denied that Philoctemon had left a will adopting Chaerestratus and claimed that Euctemon had two legitimate sons by a second wife. By the time the case came to court, Euctemon had also died, and Androcles had claimed one of his daughters in marriage as an *epiklēros*.

The speaker, a friend of the family whose name was probably Aristomenes, first produces proof that Philoctemon did leave a will in which he adopted Chaerestratus. He then turns to the identity of the two young men put forward by Androcles, and the rest of the speech is devoted to a rebuttal of their claim to be legitimate sons of Euctemon. At the preliminary hearing (*anakrisis*) before the archon, Androcles was unable to say who the boys' mother was, or to name her father. He declared that she was a Lemnian, and the hearing was adjourned so that he could seek more detailed information. At the resumed hearing, he announced that her name was Callippe and that her father, Pistoxenus, had died on campaign in Sicily. He had left her in the care of Euctemon, to whom she bore the two children while he was her guardian.

After denouncing this story as a fabrication, Aristomenes moves on to explain the true origin of the two boys. According to his story Euctemon, in old age, became infatuated with Alce, a former slave and prostitute who managed a brothel that he owned in the Cerameicus district of Athens. Eventually Euctemon abandoned his legitimate wife and family and moved in with Alce. She had two sons, whose father was reputedly one of her former clients, and she induced the senile and gullible Euctemon to introduce the older one to his phratry as his own legitimate son. His attempt to do so initially failed because of an objection by Philoctemon (his only surviving son by his wife) but Philoctemon was eventually persuaded to acquiesce in the arrangement, on condition that Alce's son would receive only a single farm from Euctemon's estate. The introduction to the phratry was then duly completed.

Some time later, after Philoctemon's death, Euctemon decided to make a form of will in which he confirmed the gift of a farm to his supposed son. He deposited the document with a relative, in the presence of his sons-in-law Chaereas and Phanostratus (the latter of whom was about to set off on a naval campaign under the command of the general Timotheus). Nearly two years later, by which time Chaereas had died, Androcles and his associate Antidorus joined forces with Alce in a conspiracy to deprive Euctemon of his property. They first persuaded him to revoke his will and sell off land, livestock, and slaves to the total value of three talents. Next, while Euctemon was still alive, they tried unsuccessfully to gain control of some of the remaining property by a fraudulent claim that Alce's sons had been adopted by two of Euctemon's deceased sons. When Euctemon died, they stripped his house of its contents and tried to prevent his wife and daughters from entering.

The legal proceedings

At the beginning of the speech there is no indication that an unusually long time has elapsed since Philoctemon's death, or that the estate in dispute was really that of Euctemon. After a brief introduction in which Aristomenes presents his credentials as *synēgoros* to the judges, he starts the first narrative with a straightforward statement: 'Philoctemon of Cephisia was on friendly terms with Chaerestratus here, and when he died he had bequeathed his property to him and adopted him as his son' (§3). Chaerestratus, he continues, 'submitted a claim for the estate, in accordance with the law' (§3). Then Aristomenes refers to the judges' task of deciding 'who should be the heir (*klēronomos*) to Philoctemon's property' (§4), and later in the speech he invites them to consider who ought to be Philoctemon's heir: Alce's son or Chaerestratus (§51). There are references elsewhere in the speech to 'Euctemon's heirs' (§17) or 'Euctemon's estate' (§46), but Isaeus is not, as some commentators have suggested, referring indiscriminately to the succession of Philoctemon or that of Euctemon.[3] Rather, as the commentary explains in more detail, he distinguishes carefully between them, making it clear that Chaerestratus was claiming the estate of Philoctemon, and there are some indications in the speech that Euctemon's estate was the subject of separate litigation.

The legal proceedings thus started in the normal way when Chaerestratus submitted a *lēxis* to the court claiming Philoctemon's estate as his son adopted by will, but the correct procedure for anyone wanting to challenge his claim would (according to Isaeus) have been to submit another *lēxis*. Instead of doing this Androcles tried to block Chaerestratus's claim with

---

3   See, e.g., Caillemer (1879. 66): 'Voilà pourquoi l'orateur parle indifféremment, tantôt de la succession d'Euctémon, tantôt de la succession de Philoctémon…'.

a formal declaration (*diamartyria*) in which he made two statements: first, that Philoctemon had died childless and not left a will, and secondly, that that Philoctemon's father, Euctemon, had two surviving legitimate sons by a second wife. Chaerestratus, plainly, disputed not only the facts as stated by Androcles, but also the latter's choice of procedure; but if he wanted to proceed with his own claim, he had no option but to prosecute Androcles for giving false testimony in his *diamartyria*. This he duly did, and the next stage in the proceedings was the *anakrisis* at which Androcles told his story about Euctemon's marriage to Callippe. Isaeus 6 is the prosecution speech from the eventual *dikē pseudomartyriōn*.

We should not necessarily take Isaeus's criticism of Androcles's *diamartyria* at face value, but both its contents and that fact that it was used at all in this case do seem extremely surprising. The *diamartyria* was a special procedure enabling a legitimate son (natural or adopted *inter vivos*) to exercise his privileged access to his deceased father's estate by blocking any claim from a collateral relative. The standard wording would be along the lines of 'X testifies that the estate of Y is not adjudicable to Z because Y left a legitimate son.'[4] Isaeus 2 provides a straightforward example of how the procedure worked, but Isaeus 6 is much more problematic. What is remarkable in this case is that Androcles's *diamartyria* does not refer to sons left by Philoctemon but to sons of his father, Euctemon (who was, if the chronology suggested below is correct, still alive at the time). This lends some plausibility to the theory that the estate in dispute was really that of Euctemon, but Androcles's litigation strategy was almost certainly an abuse of the procedure, as Isaeus repeatedly asserts.[5]

Androcles, as portrayed by Isaeus, was desperate to get his hands on both Euctemon's and Philoctemon's property by whatever means possible, legal or illegal. His litigation strategy was irregular and inconsistent: he has presented his two protégés as, on the one hand, legitimate sons of Euctemon and, on the other, the adopted sons of Euctemon's deceased sons Philoctemon and Ergamenes – but they cannot be both. Moreover, Androcles has claimed one of Euctemon's daughters (the widow of Chaereas) in marriage as an *epiklēros*, contradicting the assertion in his *diamartyria* that Euctemon had legitimate sons.

---

4 Cf. commentary on 'telling the truth', 2.17.
5 See Griffith-Williams (2018) for a detailed analysis of the procedural abuse.

Isaeus, understandably, made no attempt to present the behaviour of his clients' opponents as lawful or rational; even for the Athenian judges, who knew more than we do about the background to the case, his account of Androcles's various interventions was probably confusing. For modern readers it is even more so, and Androcles's claim to Euctemon's daughter as *epiklēros* (§46) has proved particularly problematic. In my view, as discussed in the commentary, the best explanation is that there were separate legal proceedings over the two estates: Euctemon was still alive when the litigation about Philoctemon's estate began, it was still in progress when he died, and Androcles claimed the *epiklēros* after his death. It appears, then, that Androcles was hedging his bets, expecting either to gain control of Euctemon's estate if he won the *dikē pseudomartyriōn*, or, if he lost, at least to secure a share of it by marrying the widowed daughter.

We do not know the outcome of the *dikē pseudomartyriōn*, despite some epigraphic evidence that has been taken as an indication that Chaerestratus lost the case. An inscription dating from around the middle of the fourth century identifies Chaerestratus as the son of Phanostratus, not Philoctemon, and that, if the inscription was later than the trial, might imply that the adoption was not recognized (Davies, 1971, 564). After reviewing the prosopographical evidence for the dating of the inscription, Thompson (1970, 2) concludes that it was almost certainly later than 365/4, which 'proves that Chaerestratus lost his case'. Thompson's dating of the inscription is persuasive, but it does not necessarily prove that Androcles won the *dikē pseudomartyriōn*. One possibility, suggested by Isaeus himself at §52, is that Chaerestratus won but Androcles reopened the litigation at a later date and was then successful. Another is that Chaerestratus, in accordance with the law mentioned at §44, returned to the *oikos* of his natural father Phanostratus leaving behind a son of his own as heir to Philoctemon.

The chronology of events described in the speech

The sequence of the key events leading to the trial, starting with Euctemon's successful introduction of Alce's older son to his phratry, is mostly clear, but the intervals between events are often designated by vague expressions such as 'after that' or 'some time later'. First,

Euctemon introduced Alce's son to his phratry (§24). 'After this' (§27) Philoctemon was killed in a naval battle near Chios. 'Some time later' (§27), when Phanostratus was about to set off on an expedition with Timotheus, Euctemon made a written agreement (will) about his gift of a single farm to Alce's son, and left it for safekeeping with a relative, Pythodorus. After 'almost two years' (§29) Euctemon revoked the agreement. 'In a very short time' (§33) Euctemon sold off property to the value of 3 talents. After an unspecified time, Euctemon died (§39).

The legal proceedings described in §§12–14 must have taken place in parallel with these events, although the exact timescale is not made clear in the speech. The proceedings were initiated, after Philoctemon's death, by Charestratus's submission to the court of his claim to the estate as Philoctemon's son adopted by will. The next step was Androcles's attempt to block the claim with a *diamartyria*. Then, Chaerestratus prosecuted Androcles for false testimony, and there was a preliminary hearing before the archon at which Androcles was unable to provide satisfactory evidence for his statement in the *diamartyria* that Euctemon had two legitimate sons by a second wife. The hearing was adjourned to allow him to provide further information about the identity of the boys and their mother, and at the resumed hearing he provided an explanation which Chaerestratus rejected as completely untrue. Finally, after Euctemon's death, the *dikē pseuromartyriōn* came to court for trial.

In the scenario suggested below, Euctemon died between two and three years after Philoctemon, and probably only a matter of weeks before Isaeus 6 was delivered. It may seem unlikely that the legal proceedings concerning Philoctemon's estate were still in progress two or three years after his death, but the timescale is not wholly implausible. It could have been some months before news of his death reached Athens, and it is possible that Chaerestratus was also away on military service at the time, and unable to submit his claim immediately. In any event, the adjournment of the *anakrisis* must have caused a significant delay.

The dating of the speech and the historical background

Aristomenes says (§14) that 52 years have passed since the Sicilian expedition, which left Athens in the summer of 415 BC. So, depending on the method of counting, the speech can be dated to 365/4 or 364/3.

There is no record of the naval encounter off Chios in which Philoctemon was killed, so attempts to pinpoint the date of his death have centred on the naval campaign on which Phanostratus set off 'some time later'. The expedition was commanded by the general Timotheus, who was instrumental in establishing the Second Athenian Confederacy (378–373) but was subsequently prosecuted and went into exile until 366/5, when he returned and captured Samos. Scholarly discussion focused initially on the period of the Theban war in the 370s, before Timotheus's exile, lending support to the view that Chaerestratus did not submit his claim until after Euctemon's death, which was assumed to have been ten years later than that of Philoctemon.

In fact a later date for Timotheus's expedition, after his return to Athens and closer to the date of the trial, would be more consistent with the chronology of events reported in the speech. The first problem is that Euctemon left his will with Pythodorus when Phanostratus was on the point of departure, and decided to revoke it 'nearly two years' later. If Phanostratus set off with Timotheus in 373 or earlier, Euctemon would then have lived for at least six years after the revocation of the will – an interval described by Labarbe (1953, 376) as 'invraisemblable'. Indeed, Isaeus's emphasis on the rapid progress of Androcles's and Alce's intrigues suggests an interval of (at most) months rather than years. A more specific difficulty, as both Labarbe (1953) and Thompson (1970) have pointed out, is the age of Alce's older son, whom Euctemon had introduced to his phratry before Philoctemon died, in a ceremony at which the *koureion* was sacrificed (§22). At the time of the trial, Aristomenes says that this young man is 'not yet 20' (§14). He was probably 15 or 16 when he was first introduced to the phratry,[6] so no more than two or three years have elapsed between his successful admission to the phratry (when Philoctemon was still alive) and the court hearing.

Thompson conjectures that the phratry introduction took place in 368/7. Labarbe, arguing that the regular age for the *koureion* was sixteen, suggests that Euktemon first tried to introduce the boy at the Apaturia in 367/6, after which the successful introduction followed at the Thargelia in the same year. Lambert (1993, 165) has questioned some aspects of Labarbe's hypothesis, including the contention that 16 was the standard

---

[6] On the age of admission at the koureion, see commentary on 'the sacrificial victim', §22.

age for the introduction of an adolescent boy to his father's phratry; but even if one does not accept Labarbe's detailed reasoning, a date in the early 360s is clearly more plausible than one in the 370s.

Without regard to the dating of the phratry introduction, Schweigert (1940) demonstrated the possibility of a later date for Phanostratus's naval campaign under Timotheus. Phanostratus of Cephisia is named as a trierarch in a naval record identified by Schweigert as relating to the first of three cleruchic expeditions to Samos, in 365/4. Suggesting that there could have been a skirmish near Chios during the ten-month siege of Samos, shortly before the departure of the cleruchic expedition, Schweigert (1940, 198) concludes: 'Philoktemon, then, was killed in 366/5 near Chios during a sea-battle. Shortly thereafter, Phanostratos, his kinsman, sailed out as trierarch in the cleruchic expedition to Samos (*IG* II^2 1609.92). This would have to be the expedition "under Timotheos" which is mentioned in Isaeus.'

Schweigert's dating is dismissed as 'impossible' by Davies (1971, 564), because (on the assumption that the speech was delivered in the year 364) it would not allow for the 'nearly two years' that elapsed between Phanostratus's departure and Euctemon's decision to annul his will. Davies himself, however, had argued persuasively that *IG* II^2 was 'the record published by the dockyard superintendents of the Attic year 366/5' (Davies, 1969, 330-31). concluding that the ten-month siege of Samos probably ended in the spring of 365 and that the cleruchic expedition, which followed shortly thereafter, returned 'before *c.* July 365'. If that is correct, then Euctemon could have deposited his will with Pythodorus in, say, May or June 365 and revoked it 'nearly two years later' in March or April 363. If the trial of Androcles for *pseudomartyria* took place not in 364 but in the summer of 363, there would have been an interval of three or four months during which Euctemon annulled his will, sold off much of his property, and died. This timescale is tight, but not impossible, and it is certainly more consistent than an interval of years with the 'very short time' in which Euktemon is said to have sold his property.

It is, of course, impossible to provide a definitive reconstruction of the historical background to the speech, and many details inevitably remain obscure. What I hope to demonstrate through the detailed commentary is that the suggested chronology is both feasible and consistent with the information provided by the speech itself about the nature of the legal proceedings and the sequence of events.

Family structure and family rivalry

We, of course, cannot hope to establish the true facts of the case, but it is worth at least considering the possibility that the 'Alce' story was a fiction invented by Isaeus to conceal the fact that Euctemon did have a second wife who bore him two sons. Remarriage after death or divorce was common in classical Athens, so a second marriage would not in itself have appeared implausible to an Athenian court.

The law on partible inheritance, with every legitimate son entitled to an equal share in his father's estate, created complications and potential problems when an Athenian man died leaving legitimate sons by different wives. The situation was further complicated by the freedom enjoyed by Athenian men (but not women) to engage in informal sexual liaisons either before, during, or after marriage. Some of these relationships with mistresses or prostitutes inevitably resulted in the birth of illegitimate children, who, according to the law, were strictly excluded from both citizenship and inheritance rights within the family. In practice, however, the distinction between legitimate and illegitimate status was not always clear, and much depended on the father's willingness (or refusal) to acknowledge paternity.

Clearly, then, there was potential for tension and rivalry between half-siblings (legitimate or not) in many Athenian families. One such family was that of Mantias of Thoricus, one of whose sons, Mantitheus, was the speaker of Dem. 39 and [Dem.] 40. Mantias's wife, the mother of Mantitheus, was a daughter of Polyaratus of Thoricus; but he had two other sons, Boeotus and Pamphilus, by Plangon, a daughter of the disgraced general Pamphilus, to whom he may also have been married. Mantitheus, who never really accepted Boeotus and Pamphilus as legitimate, was reluctantly obliged to share his father's estate with them because Mantias had publicly acknowledged them as his legitimate sons by introducing them to his phratry. In the bitter and protracted dispute between Mantitheus and Boeotus, both men claimed to be the legitmate first-born son of Mantias, but Mantitheus strives to create the impression that Plangon was Mantias's mistress, not his wife, and claims that it was only because of her trickery that Mantias was forced to acknowledge her sons as legitimate.

Whatever the true facts, and despite the different circumstances of the families of Mantias and Euctemon, there are some obvious parallels between the stories told, respectively, by Mantitheus and Aristomenes. In both cases someone who claims to be the only surviving son of his father's first (or perhaps only) marriage, who is indisputably legitimate and has expectations of becoming his father's sole heir, resents the arrival of later sons with whom he would have to share the paternal estate. In both cases, too, the father has acknowledged at least one of the younger sons as legitimate by introducing them to his phratry – an inconvenient fact which the other branch of the family cannot ignore and needs to explain. In both cases, the explanation involves an accusation of trickery by a scheming and unscrupulous woman ambitious on behalf of her own sons. In short, even if someone in the position of Philoctemon or Mantitheus knew that his half-brothers were indeed legitimate, it would be an obvious tactic to accuse them of being the illegitimate children of the father's concubine or mistress, not the sons of a lawfully married Athenian wife. Given the Athenians' ambivalent attitude to women, it would be equally natural to blame the mother.[7]

In Isaeus 6, the speaker does not openly admit that the boys he identifies as Alce's sons were really the sons of Euctemon at all, although the possibility that they were cannot be excluded.[8] Philoctemon is presented in Isaeus's narrative as resisting his father's introduction of Alce's son to the phratry because he sees it as an attempt to pollute the family's bloodline by the infiltration of an outsider, the son of a former slave who had no claim at all to Athenian citizenship or legitimate family status. But even if he had known that the boy introduced to the phratry was indeed Euctemon's legitimate son by a second wife, Philoctemon would still have had good reason to resist the formal recognition of a half-brother with whom he (if he had outlived Euctemon) would have been forced to share the paternal estate. Because of Philoctemon's objection, Euctemon failed in his first attempt to introduce the boy to his phratry; but he overcame Philoctemon's resistance by agreeing to limit his younger son's share in the estate to a single farm.

---

7   Cf. Griffith-Williams (2017, 42).
8   See commentary on 'she said he was the father of these boys', §20.

Philoctemon's premature death, while Euctemon was still living, changed the order of succession to Euctemon's estate significantly. It was not disputed between the parties that Euctemon died leaving two legitimate daughters by his (first?) wife: one was the wife (later widow) of Chaereas, whose only child was a daughter; while the other, the wife of Phanostratus, was the mother of Chaerestratus and his younger brother. But, in accordance with the principle of male precedence in Athenian inheritance law, Euctemon's daughters would inherit his estate only if they had no surviving legitimate brothers or half-brothers; if 'Alce's sons' were in fact Euctemon's legitimate sons by a second wife, his daughters by his first wife would have no claim to his estate at all.[9] So it was apparently in order to protect their interests (and, as argued by Humphreys (2019, 189–90) perhaps under pressure from their husbands) that Euctemon decided, afteer Philoctemon's death, to confirm his agreement with his 'younger son' in a form of written will. As discussed in the commentary, it is doubtful whether such an agreement was strictly legal, but it was executed with due formality, in the presence of witnesses, and deposited with a trusted third party, and its revocation evidently required the sanction of the archon. In practice, then, it may be that an Athenian father could exercise some influence over the distribution of his property between separate 'families' by different wives. But since Euctemon revoked his 'will', it is impossible to know whether it could have had the intended effect of preventing his younger sons from claiming the entire estate.

Conclusion

The identity of the claimants put forward by Androcles – whether they were really Euctemon's legitimate sons or the offspring of a slave – is, from a certain perspective, immaterial. Either way, their claim to Euctemon's estate was perceived as a threat to the status of those who identified themselves as Euctemon's *only* legitimate family. Chaerestratus, in the litigation, represented not only his personal interest as Philoctemon's adopted son but also the right of his mother and aunt

---

9 The principle of male precedence in Athenian inheritance law meant that a woman could only inherit the estate of her father or other male relative if she was more closely related to him than any surviving male member of the family.

to succeed to the estate of their father, Euctemon (and to that of their brother, Philoctemon, if Chaerestratus did not win his claim on the basis of the will). And that, without any deception or concealment on Isaeus's part, would be sufficient to explain why the estate of Philoctemon seems to be so inextricably connected in the speech with the succession to his father Euctemon.

Should we, then, accept Isaeus's version of the story, according to which Chaerestratus was an innocent victim, forced reluctantly to defend himself and his relatives against Androcles's abusive litigation tactics? Or should we believe that the real villains in the case were not Androcles and Antidorus but Chaerestratus and Phanostratus, who, not content with their own wealth, were scheming to deprive poorer and weaker family members of their rightful inheritance? Whatever doubts or suspicions we may have (or however persuasive we may find Isaeus's narrative and argumentation) that question is impossible to answer with certainty. For the Athenian judges who had to answer it in real life, the true facts would have been equally difficult to ascertain. As in every case their task was to decide, drawing on their own experience of life and knowledge of contemporary Athenian values, which of the stories they had heard was more likely to be true.

ISAEUS 6: ON THE ESTATE OF PHILOCTEMON

ὅτι μέν, ὦ ἄνδρες, πάντων οἰκειότατα <τυγχάνω> χρώμενος Φανοστράτῳ τε καὶ Χαιρεστράτῳ τουτῳί, τοὺς πολλοὺς οἶμαι ὑμῶν εἰδέναι, τοῖς δὲ μὴ εἰδόσιν ἱκανὸν ἐρῶ τεκμήριον· ὅτε γὰρ εἰς Σικελίαν ἐξέπλει τριηραρχῶν Χαιρέστρατος, διὰ τὸ πρότερον αὐτὸς ἐκπεπλευκέναι προῄδειν πάντας τοὺς ἐσομένους κινδύνους, ὅμως δὲ δεομένων τούτων καὶ συνεξέπλευσα καὶ συνεδυστύχησα καὶ ἑάλωμεν εἰς τοὺς πολεμίους. [2] ἄτοπον δὴ εἰ ἐκεῖνα μὲν προδήλων ὄντων τῶν κινδύνων ὅμως διὰ τὸ χρῆσθαι τούτοις καὶ φίλους νομίζειν ὑπέμενον, νῦν δὲ οὐ πειρώμην συνειπεῖν ἐξ ὧν ὑμεῖς τε τὰ εὔορκα ψηφιεῖσθε καὶ τούτοις τὰ δίκαια γενήσεται. δέομαι οὖν ὑμῶν συγγνώμην τε ἔχειν καὶ μετ' εὐνοίας ἀκροάσασθαι· ὁ γὰρ ἀγὼν οὐ μικρὸς αὐτοῖς, ἀλλὰ περὶ τῶν μεγίστων.[3] Φιλοκτήμων γὰρ ὁ Κηφισιεὺς φίλος ἦν Χαιρεστράτῳ τουτῳί δοὺς δὲ τὰ ἑαυτοῦ καὶ ὑὸν αὐτὸν ποιησάμενος ἐτελεύτησε. λαχόντος δὲ τοῦ Χαιρεστράτου κατὰ τὸν νόμον τοῦ κλήρου, ἐξὸν ἀμφισβητῆσαι Ἀθηναίων τῷ βουλομένῳ καὶ εὐθυδικίᾳ εἰσελθόντι εἰς ὑμᾶς, εἰ φαίνοιτο δικαιότερα λέγων, ἔχειν τὸν κλῆρον, [4] διεμαρτύρησεν Ἀνδροκλῆς οὑτοσὶ μὴ ἐπίδικον εἶναι τὸν κλῆρον, ἀποστερῶν τοῦτον τῆς ἀμφισβητήσεως καὶ ὑμᾶς τοῦ κυρίους γενέσθαι ὅντινα δεῖ κληρονόμον καταστήσασθαι τῶν Φιλοκτήμονος· καὶ ἐν μιᾷ ψήφῳ καὶ ἑνὶ ἀγῶνι οἴεται ἀδελφοὺς καταστήσειν ἐκείνῳ τοὺς οὐδὲν προσήκοντας, καὶ τὸν κλῆρον ἀνεπίδικον ἕξειν αὐτός, καὶ τῆς ἀδελφῆς τῆς ἐκείνου κύριος γενήσεσθαι, καὶ τὴν διαθήκην ἄκυρον ποιήσειν. [5] πολλῶν δὲ καὶ δεινῶν ὄντων ἃ διαμεμαρτύρηκεν Ἀνδροκλῆς, τοῦτ' αὐτὸ πρῶτον ἐπιδείξω ὑμῖν, ὡς διέθετο καὶ ἐποιήσατο ὑὸν τουτονὶ Χαιρέστρατον. ἐπειδὴ γὰρ τῷ Φιλοκτήμονι ἐκ μὲν τῆς γυναικὸς ᾗ συνῴκει οὐκ ἦν παιδίον οὐδέν, πολέμου δ' ὄντος ἐκινδύνευε καὶ ἱππεὺς στρατευόμενος καὶ τριήραρχος πολλάκις ἐκπλέων, ἔδοξεν αὐτῷ διαθέσθαι τὰ αὑτοῦ, μὴ ἔρημον καταλίπῃ τὸν οἶκον, εἴ τι πάθοι. [6] τὼ μὲν οὖν ἀδελφὼ αὑτῷ, ὥπερ ἐγενέσθην, ἄμφω ἄπαιδε ἐτελευτησάτην· τοῖν δὲ ἀδελφαῖν τῇ μὲν ἑτέρᾳ, ᾗ ὁ Χαιρέας συνῴκει, οὐκ ἦν ἄρρεν παιδίον οὐδὲ ἐγένετο πολλὰ ἔτη συνοικούσῃ, ἐκ δὲ τῆς ἑτέρας, ᾗ συνῴκει Φανόστρατος οὑτοσί, ἤστην ὑὼ δύο. τούτων τὸν πρεσβύτερον τουτονὶ Χαιρέστρατον ἐποιήσατο ὑόν· [7] καὶ ἔγραψεν οὕτως ἐν διαθήκῃ, εἰ μὴ γένοιτο αὐτῷ παιδίον ἐκ τῆς γυναικός, τοῦτον κληρονομεῖν τῶν ἑαυτοῦ. καὶ τὴν διαθήκην κατέθετο παρὰ τῷ κηδεστῇ Χαιρέᾳ, τῷ τὴν ἑτέραν αὐτοῦ ἀδελφὴν ἔχοντι. καὶ ὑμῖν ἥ τε διαθήκη αὕτη ἀναγνωσθήσεται καὶ οἱ παραγενόμενοι μαρτυρήσουσι. καί μοι ἀνάγνωθι.

(1) I think, gentlemen, most of you know that I am on very good terms with Phanostratus and Chaerestratus here, but for those who don't know I'll provide sufficient proof. For when Chaerestratus was about to sail off to Sicily as a trierarch, I knew from previous experience all the dangers that would arise, but nevertheless, when they asked me, I sailed out with him and shared his discomfort, and we were captured by the enemy. (2) It would surely be strange if, having endured all this when faced with obvious danger, because I was fond of them and considered them friends, I did not now try to support them so that you will vote in accordance with your oath and justice will be done to them. So I ask you to have sympathy and listen with good will, since the contest is no small matter for them but of the greatest importance.

(3) Philoctemon of Cephisia was on friendly terms with Chaerestratus here, and when he died he had bequeathed his property to him and adopted him as his son. And when Chaerestratus had submitted a claim for the estate, in accordance with the law, although it is lawful for any Athenian who so wishes to go to court and contest the claim in a direct action, and to have the estate if he seems to make the better case, (4) Androcles here testified in a *diamartyria* that the estate was not subject to adjudication, in an attempt to deprive Chaerestratus of his claim and you of the authority to decide who should be confirmed as Philoctemon's heir. And in one vote and one trial he thought he would appoint brothers for Philoctemon who were completely unrelated to him, take the estate himself without an adjudication, become the *kyrios* of Philoctemon's sister, and annul the will. (5) Of the many things that Androcles has falsely stated, I shall first prove to you that Philoctemon did make a will and adopt Chaerestratus here. For since Philoctemon had no child by his wife, and since it was wartime and he was frequently at risk both on campaign as a cavalryman and as a trierarch, he decided to dispose of his property so as not to leave his family without an heir if anything should happen to him. (6) Now both of his brothers had died childless, and one of his sisters, the wife of Chaereas, had no son although they had been married many years, but the other sister, who is married to Phanostratus here, had two sons. He adopted the older of them, Chaerestratus, as his son, (7) and wrote in his will that if he should have no child by his wife, Chaerestratus was to be his heir. And he deposited the will with his brother-in-law Chaereas, the husband of his other sister. And not only shall the will itself be read to you, but also those who were present will testify. Please read.

ΔΙΑΘΗΚΗ. <ΜΑΡΤΥΡΕΣ>

[8] ὡς μὲν διέθετο καὶ ἐφ᾽ οἷς ἐποιήσατο ὑὸν τοῦτον, ἀκηκόατε: ὡς δ᾽ ἐξὸν αὐτῷ ταῦτ᾽ ἔπραξεν, ὅθεν δικαιότατα ἡγοῦμαι τὰ τοιαῦτ᾽ εἶναι μανθάνειν, τοῦτον ὑμῖν αὐτὸν παρέξομαι τὸν νόμον. καί μοι ἀνάγνωθι.

ΝΟΜΟΣ

[9] οὑτοσὶ ὁ νόμος, ὦ ἄνδρες, κοινὸς ἅπασι κεῖται, ἐξεῖναι τὰ ἑαυτοῦ διαθέσθαι, ἐὰν μὴ παῖδες ὦσι γνήσιοι ἄρρενες, ἐὰν μὴ ἄρα μανεὶς ἢ ὑπὸ γήρως ἢ δι᾽ ἄλλο τι τῶν ἐν τῷ νόμῳ παρανοῶν διαθῆται. ὅτι δ᾽ οὐδενὶ τούτων ἔνοχος ἦν Φιλοκτήμων, βραχέα εἰπὼν δηλώσω ὑμῖν. ὅστις γὰρ καὶ ἕως ἔζη τοιοῦτον πολίτην ἑαυτὸν παρεῖχεν, ὥστε διὰ τὸ ὑφ᾽ ὑμῶν τιμᾶσθαι ἄρχειν ἀξιοῦσθαι, καὶ ἐτελεύτησε μαχόμενος τοῖς πολεμίοις, πῶς ἄν τις τοῦτον τολμήσειεν εἰπεῖν ὡς οὐκ εὐέφρόνει; [10] ὅτι μὲν οὖν διέθετο καὶ ἐποιήσατο εὖ φρονῶν, ἐξὸν αὐτῷ, ἀποδέδεικται ὑμῖν, ὥστε κατὰ μὲν τοῦτο ψευδῆ μεμαρτυρηκὼς Ἀνδροκλῆς ἀποδέδεικται: ἐπειδὴ δὲ προσδιαμεμαρτύρηκεν [ὡς]ὑὸν εἶναι γνήσιον Εὐκτήμονος τοῦτον, καὶ ταῦτ᾽ ἀποδείξω ψευδῆ ὄντα. Εὐκτήμονι γάρ, ὦ ἄνδρες, τῷ Φιλοκτήμονος πατρί, τοὺς μὲν ὄντως γενομένους παῖδας, Φιλοκτήμονα καὶ Ἐργαμένην καὶ Ἡγήμονα καὶ δύο θυγατέρας, καὶ τὴν μητέρα αὐτῶν, ἣν ἔγημεν ὁ Εὐκτήμων, Μειξιάδου Κηφισιῶς θυγατέρα, πάντες οἱ προσήκοντες ἴσασι καὶ οἱ φράτορες καὶ τῶν δημοτῶν οἱ πολλοί, καὶ μαρτυρήσουσιν ὑμῖν: [11] ὅτι δ᾽ ἄλλην τινὰ ἔγημε γυναῖκα, ἐξ ἧς τινος οἶδε αὐτῷ ἐγένοντο, οὐδεὶς τὸ παράπαν οἶδεν οὐδ᾽ ἤκουσε πώποτε ζῶντος Εὐκτήμονος. καίτοι τούτους εἰκὸς πιστοτάτους εἶναι νομίζειν μάρτυρας: τοὺς γὰρ οἰκείους εἰδέναι προσήκει τὰ τοιαῦτα. καί μοι τούτους κάλει πρῶτον, καὶ τὰς μαρτυρίας ἀνάγνωθι.

ΜΑΡΤΥΡΙΑΙ

[12] ἔτι τοίνυν καὶ τοὺς ἀντιδίκους ἐπιδείξω ἔργῳ ὑμῖν ταῦτα μεμαρτυρηκότας. ὅτε γὰρ αἱ ἀνακρίσεις ἦσαν πρὸς τῷ ἄρχοντι καὶ οὗτοι παρακατέβαλον ὡς ὑπὲρ γνησίων τῶνδ᾽ Εὐκτήμονος ὄντων,

WILL. WITNESSES

(8) You have heard that he made a will, and on what terms he adopted Chaerestratus. I shall produce for you the law itself, from which I think you will learn that this was most just. And please read it.

LAW

(9) This law, gentlemen, has been established for everyone in common, that it is permissible to dispose of one's property by will if one has no legitimate male children, provided that when one makes the will one is neither insane nor deranged through old age or through any of the other causes specified in the law. That none of these applied to Philoctemon, I shall briefly reveal to you. For how could anyone dare to say that a man was not in his right mind, when throughout his life he was such a good citizen that, thanks to your esteem for him, he was considered worthy to hold office, and died fighting against the enemy?

(10) It has been proved to you that Philoctemon did indeed make a will and adopt a son while he was in his right mind, as he was entitled to do, and it has thus been proved that Androcles gave false testimony. But since he has also said in his *diamartyria* that this man is a legitimate son of Euctemon, I shall prove that this is false as well. For, gentlemen, all his relatives and fellow phratry members, and most of his fellow demesmen, know the real sons of Euctemon, Philoctemon's father – Philoctemon, Ergamenes, and Hegemon – and his two daughters, and their mother, the daughter of Meixiades of Cephisia, and they will testify to you. (11) No-one, on the other hand, has any knowledge, or ever heard in Euctemon's lifetime, that he married any other woman by whom he had more children. Yet it is natural that they should be considered the most reliable witnesses, because relatives ought to know about such matters. Please call them first, and read out the witness statements.

WITNESS STATEMENTS

(12) I shall further demonstrate to you that my opponents have testified to these facts by their own conduct. At the preliminary hearings before the archon, when they had paid a deposit in support of their claim that these young men were legitimate sons of Euctemon, we asked them who was

ἐρωτώμενοι ὑφ᾽ ἡμῶν τίς εἴη αὐτῶν μήτηρ καὶ ὅτου θυγάτηρ οὐκ εἶχον ἀποδεῖξαι, διαμαρτυρομένων ἡμῶν καὶ τοῦ ἄρχοντος κελεύοντος ἀποκρίνασθαι κατὰ τὸν νόμον. <καίτοι ἄτοπον>, ὦ ἄνδρες, ἀμφισβητεῖν μὲν ὡς ὑπὲρ γνησίων καὶ διαμαρτυρεῖν, μητέρα δὲ ἥτις ἦν μὴ ἔχειν ἀποδεῖξαι, μηδὲ προσήκοντα αὐτοῖς μηδένα. [13] ἀλλὰ τότε μὲν Λημνίαν σκηψάμενοι ταύτην ἀναβολὴν ἐποιήσαντο: τὸ δ᾽ ὕστερον ἥκοντες εἰς τὴν ἀνάκρισιν, πρὶν καί τινα ἐρέσθαι, εὐθὺς ἔλεγον ὅτι Καλλίππη μήτηρ, αὕτη δ᾽ εἴη Πιστοξένου θυγάτηρ, ὡς ἐξαρκέσον εἰ ὄνομα μόνον πορίσαιντο τὸν Πιστόξενον. ἐρομένων δ᾽ ἡμῶν ὅστις εἴη καὶ εἰ ζῇ ἢ μή, ἐν Σικελίᾳ ἔφασαν ἀποθανεῖν στρατευόμενον, καταλιπόντα ταύτην θυγατέρα παρὰ τῷ Εὐκτήμονι, ἐξ ἐπιτροπευομένης δὲ τούτῳ γενέσθαι, πρᾶγμα πλάττοντες ἀναιδείᾳ ὑπερβάλλον καὶ οὐδὲ γενόμενον, ὡς ἐγὼ ὑμῖν ἀποφανῶ ἐκ τούτων πρῶτον ὧν αὐτοὶ ἀπεκρίναντο. [14] τῇ μὲν γὰρ στρατιᾷ, ἀφ᾽ οὗ ἐξέπλευσεν εἰς Σικελίαν, ἤδη ἐστὶ δύο καὶ πεντήκοντα ἔτη, ἀπὸ Ἀριμνήστου ἄρχοντος, τῷ δὲ πρεσβυτέρῳ τούτων, ὧν φασιν ἐκ τῆς Καλλίππης καὶ τοῦ Εὐκτήμονος εἶναι, οὔπω ὑπὲρ εἴκοσιν ἔτη. ἀφελόντι οὖν ταῦτα ἀπὸ τῶν ἐν Σικελίᾳ ὑπολείπεται πλείω ἢ τριάκοντα ἔτη: ὥστ᾽ οὔτ᾽ ἐπιτροπεύεσθαι προσῆκε τὴν Καλλίππην ἔτι, τριακοντοῦτίν γε οὖσαν, οὔτε ἀνέκδοτον καὶ ἄπαιδα εἶναι, ἀλλὰ πάνυ πάλαι συνοικεῖν, ἢ ἐγγυηθεῖσαν κατὰ νόμον ἢ ἐπιδικασθεῖσαν. [15] ἔτι δὲ καὶ γιγνώσκεσθαι αὐτὴν ὑπὸ τῶν Εὐκτήμονος οἰκείων ἀναγκαῖον ἦν καὶ ὑπὸ τῶν οἰκετῶν, εἴ πέρ γε συνῴκησεν ἐκείνῳ ἢ διῃτήθη τοσοῦτον χρόνον ἐν τῇ οἰκίᾳ. τὰ γὰρ τοιαῦτα οὐκ εἰς τὴν ἀνάκρισιν μόνον δεῖ πορίζεσθαι ἀλλὰ τῇ ἀληθείᾳ γεγονότα φαίνεσθαι καὶ ὑπὸ τῶν προσηκόντων καταμαρτυρεῖσθαι. [16] ἀποδεῖξαι τοίνυν ἡμῶν κελευόντων ὅστις οἶδε τῶν Εὐκτήμονος οἰκείων ἢ συνοικήσασαν ἐκείνῳ τινὰ [ἢ τὴν] Καλλίππην <ἢ> ἐπιτροπευομένην, καὶ παρὰ τῶν ὄντων <ἡμῖν> θεραπόντων τὸν ἔλεγχον ποιεῖσθαι, ἢ εἴ τις τῶν παρ᾽ αὐτοῖς οἰκετῶν φάσκει ταῦτα εἰδέναι, ἡμῖν παραδοῦναι, οὔτε λαβεῖν ἠθέλησαν οὔθ᾽ ἡμῖν παραδοῦναι. καί μοι λαβὲ τήν τ᾽ ἀπόκρισιν αὐτῶν καὶ τὰς ἡμετέρας μαρτυρίας καὶ προκλήσεις.

ἈΠΟΚΡΙΣΙΣ. ΜΑΡΤΥΡΙΑΙ. ΠΡΟΚΛΗΣΕΙΣ

[17] οὗτοι μὲν τοίνυν τοιοῦτο πρᾶγμα ἔφυγον: ἐγὼ δ᾽ ὑμῖν ἐπιδείξω καὶ ὅθεν εἰσὶ καὶ οἵτινες, οὓς γνησίους διεμαρτύρησαν εἶναι καὶ κληρονόμους

their mother and whose daughter she was, but they could not produce the information, although we lodged an objection and the archon ordered them to reply in accordance with the law. But is it not strange, gentlemen, to make a claim on behalf of legitimate sons, and swear a *diamartyria*, yet be unable to identify their mother or any other of their relatives? (13) But then they secured an adjournment by making a formal declaration that she was a Lemnian, and later, when the hearing resumed, before anyone had asked a question, they immediately said that the mother was Callippe, the daughter of Pistoxenus – as if it were enough merely to provide the name Pistoxenus. When we asked who he was, and whether he was still alive, they said that he had died on campaign in Sicily, leaving this daughter behind in Euctemon's house, and that she bore him these two children while he was her guardian. They have fabricated a story that is completely untrue, beyond the bounds of decency, as I shall reveal to you first of all from the answers they themselves gave. (14) It is already 52 years since the Sicilian expedition, counting from the archonship of Arimnestus, but the older of these two boys, who they say are the sons of Callippe and Euctemon, is not yet 20 years of age. If this time is deducted, there still remain more than 30 years since the Sicilian expedition, so Callippe, if she was 30, should no longer have been a ward, or unmarried and childless, but long since married, after being either lawfully betrothed or adjudicated by the court. (15) Moreover, she must inevitably have been known to Euctemon's relatives and slaves if she had really been married to him and lived for such a long time in his house. It is not sufficient for my opponents just to produce these kinds of facts at the preliminary hearing; they must also prove that the events actually happened, and have them confirmed by testimony from the relatives. (16) Well then, we ordered them to reveal which of Euctemon's relatives knew that someone called Callippe had been married to Euctemon or under his guardianship, and to put our slaves to the proof or hand over any of their slaves who said they knew these facts, but they would not take any of our slaves or hand over any of theirs. Now please read their reply and our witness statements and challenges.

REPLY. WITNESS STATEMENTS. CHALLENGES

(17) So my opponents avoided such a decisive procedure, but I shall reveal to you the origin and identity of these men who, according to them, are

ζητοῦσι καταστῆσαι τῶν Εὐκτήμονος. ἴσως μέν ἐστιν ἀηδὲς Φανοστράτῳ, ὦ ἄνδρες, τὰς Εὐκτήμονος συμφορὰς φανερὰς καθεστάναι· ὀλίγα δ᾽ ἀναγκαῖον ῥηθῆναι, ἵν᾽ ὑμεῖς τὴν ἀλήθειαν εἰδότες ῥᾷον τὰ δίκαια ψηφίσησθε. [18] Εὐκτήμων μὲν γὰρ ἐβίω ἔτη ἓξ καὶ ἐνενήκοντα, τούτου δὲ οὗ χρόνου τὸν μὲν πλεῖστον ἐδόκει εὐδαίμων εἶναι καὶ γὰρ οὐσία ἦν οὐκ ὀλίγη αὐτῷ καὶ παῖδες καὶ γυνή, καὶ τἆλλ᾽ ἐπιεικῶς εὐτύχει), ἐπὶ γήρως δὲ αὐτῷ συμφορὰ ἐγένετο οὐ μικρά, ἣ ἐκείνου πᾶσαν τὴν οἰκίαν ἐλυμήνατο καὶ χρήματα πολλὰ διώλεσε καὶ αὐτὸν τοῖς οἰκειοτάτοις εἰς διαφορὰν κατέστησεν. [19] ὅθεν δὲ καὶ ὅπως ταῦτ᾽ ἐγένετο, ὡς ἂν δύνωμαι διὰ βραχυτάτων δηλώσω. ἀπελευθέρα ἦν αὐτοῦ, ὦ ἄνδρες, ἣ ἐναυκλήρει συνοικίαν ἐν Πειραιεῖ αὐτοῦ καὶ παιδίσκας ἔτρεφε. τούτων μίαν ἐκτήσατο ᾗ ὄνομα ἦν Ἀλκή, ἣν καὶ ὑμῶν οἶμαι πολλοὺς εἰδέναι. αὕτη δὲ ἡ Ἀλκὴ ὠνηθεῖσα πολλὰ μὲν ἔτη καθῆστο ἐν οἰκήματι, ἤδη δὲ πρεσβυτέρα οὖσα ἀπὸ μὲν τοῦ οἰκήματος ἀνίσταται. [20] διαιτωμένη δὲ αὐτῇ ἐν τῇ συνοικίᾳ συνῆν ἄνθρωπος ἀπελεύθερος, Δίων ὄνομα αὐτῷ, ἐξ οὗ ἔφη ἐκείνη τούτους γεγονέναι· καὶ ἔθρεψεν αὐτοὺς ὁ Δίων ὡς ὄντας ἑαυτοῦ. χρόνῳ δὲ ὕστερον ὁ μὲν Δίων ζημίαν εἰργασμένος καὶ δείσας ὑπὲρ αὑτοῦ ὑπεχώρησεν εἰς Σικυῶνα· τὴν δ᾽ ἄνθρωπον ταύτην, τὴν Ἀλκήν, καθίστησιν Εὐκτήμων ἐπιμελεῖσθαι τὴν ἐν Κεραμεικῷ συνοικίας, τῆς παρὰ τὴν πυλίδα, οὗ ὁ οἶνος ὤνιος. [21] κατοικισθεῖσα δ᾽ ἐνταυθοῖ πολλῶν καὶ κακῶν ἦρξεν, ὦ ἄνδρες. φοιτῶν γὰρ ὁ Εὐκτήμων ἐπὶ τὸ ἐνοίκιον ἑκάστοτε τὰ πολλὰ διέτριβεν ἐν τῇ συνοικίᾳ, ἐνίοτε δὲ καὶ ἐσιτεῖτο μετὰ τῆς ἀνθρώπου, καταλιπὼν καὶ τὴν γυναῖκα καὶ τοὺς παῖδας καὶ τὴν οἰκίαν ἣν ᾤκει. χαλεπῶς δὲ φερούσης τῆς γυναικὸς καὶ τῶν υἱέων οὐχ ὅπως ἐπαύσατο, ἀλλὰ τελευτῶν παντελῶς διῃτᾶτο ἐκεῖ, καὶ οὕτω διετέθη εἴθ᾽ ὑπὸ φαρμάκων εἴθ᾽ ὑπὸ νόσου εἴθ᾽ ὑπ᾽ ἄλλου τινός, ὥστε ἐπείσθη ὑπ᾽ αὐτῆς τὸν πρεσβύτερον τοῖν παίδοιν εἰσαγαγεῖν εἰς τοὺς φράτορας ἐπὶ τῷ αὑτοῦ ὀνόματι. [22] ἐπειδὴ δὲ οὔθ᾽ ὁ υἱὸς αὐτῷ Φιλοκτήμων συνεχώρει οὔθ᾽ οἱ φράτορες εἰσεδέξαντο, ἀλλ᾽ ἀπηνέχθη τὸ κούρειον, ὀργιζόμενος ὁ Εὐκτήμων τῷ υἱεῖ καὶ ἐπηρεάζειν βουλόμενος ἐγγυᾶται γυναῖκα Δημοκράτους τοῦ Ἀφιδναίου ἀδελφήν, ὡς ἐκ ταύτης παῖδας ἀποφανῶν καὶ εἰσποιήσων εἰς τὸν οἶκον, εἰ μὴ συγχωροίη τοῦτον ἐᾶν εἰσαχθῆναι. [23] εἰδότες δ᾽ οἱ ἀναγκαῖοι ὅτι ἐξ ἐκείνου μὲν οὐκ ἂν ἔτι γένοιντο παῖδες ταύτην τὴν ἡλικίαν ἔχοντος, φανήσοιντο δ᾽ ἄλλῳ τινὶ τρόπῳ, καὶ ἐκ τούτων ἔσοιντο ἔτι μείζους διαφοραί, ἔπειθον, ὦ ἄνδρες, τὸν Φιλοκτήμονα ἐᾶσαι εἰσαγαγεῖν τοῦτον τὸν παῖδα ἐφ᾽ οἷς ἐζήτει ὁ

of legitimate birth, and whom they are trying to establish as Euctemon's heirs. Perhaps, gentlemen, it's embarrassing for Phanostratus to expose Euctemon's misfortunes in public, but it's essential to say a few words so that you know the truth and can more easily make the right decision. (18) Euctemon lived for 96 years, and for most of that time he was considered to be fortunate (since he had a substantial amount of property, children and a wife, and in all other respects was reasonably well off), but in his old age a great misfortune befell him, which ruined his entire household, lost him a great deal of money and set him in conflict with his closest relatives. (19) I shall explain as briefly as I can how and why this happened. He had a freedwoman, gentlemen, who managed his tenement house in Peiraeus and kept prostitutes. One of those she acquired was called Alce, and I think many of you know her. This Alce, after she had been purchased, worked as a prostitute for many years, but retired when she became too old. (20) While she was living in the brothel she had a relationship with a freedman, a fellow called Dion, who she said was the father of these boys; and he did, in fact, bring them up as his children. Some time later, Dion fled to Sicyon, fearing the consequences of an offence he had committed, and Euctemon installed this woman, Alce, as the manager of his tenement house in Cerameicus, near the postern gate where wine is sold. (21) Once established there, gentlemen, she became the cause of many evils. Euctemon went there frequently to collect the rent, spending most of his time in the tenement house; and he sometimes had meals with the woman, leaving behind his wife and children and the house where he lived. His wife and sons took this badly, but he didn't stop going there. In the end he was living there all the time, and so ruined by drugs or disease, or something else, that he was persuaded by the woman to introduce her older son to his phratry under his own name. (22) But his son Philoctemon objected, the phratry members refused to admit the boy, and the sacrificial victim was removed from the altar. So Euctemon was angry with his son and, wanting to insult him, betrothed himself to marry the sister of Democrates of Aphidna, threatening to produce children by her and bring them into the family unless Philoctemon agreed to let Alce's son be introduced to the phratry. (23) His relatives knew that at his age he would not father more children, but they would appear in some other way, causing yet more serious disputes. So, gentlemen, they tried to persuade Philoctemon to allow the boy to be introduced on the terms

Εὐκτήμων, χωρίον ἓν δόντα. [24] καὶ ὁ Φιλοκτήμων αἰσχυνόμενος μὲν ἐπὶ τῇ τοῦ πατρὸς ἀνοίᾳ, ἀπορῶν δ᾽ ὅ τι χρήσαιτο τῷ παρόντι κακῷ, οὐκ ἀντέλεγεν οὐδέν. ὁμολογηθέντων δὲ τούτων, καὶ εἰσαχθέντος τοῦ παιδὸς ἐπὶ τούτοις, ἀπηλλάγη τῆς γυναικὸς ὁ Εὐκτήμων, καὶ ἐπεδείξατο ὅτι οὐ παίδων ἕνεκα ἐγάμει, ἀλλ᾽ ἵνα τοῦτον εἰσαγάγοι. [25] τί γὰρ ἔδει αὐτὸν γαμεῖν, ὦ Ἀνδρόκλεις, εἴ περ οἵδε ἦσαν ἐξ αὐτοῦ καὶ γυναικὸς ἀστῆς, ὡς σὺ μεμαρτύρηκας; τίς γὰρ ἂν γνησίους ὄντας οἷός τε ἦν κωλῦσαι εἰσαγαγεῖν; ἢ διὰ τί ἐπὶ ῥητοῖς αὐτὸν εἰσήγαγε, τοῦ νόμου κελεύοντος ἅπαντας τοὺς γνησίους ἰσομοίρους εἶναι τῶν πατρῴων; [26] ἢ διὰ τί τὸν μὲν πρεσβύτερον τοῖν παίδοιν ἐπὶ ῥητοῖς εἰσήγαγε, τοῦ δὲ νεωτέρου ἤδη γεγονότος οὐδὲ λόγον ἐποιεῖτο ζῶντος Φιλοκτήμονος οὔτε πρὸς αὐτὸν ἐκεῖνον οὔτε πρὸς τοὺς οἰκείους; οὓς σὺ νῦν διαρρήδην μεμαρτύρηκας γνησίους εἶναι καὶ κληρονόμους τῶν Εὐκτήμονος. ταῦτα τοίνυν ὡς ἀληθῆ λέγω, ἀναγίγνωσκε τὰς μαρτυρίας.

ΜΑΡΤΥΡΙΑΙ

[27] μετὰ ταῦτα τοίνυν ὁ Φιλοκτήμων τριηραρχῶν περὶ Χίον ἀποθνήσκει ὑπὸ τῶν πολεμίων: ὁ δ᾽ Εὐκτήμων ὕστερον χρόνῳ πρὸς τοὺς κηδεστὰς εἶπεν ὅτι βούλοιτο τὰ πρὸς τὸν υόν οἱ πεπραγμένα γράψας καταθέσθαι. καὶ ὁ μὲν Φανόστρατος ἐκπλεῖν ἔμελλε τριηραρχῶν μετὰ Τιμοθέου, καὶ ἡ ναῦς αὐτῷ ἐξώρμει Μουνυχίασι, καὶ ὁ κηδεστὴς Χαιρέας παρὼν συναπέστελλεν αὐτόν: ὁ δ᾽ Εὐκτήμων παραλαβών τινας ἧκεν οὗ ἐξώρμει ἡ ναῦς, καὶ γράψας διαθήκην, ἐφ᾽ οἷς εἰσήγαγε τὸν παῖδα, κατατίθεται μετὰ τούτων παρὰ Πυθοδώρῳ Κηφισιεῖ, προσήκοντι αὐτῷ. [28] καὶ ὅτι μέν, ὦ ἄνδρες, οὐχ ὡς περὶ γνησίων ἔπραττεν Εὐκτήμων, ὃ Ἀνδροκλῆς μεμαρτύρηκε, καὶ αὐτὸ τοῦτο ἱκανὸν τεκμήριον: τοῖς γὰρ φύσει ὑέσιν αὐτοῦ οὐδεὶς οὐδενὸς ἐν διαθήκῃ γράφει δόσιν οὐδεμίαν, διότι ὁ νόμος αὐτὸς ἀποδίδωσι τῷ ὑεῖ τὰ τοῦ πατρὸς καὶ οὐδὲ διαθέσθαι ἐᾷ ὅτῳ ἂν ὦσι παῖδες γνήσιοι. [29] κειμένου δὲ τοῦ γραμματείου σχεδὸν δύ᾽ ἔτη καὶ τοῦ Χαιρέου τετελευτηκότος, ὑποπεπτωκότες οἵδε τῇ ἀνθρώπῳ, καὶ ὁρῶντες ἀπολλύμενον τὸν οἶκον καὶ τὸ γῆρας καὶ τὴν

that Euctemon sought, giving him a single farm. (24) And Philoctemon, ashamed by his father's folly but not knowing what to do about his present trouble, made no objection. Once such an agreement was concluded, and the boy was introduced on these terms, Euctemon abandoned his plans to marry, thus showing that they it was not his intention to produce more children, but to introduce this one to the phratry. (25) For why would he need to marry, Androcles, if these were his children by a citizen wife, as you testified in your *diamartyria*? For if they had been legitimate sons, how could anyone have prevented them from being introduced to the phratry? And why did Euctemon introduce this boy on specified terms, when the law gives all legitimate sons an equal share in their father's estate? (26) And why did he introduce the older of the boys on specified terms, without saying a word about the younger one – who had already been born – either to Philoctemon himself while living or to his other relatives? These are the young men who, as you have just testified, are Euctemon's legitimate heirs. To show that I am speaking the truth, read out the witness statements.

WITNESS STATEMENTS

(27) After this, then, Philoctemon died at the hands of the enemy while serving as a trierarch near Chios. And some time later Euctemon told his sons-in-law that he wanted to put his arrangement with his son into writing and place it in safe keeping. Phanostratus was about to set sail as a trierarch with Timotheus; his ship was lying at anchor at Munychia, and his brother-in-law Chaereas was there to see him off. Euctemon arrived with some companions at the ship's mooring place, and in their presence he deposited with one of his relatives, Pythodorus of Cephisia, the will in which he had written the terms on which he had introduced the boy to his phratry. (28) And that, gentlemen, is sufficient proof that Euctemon was not dealing with legitimate sons, as Androcles has testified in his *diamartyria*. For no-one ever makes any bequest in a will to his natural sons, because the law itself gives the father's property to the son, and does not even allow anyone who has legitimate sons to make a will. (29) When the document had been deposited for almost two years, and Chaereas had died, these men joined forces with the woman, and seeing that Euctemon was old and senile and his property

ἄνοιαν τοῦ Εὐκτήμονος, ὅτι εἴη αὐτοῖς ἱκανὴ ἀφορμή, συνεπιτίθενται. [30] καὶ πρῶτον μὲν πείθουσι τὸν Εὐκτήμονα τὴν μὲν διαθήκην ἀνελεῖν ὡς οὐ χρησίμην οὖσαν τοῖς παισί· τῆς γὰρ φανερᾶς οὐσίας οὐδένα κύριον ἔσεσθαι τελευτήσαντος Εὐκτήμονος ἄλλον ἢ τὰς θυγατέρας καὶ τοὺς ἐκ τούτων γεγονότας· εἰ δὲ ἀποδόμενός τι τῶν ὄντων ἀργύριον καταλίποι, τοῦτο βεβαίως ἕξειν αὐτούς. [31] ἀκούσας δ' ὁ Εὐκτήμων εὐθὺς ἀπῄτει τὸν Πυθόδωρον τὸ γραμματεῖον, καὶ προσεκαλέσατο εἰς ἐμφανῶν κατάστασιν. καταστάντος δὲ ἐκείνου πρὸς τὸν ἄρχοντα, ἔλεγεν ὅτι βούλοιτ' ἀνελέσθαι τὴν διαθήκην. [32] ἐπειδὴ δ' ὁ Πυθόδωρος ἐκείνῳ μὲν καὶ τῷ Φανοστράτῳ παρόντι ὡμολόγει ἀναιρεῖν, τοῦ δὲ Χαιρέου τοῦ συγκαταθεμένου θυγάτηρ ἦν μία, ἧς ἐπειδὴ κύριος καταστᾴη, τότε ἠξίου ἀνελεῖν, καὶ ὁ ἄρχων οὕτως ἐγίγνωσκε, διομολογησάμενος ὁ Εὐκτήμων ἐναντίον τοῦ ἄρχοντος καὶ τῶν παρέδρων καὶ ποιησάμενος πολλοὺς μάρτυρας ὡς οὐκέτ' αὐτῷ κέοιτο ἡ διαθήκη, ᾤχετο ἀπιών. [33] καὶ ἐν πάνυ ὀλίγῳ χρόνῳ, οὗπερ ἕνεκα οὗτοι λῦσαι αὐτὸν ἔπεισαν, ἀποδίδοται ἀγρὸν μὲν Ἀθμονοῖ πέντε καὶ ἑβδομήκοντα μνῶν Ἀντιφάνει, τὸ δ' ἐν Σηραγγίῳ βαλανεῖον τρισχιλίων Ἀριστολόχῳ· οἰκίαν δὲ ἐν ἄστει τεττάρων καὶ τεσσαράκοντα μνῶν ὑποκειμένην ἀπέλυσε τῷ ἱεροφάντῃ. ἔτι δὲ αἶγας ἀπέδοτο σὺν τῷ αἰπόλῳ τριῶν καὶ δέκα μνῶν, καὶ ζεύγη δύο ὀρικά, τὸ μὲν ὀκτὼ μνῶν τὸ δὲ πεντήκοντα καὶ πεντακοσίων δραχμῶν, καὶ δημιουργοὺς ὅσοι ἦσαν αὐτῷ. [34] σύμπαντα δὲ πλείονος ἢ τριῶν ταλάντων, ἃ ἐπράθη διὰ ταχέων πάνυ τελευτήσαντος Φιλοκτήμονος. καὶ ταῦθ' ὅτι ἀληθῆ λέγω, καθ' ἕκαστον ὑμῖν τῶν εἰρημένων πρῶτον καλῶ τοὺς μάρτυρας.

<ΜΑΡΤΥΡΕΣ>

[35] ταῦτα μὲν δὴ τοῦτον τὸν τρόπον εἶχε· περὶ δὲ τῶν ὑπολοίπων εὐθὺς ἐπεβούλευον, καὶ π-άντων δεινότατον πρᾶγμα κατεσκεύασαν, ᾧ ἄξιόν ἐστι προσέχειν τὸν νοῦν. ὁρῶντες γὰρ τὸν Εὐκτήμονα κομιδῇ ἀπειρηκότα ὑπὸ γήρως καὶ οὐδ' <ἐκ> τῆς κλίνης ἀνίστασθαι δυνάμενον, ἐσκόπουν ὅπως καὶ τελευτήσαντος ἐκείνου δι' αὐτῶν ἔσοιτο ἡ οὐσία. [36] καὶ τί ποιοῦσιν; ἀπογράφουσι τὼ παῖδε τούτω πρὸς τὸν ἄρχοντα ὡς εἰσποιήτω τοῖς τοῦ Εὐκτήμονος ὑέσι τοῖς τετελευτηκόσιν, ἐπιγράψαντες σφᾶς αὐτοὺς ἐπιτρόπους, καὶ μισθοῦν ἐκέλευον τὸν ἄρχοντα τοὺς οἴκους ὡς ὀρφανῶν ὄντων, ὅπως ἐπὶ τοῖς τούτων ὀνόμασι τὰ μὲν μισθωθείη τῆς

had been ruined, which gave them the opportunity they needed, they put together a plan. (30) First of all they persuaded Euctemon to annul the will because it was not beneficial for the boys, since after Euctemon's death no-one would have control of the real estate except his daughters and their offspring. If, on the other hand, he sold some of the property and left cash, they could take secure possession of it. (31) On hearing this, Euctemon immediately asked Pythodorus to return the document and summoned him to produce it. When Pythodorus appeared before the archon, Euctemon said that he wanted to annul the will. (32) Pythodorus agreed with him, and with Phanostratus (who was present) that the will should be destroyed, but Chaereas, who was a joint depositary, had left a daughter, so he suggested that the will should not be destroyed until a *kyrios* had been appointed for her, and the archon so decided. Euctemon agreed to this in front of the archon and his assessors, and, after calling many witnesses to the fact that the will he had deposited was no longer in existence, he left. (33) And in a very short time (which was precisely why my opponents had persuaded him to revoke the will) he sold a farm at Athmonon to Antiphanes for 75 minas and the bath-house at Serangion to Aristolochus for 3,000 drachmas, and he mortgaged a house in the city to the hierophant for 44 minas. He also sold some goats with their goatherd for 13 minas and two pairs of mules, one for eight minas and the other for 550 drachmas, and all his craftsman slaves, (34) In total, he raised more than three talents on the property he hastily sold after Philoctemon's death. And to prove that I am telling the truth, I first call witnesses to the details of my statements.

WITNESSES

(35) That, then, was how part of his property was dealt with. As to the rest, they immediately started plotting, and concocted the most dreadful scheme of all, to which you must pay careful attention. Observing that Euctemon was completely incapacitated by old age, and could not even get out of bed, they considered how to get control of all his property after his death. And what did they do? (36) They registered these two boys with the archon as the adopted sons of Euctemon's deceased sons, entering themselves as their guardians, and asked the archon to lease the estates of the 'orphans'. In that way, part of the property under the

οὐσίας, τὰ δὲ ἀποτιμήματα κατασταθείη καὶ ὅροι τεθεῖεν ζῶντος ἔτι τοῦ Εὐκτήμονος, μισθωταὶ δὲ αὐτοὶ γενόμενοι τὰς προσόδους λαμβάνοιεν. [37] καὶ ἐπειδὴ πρῶτον τὰ δικαστήρια ἐπληρώθη, ὁ μὲν ἄρχων προεκήρυττεν, οἱ δ᾽ ἐμισθοῦντο. παραγενόμενοι δέ τινες ἐξαγγέλλουσι τοῖς οἰκείοις τὴν ἐπιβουλήν, καὶ ἐλθόντες ἐδήλωσαν τὸ πρᾶγμα τοῖς δικασταῖς, καὶ οὕτως ἀπεχειροτόνησαν οἱ δικασταὶ μὴ μισθοῦν τοὺς οἴκους· εἰ δ᾽ ἔλαθεν, ἀπωλώλει ἂν ἅπασα ἡ οὐσία. καί μοι κάλει τοὺς παραγενομένους μάρτυρας.

ΜΑΡΤΥΡΕΣ

[38] πρὶν μὲν τοίνυν τούτους γνωρίσαι τὴν ἄνθρωπον καὶ μετ᾽ ἐκείνης ἐπιβουλεῦσαι Εὐκτήμονι, οὕτω πολλὴν οὐσίαν ἐκέκτητο Εὐκτήμων μετὰ τοῦ ὑέος Φιλοκτήμονος, ὥστε ἅμα τά τε μέγιστα ὑμῖν λητουργεῖν ἀμφοτέρους τῶν τε ἀρχαίων μηδὲν πραθῆναι τῶν τε προσόδων περιποιεῖν, ὥστε ἀεί τι προσκτᾶσθαι· ἐπειδὴ δ᾽ ἐτελεύτησε Φιλοκτήμων, οὕτω διετέθη ἡ οὐσία, ὥστε τῶν ἀρχαίων μηδὲ τὰ ἡμίσεα εἶναι λοιπὰ καὶ τὰς προσόδους ἁπάσας ἠφανίσθαι. [39] καὶ οὐδὲ ταῦτα ἐξήρκεσεν αὐτοῖς διαφορῆσαι, ὦ ἄνδρες, ἀλλ᾽ ἐπειδὴ καὶ ἐτελεύτησεν ὁ Εὐκτήμων, εἰς τοῦτο ἦλθον τόλμης ὥστ᾽ ἐκείνου κειμένου ἔνδον τοὺς μὲν οἰκέτας ἐφύλαττον, ὅπως μηδεὶς ἐξαγγείλειε μήτε τοῖν θυγατέροιν μήτε τῇ γυναικὶ αὐτοῦ μήτε τῶν οἰκείων μηδενί, τὰ δὲ χρήματα ἔνδοθεν ἐξεφορήσαντο μετὰ τῆς ἀνθρώπου εἰς τὴν ὁμότοιχον οἰκίαν, ἣν ᾤκει μεμισθωμένος εἷς τούτων, Ἀντίδωρος ἐκεῖνος. [40] καὶ οὐδ᾽ ἐπειδὴ ἑτέρων πυθόμεναι ἦλθον αἱ θυγατέρες αὐτοῦ καὶ ἡ γυνή, οὐδὲ τότε εἴων εἰσιέναι, ἀλλ᾽ ἀπέκλεισαν τῇ θύρᾳ, φάσκοντες οὐ προσήκειν αὐταῖς θάπτειν Εὐκτήμονα· καὶ οὐδ᾽ εἰσελθεῖν ἐδύναντο, εἰ μὴ μόλις καὶ περὶ ἡλίου δυσμάς. [41] εἰσελθοῦσαι δὲ κατέλαβον ἐκεῖνον μὲν ἔνδον κείμενον δευτεραῖον, ὡς ἔφασαν οἱ οἰκέται, τὰ δ᾽ ἐκ τῆς οἰκίας ἅπαντα ἐκπεφορημένα ὑπὸ τούτων. αἱ μὲν οὖν γυναῖκες, οἷον εἰκός, περὶ τὸν τετελευτηκότα ἦσαν· οὗτοι δὲ τοῖς ἀκολουθήσασι παραχρῆμα ἐπεδείκνυσαν τὰ ἔνδον ὡς εἶχε, καὶ τοὺς οἰκέτας πρῶτον ἠρώτων ἐναντίον τούτων ὅποι τετραμμένα εἴη τὰ χρήματα. [42] λεγόντων δὲ ἐκείνων ὅτι οὗτοι ἐξενηνοχότες εἶεν εἰς τὴν

children's names could be leased and part of it used as security, with mortgage stones placed on it, while Euctemon was still alive, and they themselves, as lessees, could take the income. (37) As soon as the courts reconvened, the archon made an announcement and they put in a bid for the lease. But some of those who were present told the family about the plot, and they went along and exposed the affair to the judges, and so the judges voted not to allow the estates to be leased. If that had not happened, the whole of the property would have been lost. Please call those who were present as witnesses.

WITNESSES

(38) Before my opponents got to know the woman and conspired with her against Euctemon, he and his son Philoctemon had acquired so much property that they could both carry out the most expensive liturgies on your behalf without selling any of their existing assets and at the same time saving out of their income, so that they were continually becoming richer. But after the death of Philoctemon the property was so reduced that not even half of the capital remains and all the profits have disappeared. (39) What's more, gentlemen, they were not content with this plundering, but when Euctemon also died they had the temerity to confine the slaves while his body was lying in the house, so that no-one could tell his daughters or his wife or his other relatives. And together with the woman they carried out his belongings into the adjoining house, which that man Antidorus, one of their people, occupied as a tenant. (40) And even when Euctemon's wife and daughters arrived, after hearing what had happened from others, they did not let them in but shut the door on them, saying it was not up to them to bury Euctemon. And they could only get in, with difficulty, around sunset. (41) When they did get inside, they found that Euctemon had been lying there dead for two days, according to the slaves, and that those people had removed everything from the house. The women were attending to the dead man, as was fitting, and my friends immediately revealed the state of affairs in the house to those who had accompanied them, first, in their presence, asking the slaves where the furniture had been taken to. (42) When the slaves replied that our opponents had taken it to the neighbouring house, my friends immediately claimed the legal right to search the house and

πλησίον οἰκίαν,καὶ ἀξιούντων παραχρῆμα τῶνδε φωρᾶν κατὰ τὸν νόμον καὶ τοὺς οἰκέτας ἐξαιτούντων τοὺς ἐκφορήσαντας, οὐκ ἠθέλησαν τῶν δικαίων οὐδὲν ποιῆσαι. καὶ ὅτι ἀληθῆ λέγω, λαβὲ ταυτὶ καὶ ἀνάγνωθι.

<ΜΑΡΤΥΡΙΑΙ>

[43] τοσαῦτα μὲν τοίνυν χρήματα ἐκ τῆς οἰκίας ἐκφορήσαντες, τοσαύτης δ᾽ οὐσίας πεπραμένης τὴν τιμὴν ἔχοντες, ἔτι δὲ τὰς προσόδους τὰς ἐν ἐκείνῳ τῷ χρόνῳ γενομένας διαφορήσαντες, οἴονται καὶ τῶν λοιπῶν κύριοι γενήσεσθαι· καὶ εἰς τοῦτο ἀναιδείας ἥκουσιν, ὥστ᾽ εὐθυδικίᾳ μὲν οὐκ ἐτόλμησαν εἰσελθεῖν, ἀλλὰ διεμαρτύρουν ὡς ὑπὲρ γνησίων ἅμα μὲν τὰ ψευδῆ ἅμα δὲ τἀναντία οἷς αὐτοὶ ἔπραξαν· [44] οἵτινες πρὸς μὲν τὸν ἄρχοντα ἀπέγραψαν αὐτοὺς ὡς ὄντας τὸν μὲν Φιλοκτήμονος τὸν δ᾽ Ἐργαμένους, νῦν δὲ διαμεμαρτυρήκασιν Εὐκτήμονος εἶναι. καίτοι οὐδ᾽ εἰ γνήσιοι ἦσαν, εἰσποίητοι δέ, ὡς οὗτοι ἔφασαν, οὐδ᾽ οὕτω προσήκει αὐτοὺς Εὐκτήμονος εἶναι· ὁ γὰρ νόμος οὐκ ἐᾷ ἐπανιέναι, ἐὰν μὴ ὑὸν καταλίπῃ γνήσιον. ὥστε καὶ ἐξ ὧν αὐτοὶ ἔπραξαν ἀνάγκη τὴν μαρτυρίαν ψευδῆ εἶναι. [45] καὶ εἰ μὲν τότε διεπράξαντο μισθωθῆναι τοὺς οἴκους, οὐκ ἂν ἔτι ἦν τοῖσδε ἀμφισβητῆσαι· νῦν δὲ ἀποχειροτονησάντων τῶν δικαστῶν ὡς οὐδὲν αὐτοῖς προσῆκον, οὐδὲ ἀμφισβητῆσαι τετολμήκασιν, ἀλλὰ πρὸς ὑπερβολὴν ἀναισχυντίας προσμεμαρτυρήκασι τούτους εἶναι κληρονόμους, οὓς ὑμεῖς ἀπεχειροτονήσατε. [46] ἔτι δὲ καὶ τοῦ μάρτυρος αὐτοῦ σκέψασθε τὴν τόλμαν καὶ ἀναίδειαν, ὅστις εἴληχε μὲν αὐτῷ τῆς θυγατρὸς τῆς Εὐκτήμονος ὡς οὔσης ἐπικλήρου, καὶ αὐτοῦ τοῦ κλήρου τοῦ Εὐκτήμονος πέμπτου μέρους ὡς ἐπιδίκου ὄντος, μεμαρτύρηκε δ᾽ Εὐκτήμονος ὑὸν εἶναι γνήσιον. καίτοι πῶς οὗτος οὐ σαφῶς ἐξελέγχει αὐτὸς αὑτὸν τὰ ψευδῆ μεμαρτυρηκότα; οὐ γὰρ δήπου γνησίου ὄντος ὑέος Εὐκτήμονι ἐπίκληρος ἂν ἦν ἡ θυγάτηρ αὐτοῦ, οὐδὲ ὁ κλῆρος ἐπίδικος. ὡς τοίνυν ἔλαχε ταύτας τὰς λήξεις, ἀναγνώσεται ὑμῖν τὰς μαρτυρίας.

asked for the slaves who had removed the furniture to be produced, but our opponents refused all their just demands. And to prove that I am telling the truth, take these documents and read them.

WITNESS STATEMENTS

(43) After having removed so much furniture from the house, and sold so much of the property at a profit, and even plundered the income that had accrued in the meantime, they thought they could also take control of the rest. And they were so shameless that they did not dare to initiate a direct action but lodged a *diamartyria* as if it were a question of legitimate sons – which is not only untrue but also contradicts their own previous conduct. (44) Those who, on the one hand, had registered the boys with the archon as being the adopted sons of Philoctemon and Ergamenes, now, on the other hand, have testified in the *diamartyria* that they are Euctemon's sons. Yet if they were his legitimate sons, but had been adopted, as our opponents claim, they still cannot be described as Euctemon's sons, because the law does not allow an adopted son to return to his natural family unless he leaves a legitimate son behind. So it is obvious, even from their own actions, that their testimony is false. (45) And if they had then successfully carried through the leasing of the estates, there would have been nothing for my friends to contest; but now that the judges have voted against them as having no right, they have not dared to submit a claim but, in an excess of effrontery, they have additionally testified that these boys, whom you voted against, are heirs. (46) Again, consider the effrontery and shamelessness of the witness, who on the one hand has claimed Euctemon's daughter as an *epikleros*, together with a fifth share of Euctemon's estate, as being adjudicable to him, while on the other hand he has testified that Euctemon left a legitimate son. Yet in doing so, does he not convict himself of having given false testimony? For it's obvious that if Euctemon did leave a legitimate son, his daughter would not be an *epikleros* and his estate would not be subject to adjudication. The clerk will read you the testimony showing that he did make these claims.

<ΜΑΡΤΥΡΙΑΙ>

[47] τοὐναντίον τοίνυν συμβέβηκεν ἢ ὡς ὁ νόμος γέγραπται: ἐκεῖ μὲν γὰρ ἔστι νόθῳ μηδὲ νόθη <μὴ> εἶναι ἀγχιστείαν μήθ' ἱερῶν μήθ' ὁσίων ἀπ' Εὐκλείδου ἄρχοντος, Ἀνδροκλῆς δὲ καὶ Ἀντίδωρος οἴονται δεῖν, ἀφελόμενοι τὰς Εὐκτήμονος θυγατέρας τὰς γνησίας καὶ τοὺς ἐκ τούτων γεγονότας, τόν τε Εὐκτήμονος οἶκον καὶ τὸν Φιλοκτήμονος ἔχειν. [48] καὶ ἡ διαφθείρασα τὴν Εὐκτήμονος γνώμην καὶ πολλῶν ἐγκρατὴς γενομένη οὕτως ὑβρίζει σφόδρα πιστεύουσα τούτοις, ὥστε οὐ μόνον τῶν Εὐκτήμονος οἰκείων καταφρονεῖ, ἀλλὰ καὶ τῆς πόλεως ἁπάσης. ἀκούσαντες δὲ ἓν μόνον σημεῖον ῥᾳδίως γνώσεσθε τὴν ἐκείνης παρανομίαν. καί μοι λαβὲ τοῦτον τὸν νόμον.

<ΝΟΜΟΣ>

[49] ταυτὶ τὰ γράμματα, ὦ ἄνδρες, ὑμεῖς, οὕτω σεμνὰ καὶ εὐσεβῆ ἐνομοθετήσατε, περὶ πολλοῦ ποιούμενοι καὶ πρὸς ταύτας καὶ πρὸς τοὺς ἄλλους θεοὺς εὐσεβεῖν: ἡ δὲ τούτων μήτηρ, οὕτως ὁμολογουμένως οὖσα δούλη καὶ ἅπαντα τὸν χρόνον αἰσχρῶς βιοῦσα, [50] ἣν οὔτε παρελθεῖν εἴσω τοῦ ἱεροῦ ἔδει οὔτ' ἰδεῖν τῶν ἔνδον οὐδέν, οὔσης τῆς θυσίας ταύταις ταῖς θεαῖς ἐτόλμησε συμπέμψαι τὴν πομπὴν καὶ εἰσελθεῖν εἰς τὸ ἱερὸν καὶ ἰδεῖν ἃ οὐκ ἐξῆν αὐτῇ. ὡς δὲ ἀληθῆ λέγω, ἐκ τῶν ψηφισμάτων γνώσεσθε ἃ ἐψηφίσατο ἡ βουλὴ περὶ αὐτῆς. λαβὲ τὸ ψήφισμα.

ΨΗΦΙΣΜΑ

[51] ἐνθυμεῖσθαι τοίνυν χρή, ὦ ἄνδρες, πότερον δεῖ τὸν ἐκ ταύτης τῶν Φιλοκτήμονος εἶναι κληρονόμον καὶ ἐπὶ τὰ μνήματα ἰέναι χεόμενον καὶ ἐναγιοῦντα, ἢ τὸν ἐκ τῆς ἀδελφῆς τοῦτον, ὃν ὑὸν αὐτὸς ἐποιήσατο: καὶ πότερον δεῖ τὴν ἀδελφὴν Φιλοκτήμονος, ἣ Χαιρέᾳ συνῴκησε, νῦν δὲ χηρεύει, ἐπὶ τούτοις γενέσθαι ἢ ἐκδοῦναι ὅτῳ βούλονται ἢ ἐᾶν καταγηράσκειν, ἢ γνησίαν οὖσαν ὑφ' ὑμῶν ἐπιδικασθεῖσαν συνοικεῖν ὅτῳ ἂν ὑμῖν δοκῇ. [52] ἡ γὰρ ψῆφός ἐστι περὶ τούτων νυνί. τουτὶ γὰρ αὐτοῖς ἡ διαμαρτυρία δύναται, ἵν' ὁ κίνδυνος τοῖσδε μὲν ᾖ περὶ πάντων, οὗτοι δὲ κἂν νῦν διαμάρτωσι τοῦ ἀγῶνος, δόξῃ δὲ ὁ κλῆρος ἐπίδικος

WITNESS STATEMENTS

(47) So what has happened is the opposite of what the law prescribes: since the archonship of Eucleides, neither an illegitimate son nor an illegitimate daughter has any right through kinship to share in family cults and property, but Androcles and Antidorus think they can take both the estate of Euctemon and that of Philoctemon, depriving Euctemon's daughters and their children. (48) And the woman who destroyed Euctemon's mind and gained control of so much property is so lawless, with the full support of our opponents, that she shows her contempt not only for Euctemon's family but for the city as a whole. When you hear one single indication, you will easily understand her criminality. Please take and read the law.

LAW

(49) You, gentlemen, enacted such solemn and pious laws, showing how highly you value reverence towards these goddesses and all other deities. But the mother of these young men, a known slave who lived a shameful life, (50) who should neither have entered the temple nor seen anything inside, had the temerity to join the procession at the sacrifices to the goddesses and to enter the temple and look at what she had no right to see. You will learn that I am telling the truth from the decrees which the Council enacted about her. Take the decree,

DECREE

(51) So now you need to consider, gentlemen, first whether that woman's son should be Philoctemon's heir and go to the family tombs to make libations and sacrifices, or whether it should be his sister's son, whom he adopted as his own son; and secondly whether Philoctemon's sister, who was married to Chaereas but is now a widow, should belong to my opponents and either be married to whoever they wish or be left to grow old as a widow; or whether, as a legitimate daughter, she should be adjudicated by you to marry whoever you think fit. (52) These are the issues on which you must now vote. The *diamartyria* gives them the advantage that all the risk falls on my friends; even if our opponents lose in the present trial, and the estate is found to be subject to adjudication,

εἶναι, ἀντιγραψάμενοι δὶς περὶ τῶν αὐτῶν ἀγωνίζωνται, καίτοι εἰ μὲν διέθετο Φιλοκτήμων μὴ ἐξὸν αὐτῷ, τοῦτ᾽ αὐτὸ ἐχρῆν διαμαρτυρεῖν, ὡς οὐ κύριος ἦν ὑὸν τόνδε ποιήσασθαι: εἰ δ᾽ ἔξεστι μὲν διαθέσθαι, ἀμφισβητεῖ δὲ ὡς οὐ δόντος οὐδὲ διαθεμένου, μὴ διαμαρτυρίᾳ κωλύειν ἀλλ᾽ εὐθυδικίᾳ εἰσιέναι. [53]νῦν δὲ πῶς ἄν περιφανέστερον ἐξελεγχθείη τὰ ψευδῆ μεμαρτυρηκὼς ἢ εἴ τις αὐτὸν ἔροιτο "Ἀνδρόκλεις, πῶς οἶσθα Φιλοκτήμον᾽ ὅτι οὔτε διέθετο οὔτε ὑὸν Χαιρέστρατον ἐποιήσατο;" οἷς μὲν γάρ τις παρεγένετο, δίκαιον, ὦ ἄνδρες, μαρτυρεῖν, οἷς δὲ μὴ παρεγένετο ἀλλ᾽ ἤκουσέ τινος, ἀκοὴν μαρτυρεῖν: [54] σὺ δ᾽ οὐ παραγενόμενος διαρρήδην μεμαρτύρηκας ὡς οὐ διέθετο Φιλοκτήμων, ἀλλ᾽ ἄπαις ἐτελεύτησε. καίτοι πῶς οἷόν τε εἰδέναι, ὦ ἄνδρες; ὅμοιον γὰρ ὥσπερ ἂν εἰ φαίη εἰδέναι, καὶ μὴ παραγενόμενος, ὅσα ὑμεῖς πάντες πράττετε. οὐ γὰρ δὴ τοῦτό γε ἐρεῖ, καίπερ ἀναίσχυντος ὤν, ὡς ἅπασι παρεγένετο καὶ πάντ᾽ οἶδεν ὅσα Φιλοκτήμων ἐν τῷ βίῳ διεπράξατο. [55] πάντων γὰρ αὐτὸν ἐκεῖνος ἔχθιστον ἐνόμιζε διά <τε> τὴν ἄλλην πονηρίαν, καὶ διότι τῶν συγγενῶν μόνος μετὰ τῆς Ἀλκῆς ἐκείνης τούτῳ καὶ τοῖς ἄλλοις συνεπιβουλεύσας τοῖς τοῦ Εὐκτήμονος χρήμασι τοιαῦτα διεπράξατο, οἷά περ ὑμῖν ἀπέδειξα. [56] πάντων δὲ μάλιστα ἀγανακτῆσαί ἐστιν ἄξιον, ὅταν οὗτοι καταχρῶνται τῷ Εὐκτήμονος ὀνόματι τοῦ τουδὶ πάππου. εἰ γάρ, ὡς οὗτοι λέγουσι, τῷ μὲν Φιλοκτήμονι μὴ ἐξῆν διαθέσθαι, τοῦ δ᾽ Εὐκτήμονός ἐστιν ὁ κλῆρος, πότερον δικαιότερον τῶν Εὐκτήμονος κληρονομεῖν τὰς ἐκείνου θυγατέρας, ὁμολογουμένως οὔσας γνησίας, καὶ ἡμᾶς τοὺς ἐκ τούτων γεγονότας, ἢ τοὺς οὐδὲν προσήκοντας, οἳ οὐ μόνον ὑφ᾽ ἡμῶν ἐλέγχονται, [57] ἀλλὰ καὶ ἐξ ὧν αὐτοὶ ἐπίτροποι διαπεπραγμένοι εἰσί; τοῦτο γὰρ ὑμῶν δέομαι καὶ ἱκετεύω σφόδρα μεμνῆσθαι, ὦ ἄνδρες, ὅπερ ὀλίγῳ πρότερον ἀπέδειξα ὑμῖν, ὅτι Ἀνδροκλῆς οὑτοσὶ φησὶ μὲν εἶναι ἐπίτροπος αὐτῶν ὡς ὄντων γνησίων Εὐκτήμονος, εἴληχε δ᾽ αὐτὸς ἑαυτῷ τοῦ Εὐκτήμονος κλήρου καὶ τῆς θυγατρὸς αὐτοῦ ὡς οὔσης ἐπικλήρου: καὶ ταῦτα μεμαρτύρηται ὑμῖν. [58] καίτοι πῶς οὐ δεινόν, ὦ ἄνδρες, πρὸς θεῶν Ὀλυμπίων, εἰ μὲν οἱ παῖδές εἰσι γνήσιοι, τὸν ἐπίτροπον ἑαυτῷ λαγχάνειν τοῦ Εὐκτήμονος

they can put forward a second claim and contest the same property twice. Yet if Philoctemon made a will that he had no legal right to make, they ought to have stated in their *diamartyria* that he was not entitled to adopt Chaerestratus as his son. If, on the other hand, he was entitled to dispose of his property by will, and their claim is that he did not do so, then they ought not to have barred the proceedings with a *diamartyria* but entered on a direct action. (53) As it is, how could anyone more plainly convict him of false testimony than by asking, 'Androcles, how do you know that Philoctemon did not make a will or adopt Chaerestratus?' For it is right, gentlemen, that one should give witness testimony about matters when one was present, or testify by hearsay when one was not present but has heard from someone else. (54) But you have expressly testified, although you were not present, that Philoctemon did not make a will but died childless. How on earth can he know this, gentlemen? It's as if he were to say that he knew everything you were all doing, without having been present. Of course he won't say that, but he's shameless enough, as if he had been present and knew about everything that Philoctemon had ever done in his life. (55) In fact Philoctemon considered him his worst enemy, both because of all his other wickedness and because he was the only one in the family to conspire with that woman Alce and this man and the others against Euctemon's property, and who did all the things I've described to you. (56) But what is most aggravating of all is the way in which our opponents abuse the name of Euctemon, Chaerestratus's grandfather. For if, as they say, Philoctemon was not entitled to make a will and the estate was Euctemon's, is it more just for his estate to go to his daughters, who are acknowledged to be legitimate, and us as their descendants, or to people who are not related to him at all, who have been condemned not only by us but also by their own actions as guardians? (57) I earnestly beg and implore you, gentlemen, to remember what I told you a little earlier, that Androcles here says on the one hand that he is the guardian of these boys, who are legitimate sons of Euctemon, while on the other hand he himself has claimed Euctemon's estate, and his daughter as an *epikleros*, on his own behalf, and witnesses have testified to you on these matters. (58) Yet by the gods of Olympus, gentlemen, how extraordinary is it, if they are legitimate sons, for the guardian to claim Euctemon's estate and daughter as being subject to adjudication; or, if they are not legitimate, for him now to have testified in his *diamarryria*

κλήρου καὶ τῆς θυγατρὸς αὐτοῦ ὡς οὔσης ἐπιδίκου, εἰ δὲ μή εἰσι γνήσιοι, νῦν διαμεμαρτυρηκέναι ὡς εἰσὶ γνήσιοι; ταῦτα γὰρ αὐτὰ ἑαυτοῖς ἐναντία ἐστίν. ὥστ᾽ οὐ μόνον ὑφ᾽ ἡμῶν ἐλέγχεται τὰ ψευδῆ διαμεμαρτυρηκώς, ἀλλὰ καὶ ἐξ ὧν αὐτὸς πράττει. [59] καὶ τούτῳ μὲν οὐδεὶς διαμαρτυρεῖ μὴ ἐπίδικον εἶναι τὸν κλῆρον, ἀλλ᾽ εὐθυδικίᾳ εἰσιέναι <ἐξῆν>, οὗτος δ᾽ ἅπαντας ἀποστερεῖ τῆς ἀμφισβητήσεως. καὶ διαρρήδην μαρτυρήσας γνησίους τοὺς παῖδας εἶναι, οἴεται ἐξαρκέσειν ὑμῖν παρεκβάσεις, ἐὰν δὲ τοῦτο μὲν μηδ᾽ ἐγχειρήσῃ ἐπιδεικνύναι ἢ καὶ κατὰ μικρόν τι ἐπιμνησθῇ, ἡμῖν δὲ λοιδορήσηται μεγάλῃ τῇ φωνῇ καὶ λέγῃ ὡς εἰσὶν οἵδε μὲν πλούσιοι αὐτὸς δὲ πένης, διὰ δὲ ταῦτα δόξειν τοὺς παῖδας εἶναι γνησίους. [60] τῆς δὲ τούτων οὐσίας, ὦ ἄνδρες, εἰς τὴν πόλιν πλείω ἀναλίσκεται ἢ εἰς αὐτοὺς τούτους. καὶ Φανόστρατος μὲν τετριηράρχηκεν ἑπτάκις ἤδη, τὰς δὲ λῃτουργίας ἁπάσας λελῃτούργηκε καὶ τὰς πλείστας νίκας νενίκηκεν· οὑτοσὶ δὲ Χαιρέστρατος τηλικοῦτος ὢν τετριηράρχηκε, κεχορήγηκε δὲ τραγῳδοῖς, γεγυμνασιάρχηκε δὲ λαμπάδι· καὶ τὰς εἰσφορὰς εἰσενηνόχασιν ἀμφότεροι πάσας ἐν τοῖς τριακοσίοις. καὶ τέως μὲν δύ᾽ ὄντες, νῦν δὲ καὶ ὁ νεώτερος οὑτοσὶ χορηγεῖ μὲν τραγῳδοῖς, εἰς δὲ τοὺς τριακοσίους ἐγγέγραπται καὶ εἰσφέρει τὰς εἰσφοράς. [61] ὥστ᾽ οὐ φθονεῖσθαί εἰσιν ἄξιοι, ἀλλὰ πολὺ μᾶλλον νὴ Δία καὶ τὸν Ἀπόλλω οὗτοι, εἰ λήψονται ἃ μὴ προσήκει αὐτοῖς. τοῦ γὰρ Φιλοκτήμονος κλήρου ἂν μὲν ἐπιδικάσηται ὅδε, ὑμῖν αὐτὸν ταμιεύσει, τὰ προσταττόμενα λῃτουργῶν ὥσπερ καὶ νῦν καὶ ἔτι μᾶλλον· ἐὰν δ᾽ οὗτοι λάβωσι, διαφορήσαντες ἑτέροις ἐπιβουλεύσουσι. [62] δέομαι οὖν ὑμῶν, ὦ ἄνδρες, ἵνα μὴ ἐξαπατηθῆτε, τῇ διαμαρτυρίᾳ τὸν νοῦν προσέχειν περὶ ἧς τὴν ψῆφον οἴσετε· καὶ πρὸς ταύτην αὐτὸν κελεύετε τὴν ἀπολογίαν ποιεῖσθαι, ὥσπερ καὶ ἡμεῖς κατηγορήσαμεν. γέγραπται ὡς οὐκ ἔδωκεν οὐδὲ διέθετο Φιλοκτήμων· τοῦτο ἐπιδέδεικται ψεῦδος ὄν· καὶ γὰρ μαρτυροῦσιν οἱ παραγενόμενοι. [63] τί ἔτι; τελευτῆσαι ἄπαιδα Φιλοκτήμονα. πῶς οὖν ἄπαις ἦν ὅστις τὸν ἑαυτοῦ ἀδελφιδοῦν υἱὸν ποιησάμενος κατέλιπεν, ᾧ ὁμοίως ὁ νόμος τὴν κληρονομίαν ἀποδίδωσι καὶ τοῖς ἐξ αὐτοῦ γενομένοις; καὶ διαρρήδην ἐν τῷ νόμῳ γέγραπται, ἐὰν ποιησαμένῳ παῖδες ἐπιγένωνται, τὸ μέρος ἑκάτερον ἔχειν τῆς οὐσίας καὶ κληρονομεῖν ὁμοίως ἀμφοτέρους. [64] ὡς οὖν εἰσὶ γνήσιοι οἱ παῖδες οἵδε, τοῦτ᾽ αὐτὸ ἐπιδεικνύτω, ὥσπερ ἂν

that they are legitimate? These things are self-contradictory. So his false testimony in the *diamartyria* has been condemned not only by us but also by his own actions. (59) And no-one is testifying against him that the estate is not subject to adjudication, and it is open to him to initiate a direct action, but he is trying to deprive everyone else of their claim. Having expressly testified that the boys are legitimate, he thinks you will be satisfied with digression, and that if he doesn't try to prove a point or only mentions something briefly, but insults us in a loud voice saying that my friends are rich but he is poor – by all these means it will seem that the boys are legitimate. (60) Most of my friends' wealth, gentlemen, has been spent on the city rather than themselves; Phanostratus has already acted as trierarch seven times, performed all the liturgies, and for the most part won victories, while Chairestratus here, young as he is, has acted as a trierarch and as a *choregos* at the tragic festivals and a gymnasiarch at the torch-races. And both of them, as members of the Three Hundred, have paid all the war-taxes. And while it was previously only the two of them, now the younger son here is also a *choregos* at the tragic festivals and, having been enrolled in the Three Hundred, pays the war-taxes. (61) So you should bear no grudge against them, but rather (by Zeus and Apollo!) against our opponents, if they get hold of what does not belong to them. For if you award Philoctemon's estate to my friend, he will manage it for you, continuing to perform his allotted liturgies as he now does, and even more. But if our opponents get hold of it, they will squander it and then conspire against others.

(62) So I beseech you, gentlemen, in order that you are not deceived, to pay close attention to the *diamartyria* about which you are going to vote. Tell my opponent to make it the subject of his defence, as we have made it the subject of our accusation. It says that Philoctemon did not dispose of his property by will; this has been shown to be untrue, for those who were present testify that he did. (63) What else does it say? That Philoctemon died childless. How could someone be childless if he has left his own nephew as his adopted son, to whom the law gives the right of inheritance just as it does to biological children? And it is explicitly written in the law that if someone who has adopted a son later has children of his own, each of them shall have a share of the estate and both inherit in the same way. (64) Let him therefore prove that the children are legitimate, as each of you would have to do. For they are not

ὑμῶν ἕκαστος. οὐ γὰρ ἂν εἴπῃ μητρὸς ὄνομα, γνήσιοί εἰσιν, ἀλλ᾽ ἐὰν ἐπιδεικνύῃ ὡς ἀληθῆ λέγει, τοὺς συγγενεῖς παρεχόμενος τοὺς εἰδότας συνοικοῦσαν τῷ Εὐκτήμονι <καὶ> τοὺς δημότας καὶ τοὺς φράτορας, εἴ τι ἀκηκόασι πώποτε ἢ ἴσασιν ὑπὲρ αὐτῆς Εὐκτήμονα λῃτουργήσαντα, ἔτι δὲ ποῦ τέθαπται, ἐν ποίοις μνήμασι, [65] <καὶ> τίς εἶδε τὰ νομιζόμενα ποιοῦντα Εὐκτήμονα· ποῖ δ᾽ ἔτ᾽ ἰόντες οἱ παῖδες ἐναγίζουσι καὶ χέονται, καὶ τίς εἶδε ταῦτα τῶν πολιτῶν ἢ ὧν οἰκετῶν <τῶν> Εὐκτήμονος. ταῦτα γάρ ἐστινἔλεγχος ἅπαντα, καὶ οὐ λοιδορία. καὶ ἐὰν περὶ αὐτοῦ τούτου κελεύητε ἐπιδεικνύναι ὥσπερ καὶ διεμαρτύρησεν, ὑμεῖς τε τὴν ψῆφον ὁσίαν καὶ κατὰ τοὺς νόμους θήσεσθε, τοῖσδέ τε τὰ δίκαια γενήσεται.

legitimate simply because he tells you their mother's name, but only if he proves that he is telling the truth, producing the relatives who know that she was married to Euctemon and the demesmen and phratry members if they have any knowledge or have ever heard that Euctemon performed liturgies on her behalf; also where she is buried and in what kind of tomb, (65) and who has seen Euctemon carrying out the customary rites for her; and whether her sons still go to make sacrifices and libations, and which of the citizens or Euctemon's slaves have seen this. All these things, not insults, are proof. And if you tell him to prove what he has said in his *diamartyria*, you will cast a just and appropriate vote, and justice will be done to my friends.

COMMENTARY

1–2. Introduction
Since this is the prosecution speech from an adversarial trial (in this case a *dikē pseudomartyriōn* or suit for false testimony) it would have been the first to be delivered in court, before the defendant's response. The speech begins with a brief introductory passage in which the speaker presents his credentials as a supporting speaker (*synēgoros*) of Chaerestratus. His identity is not known for certain, but he may have been Aristomenes of Porus, who is named at *IG.* II², 1609.82 as a syntrierarch with Phanostratus (see on 'about to set sail as a trierarch', §27), and I shall use that name for convenience. The absence of a longer, more formal introduction probably suggests that Chaerestratus himself had made a short speech to introduce his case before handing over to his *synēgoros*.

1 gentlemen: On addresses to the judges in general, and in particular at the beginning of a speech, see on 'gentlemen', 1.1. In this speech Isaeus uses only his preferred form, 'gentlemen' (*ō andres*), which occurs 18 times. Following this introductory address to engage the judges' attention, seven more have a structural function, marking the resumption of the speech after the reading of a law or decree (§§9, 49, 51) or the transition between narrative and argumentation or between different stages of the argument (§§10, 19, 28 60). The remaining 10 are used to engage the judges in the speaker's argumentation or narrative (§§12, 17, 21, 23, 39, 53, 54, 57, 58, 62).

most of you know: Whether or not most of the judges did know who Aristomenes was, this was probably designed to have a psychological impact on them: common knowledge is an aspect of group identity, and no-one wants to risk exclusion from the group by admitting ignorance. Cf. on 'everyone knows', 1.37.

sufficient proof: On the meaning of *tekmērion* (here translated as 'proof') see on 'strongest indication', 1.12.

Chaerestratus: Two manuscripts (M, Ald.) have 'Menestratus' for 'Chaerestratus'. This is obviously a mistake, but since Chaerestratus was too young to have been involved in the disastrous Sicilian expedition of 415–13 BC, some editors have proposed an emendation to 'Phanostratus'. Others, including Wyse (1904) *ad loc.* have pointed out that the speaker could be referring to a later campaign to Sicily, the date of which is not known.

trierarch: A trierarch was the commander of a trireme, appointed by the generals. By the late 5th century his functions included the payment of a ship's running costs as well as commanding it in the fleet (Rhodes, 1981, 680). The trierarchy, which cost up to a talent for a year's service, became the most prestigious and expensive of the public services (liturgies) performed as a duty by the wealthiest Athenians. (Cf. on 'liturgies', §38.)

Chaerestratus had apparently served as trierarch only once before the trial (§60). If the restoration [Χαρέστρ]ατος Κηφι, at *IG* II^2 1609.81–2 is correct, and if this inscription is correctly identified as a record of Timotheus's cleruchic expedition to Samos (see Schweigert, 1940, and cf. on 'Timotheus', §27), then the text must be corrupt.

2 vote in accordance with your oath: For the system of voting at Athenian trials, and the oath sworn by the judges (the dicastic oath), see on 2.47.

So I ask you to have sympathy and listen with good will: For the conventional *captatio benevolentiae*, see on 'I beg, entreat and beseech you all to receive my speech with good will', 2.2; and cf. on 'I earnestly beg and implore you, gentlemen', 6.57.

the contest is no small matter for them but of the greatest importance: It will become clear in the course of the speech that, according to Isaeus, what is at stake for Chaerestratus and his father Phanostratus is not just the material value of Philoctemon's estate but the integrity of their family's bloodline. Cf. Griffith-Williams (2022).

3–9. *Philoctemon's will (narrative and testimony)*

Aristomenes first sets out to prove that Philoctemon made a valid will adopting his nephew Chaerestratus (which his opponent Androcles has denied): the will is read out, along with the testimony of witnesses who were present when it was made. He complains that Androcles has not only testified falsely in his *diamartyria* but failed to follow the correct legal procedure, hinting at an unfair attempt to conflate the issue of Philoctemon's will with that of the succession to Euctemon. This will become a recurrent theme in the course of the speech.

Wyse (1904, 491–92) allows his hostility to Isaeus to override his critical judgment in his commentary on §§3–9: 'What judge listening to these artful paragraphs could have suspected that Philoctemon had been dead at least ten years, and that Chaerestratus only applied to the Archon after the death of Euctemon?' In fact (as discussed in the introduction to this speech, pp. 168–71) the hypothesis that Philoctemon died at least ten years before Euctemon rests on a misunderstanding of the historical background; there is ample internal evidence that the interval was much shorter, and no reason to believe that Chaerestratus delayed his claim to Phioctemon's estate.

3 Philoctemon of Cephisia: Literally meaning 'loving possessions' or 'covetous', the name Philoctemon seems peculiarly appropriate for someone who had accumulated a large amount of property (§38). It is possible that the testator's real name was replaced by a *nom parlant* in order to protect his identity in the published version of the speech. (Cf. on 'Euctemon', §10.)

Cephisia (modern Kifisia), located about 12 km. northeast of central Athens, was one of the 139 demes (local districts) of Athens and the surrounding countryside. For demes and demotics more generally, see on 'Eponymus of Acharnae', 2.3.

on friendly terms: The Greek word *philos* can be either a noun ('friend') or an adjective ('friendly', 'on friendly terms'). In this context I think it is preferable to treat it as an adjective, because to say that Philoctemon was 'a friend of Chaerestratus' might imply that they were unrelated.

Chaerestratus here: On the deictic pronoun *houtosi* ('this man here') to indicate someone who was present in court, see on 'my uncle here', 2.35.

submitted a claim for the estate: As a son adopted by will (see §5) Chaerestratus could not enter directly onto the estate like a natural son or one adopted *inter vivos*, but had to make a claim to the court for *epidikasia*. For details of the procedure, see on 'claim', 4.2.

although it is lawful: The Greek construction is an accusative absolute (*exon*, lit. 'it being lawful'), the meaning of which could be either causal or concessive. Most translators and commentators have taken it as causal: 'since it is lawful for any Athenian who wishes to do so to dispute an inheritance by bringing a direct action before you... Androcles here put in a protestation...' (Forster, 1927); 'But any Athenian who wished could make a claim... Androcles here thus made a declaration...' (Edwards, 2007); 'because it is permitted' (Kamen, 2000). These versions, however, miss Isaeus's point that Androcles had followed the wrong procedure by issuing a *diamartyria* instead of initiating a direct action (*euthydikia*). This is accurately reflected by Roussel (1926): 'bien qu'il fût loisible à tout Athénien qui le voulait d'élever une revendiquation ... c'est à la procédure d'opposition par attestation qu'eut recours Androklès...'.

direct action: The term (Gk. *euthydikia*) is here contrasted with *diamartyria*, the first of several points at which Aristomenes complains that the procedure adopted by Androcles is inappropriate. Cf. §§43, 52, 59.

4 Androcles here: The defendant in the trial, Androcles, was apparently Euctemon's closest collateral relative (next of kin), but Isaeus does not specify their exact relationship (see on '*epiklēros*', §46). Given Euctemon's advanced age, it is perhaps more likely that Androcles was a nephew, or possibly a cousin, but he could have been a younger brother. On the deictic pronoun *houtosi* ('this man here'), cf. on 'Chaerestratus here', §3.

diamartyria: See on '*diamartyria*', 2.1. In this case, the existence of a son of Euctemon could legitimately have been used to block a rival claim to Euctemon's estate, but not to Philoctemon's. If the claimants put forward by Androcles really were Euctemon's sons, and therefore patrilineal half-brothers of Philoctemon, they were entitled to claim Philoctemon's estate as his next of kin, but the correct procedure would have been for them to contest Chaerestratus's claim in a *diadikasia*. On this case as an example of procedural abuse, see Griffith-Williams (2018).

We do not have the text of the *diamartyria*, and it is not recorded among the documents read out by the court clerk in the course of the speech. Its contents must, presumably, have been disclosed to the judges, so it was probably read out to them in the course of the prosecution speech, or before it began.

not subject to adjudication: At this stage, Isaeus does not specify Androcles's reasons for declaring that Philoctemon's estate is not subject to adjudication; he starts to discuss the contents of the *diamartyria* at §10.

deprive Chaerestratus of his claim: The aim of the *diamartyria* was to block further legal proceedings in relation to the estate. In practice, however, Chaerestratus did not lose the opportunity to pursue his claim; he did so by prosecuting Androcles for false testimony.

and you of the authority to decide: This implies that Androcles has shown disrespect for the judges: if Chaerestratus had not opposed the *diamartyria* by prosecuting Androcles for fasle testimony, the case would not have come to court for a judicial decision.

Philoctemon's heir: This establishes that the estate in dispute is that of Philoctemon, not Euctemon. Cf. on 'Philoctemon's heir', §51 and 'Philoctemon's esate' §61; also 'Euctemon's heirs', §17.

take the estate himself without an adjudication: Androcles aimed, by using the *diamartyria*, to avoid a formal adjudication of his claim.

become the *kyrios* of Philoctemon's sister: It appears that Androcles, in a separate legal action, has claimed one of Euctemon's daughters in marriage, along with a share of his estate (see on '*epiklēros*' §46). By marrying her, he would become her *kyrios* (legal guardian or representative).

5 falsely stated: A reference to the statements made by Androcles in the *diamartyria*.

had no child by his wife: The fact that Philoctemon and his wife were childless entitled him to make a will adopting a son. (On Solon's law, which restricted freedom of testamentary disposition to those without legitimate sons, see General Introduction, p. 3.)

since it was wartime: For a childless man facing imminent danger, such as a military campaign, testamentary adoption was particularly appropriate because the adoption would not take effect if the testator survived to father a natural son. According to Rubinstein (1993, 23) six of the ten attested Athenian cases of testamentary adoption were carried out by men who later died in war or while travelling.

as a cavalryman: This is an indication of Philoctemon's wealth, since only the richer Athenians could afford horses.

as a trierarch: On the trierarchy, see on 'as a trierarch', §1. The fact that Philoctemon was serving as a trierarch when he made his will, and at the time of his death (§27), again emphasizes his wealth.

Athens was at war for much of the first half of the fourth century, notably in the Corinthian War of 395–386 and the Theban War of 378–371. When he died, probably around 367/6 (see on 'Timotheus', §27), Philoctemon must have been under 60, the maximum age for military service; but if he was born in the 420s he could have been active as a cavalryman and trierarch, and already married, during the Corinthian War.

not to leave his family without an heir: Literally 'not leave his house empty'; on the Athenians's fear of leaving an 'empty house' as a motive for adoption, see on 'leave his family without heirs', 2.15.

6 both of his brothers had died childless: This implies that if one of Philoctemon's brothers had left a son, that son would have been his first choice for adoption. (Cf. commentary on 2.10–17, where one of the aims of the narrative is to explain why Menecles did not adopt his brother's son.) On the choice of a close blood relation, or intestate heir, as an Athenian's adopted son, see Rubinstein, (1993, 79).

who is married to Phanostratus here: A Phanostratus of Cephisia, who may have been the younger son of Philoctemon's brother-in-law Phanostratus, is mentioned at Dem. 54.7 as a friend of the speaker Ariston. On the deictic pronoun *houtosi* ('this man here') see on 'my uncle here', 2.35, and cf. 'Androcles here', §4.

According to Raubitschek (1954, 69) the speaker of Antiphon 6, who refers to his son-in-law, Phanostratus (Ant. 6.12), may have been Euctemon.

But as Davies (1971, 564) points out, this identification is impossible on chronological grounds: although the precise date of Antiphon 6 has been disputed, it cannot have been later than 412 BC, while the marriage of Phanostratus to Euctemon's daughter probably took place in the 390s.

had two sons: By adopting one of his sister's two sons, Philoctemon left the other to inherit the estate of his natural father. (Cf. Menecles's reluctance to adopt his brother's only son, 2.10.)

7 if he should have no child by his wife: A provisional testamentary adoption would have been an attractive option for a childless Athenian who still had some prospects of fathering natural sons, especially if he was facing imminent danger such as military service. An adoption *inter vivos* might have provided greater certainty for the adopted son after the father's death, but it could not be revoked, and the adopted son would have had to share the father's estate with any natural legitimate sons born after the adoption. See on 'it is explicitly written in the law...', §63, and cf. Todd (1993, 223–24).

with his brother-in-law Chaereas: It was customary for an Athenian to deposit his will with a trusted relative or friend who had no material interest in the contents. Cf. 'with his kinsman Pythodorus of Cephisia', §27. Another example of this practice occurs in Isaeus 9, where (according to the speaker's opponent) Astyphilus left his will for safekeeping with his uncle Hierocles before leaving Athens on military service.

the will itself: The text of Philoctemon's will is not preserved, and it is not clear whether the document produced and read in court was the original will or a transcript. There are only two other extant speeches (Isoc. 19 and [Dem.] 45) in which the documentary evidence produced by the speaker includes a will. (The significance of this is explained in the introduction to Isaeus 1, p. 21) The speakers of Isaeus 1, 4, 9, and 10 are challenging wills, so presumably the will was read on behalf of the opposing party. (On the production of wills in court, cf. the introduction to Isaeus 1, p. 20.) The purported text of Pasion the banker's will is preserved at [Dem.] 45.28; otherwise there are no extant wills from the classical period, but the wills of several Greek philosophers, including Plato and Aristotle, are preserved in the *Vitae philosophorum* of Diogenes Laertius (third century AD).

those who were present will testify: According to Apollodorus, in his prosecution of Stephanus for false testimony, it was illegal to testify to an event at which one was not actually present: 'Yet the laws ... enjoin that a man is to testify to what he knows and to events at which he was present and that these details are to be written on a tablet so that it's impossible to add or subtract anything to what has been recorded' ([Dem.] 46.7, trans. Scafuro).

There was no legal requirement for an Athenian will to be witnessed, but, as in the case of any other significant transaction, an Athenian would normally make his will in the presence of witnesses who could give evidence in court in the event of a dispute. Given that the Athenian courts had been using written testimony since the early fourth century (see on 1.1.), 'will testify' (Gk. *martyrēsousi*) cannot mean literally that the witnesses were about to speak; rather, their statements would be read out by the clerk.

Please read: This instruction to the clerk covers both the will and the witness statements. There are seven more items of witness testimony in this speech, of which five (§§11, 16, 26, 42, and 46) are introduced by instructions to the clerk to read them, while the formulae introducing the remaining two (§§34 and 37) refer to the witnesses in person rather than the documents.

8 You have heard that he made a will: Because this part of the story is taken out of sequence, it is impossible to tell exactly when Philoctemon made his will in relation to the series of events narrated later in the speech, and it is not clear whether the witnesses' testimony mentioned the date of the will. It would be particularly interesting to know whether Philoctemon made it before or after his quarrel with Euctemon about the introduction of Alce's son to Euctemon's phratry (§§22–24). (Cf. Wyse, 1904, 494). A will made after the quarrel might, perhaps, have resulted from a wider agreement among the family about the disposition of property and questions of succession.

on what terms he adopted Chaerestratus: The will was provisional, and the adoption would not come into effect if Philoctemon later fathered a natural legitimate son. (Cf. on 'if he should have no child by his wife', §7.)

the law itself: See on 'the law itself', 2.16.

9 This law, gentlemen: The law in question was Solon's law on wills, cited at [Dem.] 46.14 (Leão and Rhodes 2016: fr. 49a); cf. on 'so ruined by drugs or disease or something else', §21.

permissible to dispose of one's property by will: It would have been essential for any Athenian litigant claiming an estate on the basis of a will to refer to Solon's law in support of his claim, but the law in itself does not prove that Philoctemon actually did leave a valid will.

10–16. The issue of legitimacy (narrative, argumentation, and testimony)
Having disposed relatively briefly of the issue of Philoctemon's will, Isaeus now turns to the main topic of the speech: Androcles's claim that Euctemon had two legitimate sons by a second wife. His initial focus is on the inadequacy of Androcles's evidence: when questioned at the preliminary

hearing, Androcles was unable to give a satisfactory account of Euctemon's second marriage or the identity of the second wife who was supposedly the mother of the two boys put forward as Euctemon's legitimate sons. This part of the speech is an important source of information about pre-trial procedure in the Athenian courts. The *anakrisis* (lit. 'enquiry') was a preliminary hearing before the presiding official (archon) at which each party swore an oath as to the truth of his case and the litigants were questioned by the archon and by one another. Kremmydas (2018) provides a useful discussion of the *anakrisis* based on the available primary source material.

10 It has been proved to you: It now becomes clear that Androcles made two statements in his *diamartyria*: the first denying that Philoctemon had left a will adopting Chaerestratus, and the second about Euctemon's sons by a second marriage.

that this man is a legitimate son of Euctemon: At this stage, Aristomenes mentions only one of Euctemon's supposed sons (presumably the older one, who, as we learn at §21, had been introduced to Euctemon's phratry).

Euctemon: Like Philoctemon (see §3), the name Euctemon (lit. 'with fair possessions') is descriptive.

all his relatives and fellow phratry members, and most of his fellow demesmen: Aristomenes is about to produce witnesses who are not identified individually but as members of the civic or kinship groups who were most likely to have knowledge of family matters such as the subsistence of a marriage or the legitimacy of children. Cf. Brock (2020, 21) on the 'sense of community solidarity' in the Attic demes that was 'most conspicuous in the provision of witnesses for fellow demesmen'.

the daughter of Meixiades of Cephisia: Euctemon's wife is not identified by name, but only by her relationship to her husband or father; his daughters, similarly, are 'the wife of Phanostratus' and 'the wife of Chaereas'. Their anonymity reflects the general convention that women of citizen status are not named in forensic speeches, especially while they are still alive. Women who *are* named, including Alce in this speech (see §19), are likely to be non-citizens or of dubious reputation (or characterized by an opponent as such) unless there is a compelling reason for naming them (cf. on 'Callippe', §13). As discussed by Schaps (1977), the Athenians' reluctance to name respectable women in court may have been more than simply a mark of respect; in a society where female citizens had no public rôle in civic affairs, it is likely that a respectable woman was more easily identifiable by her relationship to a husband, father or brother than by her own name.

11 Please read out the witness statements: See on 'please read', §7.

12 my opponents: As Kamen (2000) *ad loc.* points out, the plural gives the first indication that Androcles has an associate: Antidorus, who is not mentioned by name until §39.

by their own conduct: The idea that an opponent has, by his own actions, 'testified' in favour of the speaker is also found at Isae. 7.18 and 8.14.

the archon ordered them to reply in accordance with the law: According to Kremmydas (2018, 116): 'This passage suggests that the *archōn* did have an active role [at the *anakrisis*] and could press a party to respond to a question ('in accordance with the law') that they might be tempted to duck (or might be unable to answer). Aristomenes is seeking to present the ignorance on the part of Androkles and Antidoros as part of a wider attempt to deceive the court through an improbable story ... which was presented to the court after the adjournment.'

paid a deposit: Anyone issuing a *diamartyria* to the effect that an estate was not adjudicable was required to pay into court a deposit of 10% of the value of the estate, which would be forfeited if (as in this case) his opponent prosecuted him for false testimony. On the deposit in inheritance claims more generally, see on 'deposit', 4.4.

But is it not strange, gentlemen, ... or any other of their relatives?: The combination of a rhetorical question and a direct address to the judges makes the speaker's point more strongly than a simple statement, inviting them to agree with his conclusion.

unable to identify their mother: According to a Solonian law cited at [Dem.] 46.18 (Leão and Rhodes, 2016, fr. 48b), a legitimate child was one born to parents who were lawfully married; and, while Pericles's citizenship law of 451/50 was in force, both parties to a lawful marriage had to be Athenian citizens. So, to prove that the boys really were Euctemon's legitimate sons, Androcles would need to show that their mother was an Athenian citizen to whom Euctemon was legally married.

13 Lemnian: An Athenian cleruchy (a colony in which the settlers retained their original citizenship) was founded on the north Aegean island of Lemnos *c.* 450 BC. After the defeat of Athens in the Peloponnesian War it was ruled by Sparta 404–393, then returned to Athens.

Callippe: On the identification of women by name in Athenian forensic oratory, see on 'the daughter of Meixiades of Cephisia', §10. In this instance, Androcles's naming of Callippe was not a sign of disrespect, but a recognition of the need to identify her unequivocally.

before anyone had asked a question: Kremmydas (2018, 116) comments:

'It is obvious that the important issue of the woman's paternity was not going to go away after the adjournment, hence Aristomenes's comment that the opponents stated the facts even though no one asked them. However, it is striking that the *archōn*'s role is minimised in this second "phase". Both the mention of his intervention before the adjournment and his apparent silence at the resumption of the *anakrisis* are rhetorically significant as they help to demonstrate the weakness of the opponent's case.'

a story that is completely untrue: No doubt the opponents made a similar accusation about the story told by Aristomenes at §§17–24. By attacking the credibility of the opponents' version of events before they had had the opportunity to speak for themselves, Isaeus no doubt hoped to predispose the judges in favour of his clients' story. It is, in fact, quite likely that Isaeus's summary of the opponents' case involved some misrepresentation, and it was the task of the judges, when they had heard both sides, to decide which was more likely to be true.

14   52 years since the Sicilian expedition: The disastrous Athenian expedition to Sicily (described in Thuc. 7) set sail in the summer of 415 BC, so the trial at which the speech was delivered can be dated to 365/4 or 364/3, depending on the method of counting.

the archonship of Arimnestus: In classical Athens the most important state official, the archon (sometimes called the 'eponymous archon'), was appointed on an annual basis, and each year was identified by the name of its archon. Arimnestus was the archon in 416/5.

not yet 20 years of age: As Labarbe (1953) and Thompson (1970) have pointed out, this has implications for the dating of the naval expedition on which Phanostratus served with Timotheus (§27). If the expedition took place *c.* 375–373, before Timotheus's exile, the boy would have been no more than ten, but in fact he must have been in his teens because he had already been introduced to Euctemon's phratry, some time before Phanostratus set sail, in a ceremony at which the *koureion* was sacrificed (see on 'the sacrificial victim', §22). There cannot, therefore, have been an interval as long as ten years between the phratry introduction and the trial. For the dating of the naval campaign, see on 'Timotheus', §27.

long since married: An Athenian girl would normally have expected to marry around the age of 16.

lawfully betrothed or adjudicated by the court: The normal procedure for an Athenian marriage was by betrothal (*engyē*), a formal contract between the bride's father (or other male relative, if her father was dead) and her prospective husband. A woman who was left with no living father or brothers became an 'heiress' or *epiklēros* (see on §46) and could be claimed for adjudication by the court (*epidikasia*), along with her paternal estate, by her father's nearest male relative.

known to Euctemon's relatives and slaves: Women were largely invisible in the public life of Athens, so the best witnesses to a woman's existence would be members of the household in which she lived.

15 testimony from the relatives: Cf. on 'the most reliable witnesses', §11.

16 put our slaves to the proof: In a dispute involving family relationships and events within a private household, the domestic slaves might have significant knowledge, but slaves could not formally act as witnesses in the Athenian courts and their evidence could not be used unless they had been questioned under torture. The consent of both parties was required to the submission of slaves for torture, so a litigant who wanted to use their evidence had to issue a formal challenge to his opponents to produce them (or, in appropriate circumstances, an offer to produce his own slaves). In the extant speeches of the Attic orators, such challenges and offers are always refused, and the procedure seems to have been reduced to little more than a rhetorical device used by litigants and speechwriters to put their opponents in the wrong. ('He wouldn't dare to produce his slaves, or have mine interrogated, so he must have something to hide.') Cf. on 'avoided such a decisive procedure', §17. For an outline of the procedure, with references to the relevant cases, see Harrison (1971, 147–50); and, for a summary of more recent scholarly discussion, Griffith-Williams (2013, 113–15).

Now please read See on 'please read', §7.

17–26. *The plot against Euctemon (narrative and testimony)*

If an Athenian man died leaving legitimate sons by more than one wife, they were all entitled to an equal share in their father's estate, but illegitimate children were excluded from the inheritance. This could lead to rivalry and disputes between half-brothers, especially if an estate had to be divided into several small shares, and an obvious tactic was for one party to identify his opponent as the illegitimate child of his father's concubine or mistress, not a legally married wife (cf. Griffith-Williams, 2020a, 34). So, having cast doubt on Androcles's account of Euctemon's second marriage, Aristomenes now provides his own explanation of the true origins of the boys put forward as Euctemon's legitimate sons: they were really the children of Alce, a former slave and prostitute with whom the elderly and senile Euctemon had become infatuated, and who persuaded him to introduce one of her sons to his phratry.

In classical Athens, where there was no central birth registration system, the introduction of a child to his father's phratry created a strong presumption of legitimacy, so the fact that Euctemon had introduced one of his 'sons' must have been a significant point in Androcles's favour. This part of the narrative is therefore crucial to the success of Isaeus's case. Chaerestratus was clearly unable to deny the fact of the introduction, so Isaeus had to counter it as effectively as he could by emphasizing the influence of Alce and the embarrassment of Euctemon's family which had forced their reluctant concurrence. Stereotypes of the scheming woman and gullible old man are likely to have been known to the judges from the comic stage, and even if his account was based on the truth, Isaeus may well have embellished the facts by exploiting familiar story patterns to enhance his client's credibility. (Cf. Griffith-Williams, 2019, 385.)

17 avoided such a decisive procedure: Testimony from the slaves would have been decisive if, as is likely, the challenge to produce them had included a demand for Androcles to withdraw his claim if their testimony did not support his case. It would, of course, have been entirely predictable that Androcles would not accept such a challenge. Cf. on 'put our slaves to the proof', §16.

trying to establish as Euctemon's heirs: Read in isolation, these words might be taken to support the view that the estate at issue in the litigation was that of Euctemon rather than Philoctemon; but if the boys identified by Aristomenes as Alce's sons were really 'Euctemon's heirs', they would also have a claim to Philoctemon's estate as his legitimate half-brothers and next of kin. (See discussion in the introduction to this speech, p. 172, and cf. on 'Philoctemon's heir', §§4 and 51, and 'Philoctemon's estate', §61.)

Perhaps, gentlemen, it's embarrassing for Phanostratus: Isaeus no doubt hoped to attract the attention of the judges by emphasizing the distressing nature of the story Aristomenes was about to tell with this elaborate introduction, including an address in the vocative which draws them into the speaker's argument and invites them to sympathize with Phanostratus's embarrassment. The potential for embarrassment to Euctemon's family may also explain why the speech was delivered by a family friend as supporting speaker, rather than Chaerestratus himself (Rubinstein, 2000, 29).

18 lived for 96 years: It has been estimated, on the basis of a study of skeletal remains, that the median age at death for men in classical Athens was 44. 'Probably less than one per cent of the population attained the age of 80 and anyone who did so was judged remarkable, as [Lucian's] catalogue of octogenarians in *Macrobii* suggests' (*OCD*, under 'age'). Descriptions of old age in classical Greek literature are generally negative, and Euctemon's story is no exception.

a great misfortune befell him: The impersonal expression avoids attributing any personal blame to Euctemon for his misfortune (cf. on 'so ruined by drugs or disease or something else' and 'persuaded by the woman', §21). This section builds up the expectations of the judges, whetting their appetites for the detailed story to follow.

19 I shall explain to you as briefly as I can: A rhetorical commonplace, showing respect for the judges and demonstrating a businesslike approach on the part of the speaker (who may in some cases also have an eye on the *klepsydra*, the water-clock used to ensure that Athenian litigants observed the time limits for their speeches). Cf. Isae. 7.4; Isoc. 21.2; Lys. 12.62; 24.4; Dem. 27.3, 12; 36.3; 37.3; 43.18; 45.2; 54.2.

He had a freedwoman: More literally, 'there was a freedwoman of his'. The genitive construction indicates that Euctemon himself was the former owner of the unnamed freedwoman. Her continuing employment by her former owner (in this case as the manager of his brothel) seems typical of relations between ex-slaves and their former owners in Athens, but it is not clear whether this was a legal requirement or simply a matter of convenience for the parties involved. (Cf. Glazebrook, 2014, 59–61.) On the status of freed slaves in Athens, cf. on 'their freedman', 4.9.

tenement house: From the ensuing description, Euctemon's house in Piraeus was clearly a brothel, but the Greek word *synoikia* could have been applied to any house in multiple occupation. Kapparis (2017, 290) draws attention to the 'rather dispassionate' way in which Euctemon is described as a brothel-keeper: 'There is no judgment or inherent stigma attached to the fact that this respectable Athenian, a man once considered happy and fortunate, was a brothel-owner. Keeping prostitutes is presented simply as a business enterprise perfectly appropriate for a well-off Athenian family man, and could have continued without ill consequences if he had not crossed the line and put a retired prostitute ahead of his family, his property and the laws of the city.'

One ... was called Alce, and I think many of you know her: A citizen woman would not have been named unless there was a special reason (cf. on 'the daughter of Meixiades of Cephisia, §10), and would certainly not have been widely known outside her family. So the manner in which Alce is introduced, implying that many of the judges would have been her clients, underlines her status as a slave and a prostitute. Kapparis (2017, 291) points out that Apollodorus makes a similar assumption about the judges' familiarity with Neaera in [Dem.] 59. The significance of Alce's status is not that being a prostitute was inherently shameful (cf. preceding note and Kamen, 2000, *ad loc.*); what is disgraceful about her alleged behaviour is that by passing off her son as the legitimate child of an Athenian citizen, she transgresses the proper boundary between citizens and non-citizens. Cf. on 'to introduce the older of the two boys to his phratry under his own name', §21.

too old: The text does not make it clear whether Alce 'retired' of her own volition, or whether there was a standard age beyond which prostitutes were no longer considered desirable. (Cf. Kamen, 2000, *ad loc.*)

20   freedman: Dion is simply described as a 'freedman', with no indication of the identity of his former owner. Cf. on 'he had a freedwoman', §19, and see Glazebrook (2014, 60, n.29).

fellow: The Greek word *anthrōpos* (lit. 'man' or 'mankind'; cf. Latin *homo*), when used of an individual (instead of *anēr*; cf. Latin *vir*) expresses contempt.

who she said was the father of these boys: Isaeus neither confirms nor denies Alce's claim that Dion was the father of her two sons, leaving open the possibility that they were in fact Euctemon's illegitimate offspring. In legal terms this makes no difference to the speaker's case: the boys would have no claim to the property of Euctemon and his family unless they were his *legitimate* sons. (Cf. on 'neither an illegitimate son nor an illegitimate daughter', §47.) Perhaps Aristomenes was reluctant to add to the family's embarrassment by explicitly admitting that Euctemon had fathered illegitimate sons (cf. on 'embarrassing for Phanostratus', §17).

some time later: Typically in Isaeus's speeches, the vague expression gives no indication how much time elapsed. In this part of the narrative precise chronology may not be particularly important, but cf. on 'some time later', §27.

this woman, Alce: Isaeus uses *anthrōpos* (see on 'fellow', above) five times as a feminine noun, with reference to Alce. (Cf. §§21, 29, 38, 39.) The term is strongly pejorative, emphasizing her servile origin (and, in combination with her personal name and the demonstrative pronoun *autē*) her identity as a prostitute. In this instance, Glazebrook (2005, 177) suggests the translation 'this creature here, Alce', pointing out that *anthrōpos* is also used pejoratively of Neaira's daughter Phano, in [Dem.] 59.

his tenement house in Cerameicus: Situated in the north-west of the city, and originally the potters' district, Cerameicus became known as the red-light district of Athens. The outer Cerameicus, beyond the Dipylon Gate (the main entrance to the city) was the main burial area. So the location of this second tenement house suggests that it may have been another brothel, but as Kapparis (2017, 289) points out, nothing in the text positively confirms this; it could have been just 'an apartment complex which included a wine shop'.

21 so ruined by drugs or disease or something else: The judges would have recognized this wording as a reference to Solon's law on wills, which had been read out to them in relation to Philoctemon's testamentary adoption of Chaerestratus (§9). This law, which provides that a will is not valid if the testator's mind is impaired 'by lunacy or drugs or disease or old age or if he is acting under the influence of a woman', was of course not directly relevant to Euctemon's introduction of Alce's son to his phratry. The allusion was, nevertheless, no doubt deliberate, intended to mitigate Euctemon's culpability by implying that he could not be held responsible for his actions. (Cf. Griffith-Williams, 2017, 51.)

persuaded by the woman: Again, Euctemon's personal responsibility for the allegedly fraudulent introduction of a 'son' to his phratry is mitigated by the claim that he acted under the influence of Alce.

to introduce her older son to his phratry under his own name: In persuading Euctemon to introduce her son into his phratry, Alce's intention was to establish the boy as a legitimate Athenian citizen, as well as to give him a claim to a share of Euctemon's estate. Her younger son, presumably, was not yet old enough to be admitted to the phratry (cf. on 'the sacrificial victim', §22). At the admission ceremony Euctemon would have been required to swear on oath that the son he was introducing was the child of a lawfully married Athenian mother (cf. Isae. 7.16, 8.19.) Isaeus, understandably, does not mention the oath at this point, because it would have been prejudicial to his client's case to admit that Euctemon did swear it.

22 objected ... removed from the altar: At this stage, Philoctemon, as Euctemon's only surviving son, expected to become his father's sole heir, so he would naturally object to the introduction of another son with whom he would have to share the estate. (Cf. on 'a single farm', §23.)

Isaeus passes very briefly over the details of the admission ceremony, focussing on its negative outcome. After approaching the altar with the sacrificial victim (see following note) Euctemon would have been received by the priest or phratriarch and invited to identify the candidate for admission. When the opportunity arose for phratry members to object to the candidate, Philoctemon would have interrupted the proceedings by taking hold of the victim and leading it away from the altar. The phratry members then took a vote, and decided against the admission of the candidate. (For details of the procedure, see Lambert, 1993, 170–71.)

the sacrificial victim: The sacrificial victim (*koureion*), a sheep or goat, was removed from the altar as a sign that the ceremony had been aborted.

Two sacrifices celebrated by the phratries, the *meion* and the *koureion*, were associated with the admission of boys. Although the evidence is not entirely conclusive, it appears likely that an Athenian son would normally be introduced twice to his father's phratry: at the *meion* as a baby or in early childhood, and at the *koureion* during adolescence. Labarbe (1953, 376) argues that the regular age for admission at the *koureion* was 16, but according to Lambert (1993, 167) it is more likely that there was no fixed age; the *koureion* was apparently linked with the attainment of physical maturity, which is variable. The regular date for the *koureion* was Koureotis, the third day of the annual festival of Apaturia, which took place in the month of Pyanepsion (October/November). On the age of the candidate introduced by Euctemon, see on 'not yet 20 years of age', §14, and for a full discussion of the evidence on phratry admission, see Lambert (1993, 161–78).

betrothed himself to marry: This passage has proved difficult for modern commentators because it appears inconsistent with the narrative in which Euctemon remained married to the daughter of Meixiades while he was living with Alce. There is, however, no suggestion in the speech that Euctemon actually divorced his wife and married Democrates's sister; since divorce was easy in Athens he could presumably have planned a second marriage while his first was still subsisting. The search for a logical explanation of his actions may, in any event, be futile, since the behaviour of a senile nonagenarian need not have been rational or even legal.

Democrates of Aphidna: A descendant of one of the tyrannicides, thought to have been born towards the end of the fifth century, he was a politician of the anti-Macedon faction, known primarily from references at Aesch. 2.17, Hyp. 2.3–4, and Arist. *Rhet.* 3.4.3. (See Whitehead, 2000, 46–51.) If Democrates was already a public figure by the 360s, it is possible that Euctemon did not really know him or his sister, but was merely using their name to maximize the embarrassment of his family. In any event, the reference to Democrates as Euctemon's intended brother-in-law may have been designed to provoke some kind of reaction (perhaps of sympathy, hostility, or even amusement) from the audience; cf. Griffith-Williams (2017, 52).

23 His relatives: It is not clear whether Androcles was among the relatives who participated in this discussion, or, if so, what position he took. Cf. on 'the only one in the family', §55.

So, gentlemen, they tried to persuade Philoctemon: Isaeus seeks to mitigate Philoctemon's complicity in the illegal phratry introduction by placing the blame for his change of mind on the persuasion of other, unnamed family members. At this sensitive point in the narrative, the address to the judges engages them with the speaker's point of view; cf. Griffith-Williams (2017, 53).

a single farm: Euctemon persuaded his relatives to accept the introduction of his younger 'son' to the phratry on condition that the boy would receive only one farm out of his estate. Indeed, this was probably the decisive factor in securing Philoctemon's agreement, since it ensured that (if he survived) he would still inherit the major share of Euctemon's eatate. But, as Isaeus points out later in the speech (§28), the gift of a single farm was anomalous if the boy introduced to Euctemon's phratry really was his legitimate son.

24 ashamed by his father's folly: Isaeus makes the story more convincing by using Philoctemon as focalizer, and is careful to put him in a sympathetic light, but Chaerestratus and his supporting speaker cannot really have known Philoctemon's motivation. No doubt Androcles gave a completely different account.

the boy was introduced: After Euctemon's failed attempt to introduce Alce's son to his phratry, the next opportunity would have been at the festival of Apaturia in the following year (cf. on 'the sacrificial victim', §22). Isaeus mentions the successful introduction only in passing, again giving no details of the procedure.

25 For why did he need to marry, Androcles...?: Apostrophe (direct address to an opponent in the vocative) is a rhetorical device used sparingly by Isaeus. There are two examples in this speech (cf. §54); the only others are 3.40, 69–71 and 5.43. (Cf. Denommé, 1974, 137–38.) The string of four rhetorical questions directed at Androcles in §§25–26 creates a strongly dramatic effect, creating the illusion of a dialogue with the opponent. The speaker not only makes his own points more effectively than through direct statements, but also makes the story told by Androcles sound absurd; cf. Griffith-Williams (2017, 54).

when the law gives all legitimate sons an equal share in their father's estate: Partible inheritance (i.e. an equal share for everyone related to the

Oration 6 217

deceased in the same degree) was a fundamental principle of the Athenian system. So if Philoctemon had survived, he would have had to share Euctemon's estate equally with any half-brothers by a different mother. Here, Isaeus's point is that by making a specific and limited bequest to his supposed son, Euctemon has implied that the boy was in fact illegitimate.

26 read out the witness statements: For the formulae used in this speech to introduce witness testimony, see on 'please read', §7. Since the text of these depositions has not survived, and their content is not detailed in the speech, we cannot be sure how much of the preceding narrative was supported by witness testimony. The Athenian trial format, where each party presented his case in a single speech and witnesses were not questioned, made it much easier than it would be in a modern trial for litigants to include unsubstantiated 'facts' in their account of events.

27–34. Philoctemon's death and the conspiracy against Euctemon's property (narrative and testimony)

This part of the narrative starts with Philoctemon's death and then deals relatively summarily with subesquent events. Euctemon, with the agreement of his sons-in-law Chaereas and Phanostratus, decided to confirm the gift of a farm to his 'son' in a written document, a form of will, which he deposited for safekeeping with a relative. But after nearly two years, when Chaereas had died, Androcles and Antidorus joined forces with Alce in a conspiracy to take control of Euctemon's property. They began by persuading him to revoke the will, so that the value of the land could be converted into cash, and after doing so he quickly sold off enough property to raise three talents.

27 After this: Another vague phrase indicating the passage of an unspecified length of time (cf. 'some time later', §§20 and 27).

at the hands of the enemy: This makes it clear that Philoctemon was killed in action, and did not simply die from some other cause in the course of his military service. He would therefore have been entitled to a state funeral, but nothing is said in this speech about the return of his remains to Athens or the burial arrangements.

serving as a trierarch near Chios: On the trierarchy, cf. on 'as a trierarch', §1. There is nothing in the historical record to identify the naval action near Chios during which Philoctemon was killed.

some time later: Once again (cf. on 'some time later', §20 and 'after this', §17) Isaeus uses a vague temporal phrase, not specifying how much time elapsed between Philoctemon's death and Euctemon's decision to record his agreement with his younger 'son' in a written document. But, given the need to protect his daughters' interest in his estate (see following note) neither they and their husbands nor Euctemon himself would have wanted a long delay, and it is certainly not plausible that he would have waited several years after Philoctemon's death.

told his sons-in-law: The conditions on which Euctemon introduced his younger 'son' to his phratry had been intended to protect Philoctemon's share of his paternal inheritance (cf. on 'a single farm', §23). After Philoctemon's death, it was Euctemon's two daughters who would have inherited their father's estate in the absence of any living brothers, so he now consulted their husbands, Phanostratus and Chaereas, about the terms of the agreement that he wanted to put into writing.

about to set sail as a trierarch: Phanostratus of Cephisia is named as a trierarch at *IG* II^2 1609.92.

Timotheus: An Athenian general who was instrumental in the establishment of the Second Athenian Confederacy (378–373 BC), after which he went into exile; then, following his return, captured Samos in 366/5. As discussed in the introduction to this speech (pp. 169–70) the expedition on which Phanostratus served with him probably took place after his return from exile in the mid 360s (not, as earlier scholars often suggested, in the 370s). The later date is more consistent with the internal chronology of the speech, and indicates that the interval between Philoctemon's death and that of Euctemon was no more than two or three years. (Cf. on 'not yet 20 years of age', §14 and 'in a very short time', §33, and for fuller discussion see the introduction to this speech, pp. 167–68.)

Munychia: The name of both a steep, fortified hill to the north-east of Piraeus (modern Kastella) and the port lying immediately below it, which played an important strategic role in Athenian history.

with some companions: These unnamed companions were probably relatives or friends of Euctemon, invited by him to witness his deposition of the will with Pythodorus so that they could testify in the event of a dispute. For the Athenian practice of using friends or family members to witness legal or business transactions, cf. Isae. 3.19 with Hatzilambrou (2018a) *ad loc.*

with one of his relatives, Pythodorus of Cephisia: Pythodorus of Cephisia, whose exact relationship to Euctemon is not specified, was, according to Davies (1971, 564), 'eponym of a naval symmory between 356 and 340..., and is no doubt the Pythodoros son of Aristion (1) of Cephisia who was councillor in 367/6.' On the practice of depositing a will with a trusted kinsman, see on 'with his brother-in-law Chaereas', §7.

the will: The Greek word *diathēkē* is regularly used of a will in the sense of 'last will and testament'. Todd (1993, 224) points out that 'the etymology of the word suggests a "settlement between"', and describes the document drawn up by Euctemon as 'a family compact which is not a will'. It is tempting to agree with Todd, given that Euctemon's *diathēkē* did not take the form of a typical Athenian will adopting a son (such as that of Philoctemon, §7), but wills without adoption were not unique in fourth century Athens (cf. Rubinstein, 1993, 81–86). And if the defining feature of a 'will' is that it sets out the testator's wishes for the disposal of (all or part of) his property after his death, then Euctemon's 'will' does fall within that definition. In the circumstances, nevertheless, the legality of such a will may have been questionable; cf. on 'because the law itself...', §28.

28 The narrative is interrupted at this point with a brief passage of argumentation, intended to reinforce the point that Alce's sons could not have been Euctemon's legitimate offspring. The narrative resumes at the beginning of §29.

no-one ever makes any bequest in a will to his natural sons: There is some force in this argument: since all natural legitimate sons were entitled to an equal share in their father's estate, an attempt to limit the share of one of them with a specific bequest would have been pointless (if not actually illegal). It might, nevertheless, have been possible for the father to specify in a will which of his sons should receive a particular part of his property.

because the law itself gives the father's property to his son: Cf. on 'the law itself', 2.16. After Euctemon's three legitimate sons had died, he was free to 'dispose of his property as he wished', subject to the conditions set out in Solon's law. But if his intention was to protect the interests of his daughters by limiting the amount of property to be inherited by a legitimate son, then Isaeus was right to point out that his actions were legally questionable. As Ogden (1996, 118) explains: 'This agreement, sanctified by a written document, is presented in quasi-legal terms, but it was surely quite illegal, since it either cheated the son of Alce out of his rightful share of the inheritance, if he was indeed the legitimate son of Euctemon, or it connived at the usurpation of citizenship if he was indeed illegitimate.' It is possible, nevertheless, that such informal agreements were relatively common in families where there was the potential for conflict between children of the same father by different mothers. According to Humphreys (2019, 250), 'A blind eye could generously be turned to doubtful birth, provided that the distribution of property was not seriously affected'.

does not even allow anyone who has legitimate sons to make a will:

Despite this provision of the law, some Athenians who did have legitimate sons are known to have made wills dealing with matters such as the marriage of a widow or daughter, and sometimes including bequests of property. Such wills were probably accepted as legal provided any disposition of property was limited and did not amount to the disinheritance of a legitimate son. (The Greek verb *diathesthai*, translated here as 'make a will', might alternatively be rendered as 'dispose of his property'.) For further discussion see Rubinstein (1993, 83–84).

29 the document: The more general term (Gk. *grammateion*) is used here and at §29 instead of *diathēkē* to refer to Euctemon's will. (Cf. on 'the will', §27.)

almost two years: A more precise expression than 'some time later' (§27), but we still do not know exactly how much time has elapsed since Euctemon deposited his will with Pythodorus.

these men: Androcles and Antidorus. Athenian litigants often refer to their opponents as 'this man' or 'these men' rather than by name. Androcles was identified at the beginning of the speech (§3) as the deponent of the *diamartyria*, and he is frequently mentioned by name as a participant in the litigation, but this is his first appearance (albeit anonymously) as a protagonist in the narrative that started at §19 with the introduction of Alce. It would be interesting to know whether he was one of the 'relatives' who persuaded Philoctemon to acquiesce in the phratry introduction (§23) and whether he was among the 'companions' who witnessed Euctemon's deposition of the will with Pythodorus (§27).

joined forces with the woman: Once again, the Greek noun translated as 'woman' is *anthrōpos* (see on 'this woman, Alce', §20). It may be significant that this part of the story is not substantiated by witness testimony; Isaeus produces no evidence, or even any explanation, of the alleged association between Alce and Androcles. Alce's motivation, as an ambitious mother wanting her sons recognized as legitimate Athenians, is obvious enough, but it is less clear why Androcles would choose to support her and her sons rather than pursue his own claim to the estate as Euctemon's next of kin.

30 annul the will: On the revocation of Athenian wills, see the introduction to Isaeus 1, p. 16.

not beneficial for the boys ... except his daughters and their offspring: If the will remained in force at Euctemon's death, his 'sons' would receive only the single farm while the rest of his property would go to his daughters. With the addition of 'and their offspring', Isaeus reminds the judges of Chaerestratus's personal interest: if he was not recognized as Philoctemon's

Oration 6 221

adopted son, he could still expect to inherit part of Euctemon's estate through his mother. (Cf. on 'depriving Euctemon's daughters and their offspring', §47.)

31 the document: Cf. on 'the document', §29.

32 destroyed: This implies that the only way of revoking an Athenian will was by physically destroying it. (Cf. on 'For the only document he could revoke, gentlemen', 1.25.)

assessors: 'The Archon, the King Archon, and the Polemarch each have two assessors of their own choice', *Ath. Pol.* 56.1 (cited by Kamen, 2000, *ad loc.*, as *Ath. Pol.* 159).

kyrios: See on 'become the *kyrios* of Philoctemon's sister', §4.

33 in a very short time: Yet another vague temporal expression (cf. on 'some time later', §20, 'after this' and 'some time later', §27, 'nearly two years', §29) making it impossible to know precisely how long it took for Euctemon to dispose of the property specified. According to the timescale proposed in the introduction to this speech (p. 168) it is likely that the interval between the annulment of the will and Euctemon's death was no more than a few months.

hierophant: The holder of a hereditary office (belonging to the Eumolpid family) who displayed the sacred emblems at the Eleusinian mysteries.

34 I first call witnessses: Formulae referring to witnesses in person were still sometimes used in the Athenian courts, even after the transition to written testimony. (See on 'those who were present will testify' and 'please read', §7.) The witnesses were clearly still required to attend the trial, and come forward when the clerk read their testimony.

35–37. 'The most dreadful scheme of all' (narrative and testimony)

In this brief but vivid section of narrative, Aristomenes accuses Androcles and Antidorus of attempting an ambitious fraud. After they had fleeced Euctemon of most of his property, and unwilling to wait until his death to get their hands on the rest, they claimed that the two boys identified by Aristomenes as Alce's sons had been adopted by two of Euctemon's deceased sons. Purporting to be the children's guardians, they then asked the archon to put the lease of the orphans' property up for auction so that they could take the proceeds. But the fraud was exposed when members of the family found out about it and denounced it to the court.

36 registered these two boys with the archon as the adopted sons of Euctemon's deceased sons: 'Euctemon's deceased sons' might be taken to refer to those who had predeceased Philoctemon, but they are identified at §44 as Philoctemon and Ergamenes, and the conjectural substitution by some early editors of 'Hegemon' for 'Philoctemon' has been rejected by Wyse and more recent commentators. It is difficult, in any event, to make sense of the episode, but perhaps that was Isaeus's point: it was simply another example of Androcles's procedural abuse, and inconsistent with his claim that Philoctemon had died childless (§63).

Registration with the archon was not part of the adoption procedure, but Androcles and Antidorus had to register the boys as the adopted sons of their deceased half-brothers, representing themselves as their appointed guardians, in order to request the leasing of the estates. (See on 'entering themselves as guardians', below.)

Rubinstein, (1993, 26) interprets Androcles's action as a failed attempt at posthumous adoption, but there is nothing in the text to indicate the procedure by which he claimed that the two boys had been adopted by their supposed half-brothers. Wyse (1904, 524) is, therefore, right that the wording might have been used of a testamentary adoption, but his inference that they had in fact been adopted by will (and that Isaeus was trying to suppress this fact) is harder to sustain. A son adopted by will could not take possession of his adoptive father's property without applying to the court for *epidikasia*, which would have made a fraudulent claim by a supposed guardian more difficult. An alternative possibility is that Androcles claimed they had been adopted *inter vivos*.

while Euctemon was still alive: If the two boys really were Euctemon's natural sons and had been adopted by their half-brothers, whose property was now being put up for lease, it would make no difference whether their natural father was alive or dead. The implication is that it was actually Euctemon's property, rather than that of his sons, that Androcles was trying to obtain by fraud.

entering themselves as their guardians: On the appointment of guardians for Athenian orphans, see on 'Our uncle Deinias, our father's brother, became our guardian', 1.9. The age of majority in Athens, when a guardianship would cease, was probably 17, or possibly 18, which implies that Androcles made his application at least two years before the trial, at the time of which the older of the two boys was 'not yet 20 years of age' (§14).

asked the archon to lease the estates of the 'orphans': The supervision of orphans' estates is among the functions of the archon listed at *Ath. Pol.* 56,7; his specific duties included granting leases and receiving the rents. This, as Todd (1993, 250) points out, 'is one of the rare cases in which the state interfered to publicize land transactions, presumably with the aim of preventing fraudulent maladministration of the estate.' For discussion of the procedure, see Harrison (1968, 105–107).

used as security, with mortgage stones placed on it: When an orphan's property was leased, the lessee was required to provide security in the form of land which had been assessed to be of equivalent value. 'Mortgage stones' (Gk. *horoi*) indicated that the land used as security was not available for sale. For further details and discussion, see Harrison (1968, 293-96) and Todd (1993, 252–53).

37 As soon as the courts were reconvened ... the judges voted not to allow the estates to be leased: The condensed narrative might give the impression that all of this happened on the same day, but that cannot have been the case. After the archon had put up the lease for auction, and Androcles had made his offer, there must have been a fixed interval during which other claimants could come forward or objections be made. In this case, Euctemon's family found out what was going on and put their objections to the judges in a formal hearing (presumably a *diadikasia*). In an uncontested case, it is possible that the archon could have awarded the lease without a court hearing.

put in a bid for the lease: This passage makes it clear that the guardians themselves could bid for the lease of an orphan's estate; and that, if they did so, they still had to provide security.

told the family: Isaeus does not identify the members of Euctemon's family who objected to Androcles's 'plot', but it is likely that Phanostratus, perhaps supported by his sons, was involved.

Please call those who were present as witnesses: On the identification of witnesses as 'those who were present', see on 'those who were present will testify', §7; and on the formula for the introduction of this testimony, 'I first call witnesses', §34.

38–42. *Euctemon's death (narrative and testimony)*

The actions of Androcles, Antidorus, and Alce after Euctemon's death – leaving his body in the house while removing all its contents and shutting his wife and daughters out – are presented as another episode in their shameless conspiracy to take possession of Euctemon's property. Androcles, no doubt, offered a completely different version of these events, and the true facts are impossible to ascertain. Conflicts between different branches of a dead man's family over the preparations for and conduct of the burial were probably not uncommon in Athens. Another such conflict is described at Isae. 8. 21–24, where the deceased Ciron's grandson (the son of his daughter by his first wife) tries to remove the body for burial but is obstructed by Ciron's widow (second wife) and her brother.

38 got to know the woman and conspired with her against Euctemon: On the association between Androcles and Alce, see on 'joined forces with the woman', §29. Here, again, Isaeus uses the insulting word *anthrōpos* with reference to Alce. (See on 'this woman', §20.)

he and his son Philoctemon had acquired so much property...: According to Wyse, *ad loc.*, 'Although in fact Philoctemon shared the property with his father, Euctemon alone was the legal owner. "The estate of Philoctemon" is a fiction of the orator.' (Cf. Caillemer, 1879, 65.) But the wording here is too vague to justify that conclusion, and although Isaeus never makes clear exactly what Philoctemon's estate comprised, there is nothing in the speech to suggest that he did not have any property of his own. If, for example, father and son were in business together, Philoctemon might have kept his own share of the profits, and bought his own house or other real estate, without having inherited the ancestral estate from his father. Wyse, as usual, is simply assuming that Isaeus is in the wrong and his opponent's version of the facts is the correct one.

liturgies: Public services performed by the richest Athenians as a form of taxation (cf. on 'as a trierarch', §1). The minimum property qualification for membership of the liturgical class is thought to have been at least three talents (cf. Davies, 1971, xxiii–xxiv).

together with the woman: This is the final instance of *anthrōpos* in the speech. (See on 'this woman', §20, and, on the alleged association between Alce and Androcles, cf. on 'joined forces with the woman', §29 and 'got to know...'. . §38.

that man Antidorus: This is the first reference by name to Antidorus, an associate of Androcles whose identity is not clear (cf. on 'my opponents', §12). He may have been another collateral kinsman of Euctemon, especially if he put himself forward as the guardian of one of the boys. He is named only once again, at §47. The late antique writer of the *hypothesis* to the speech mistakenly thought that Antidorus was the name of the 'son' introduced by Euctemon to his phratry.

40 wife and daughters: Euctemon's legitimate wife and daughters would have expected to prepare his body for burial (like the widow of Ciron; see Isae. 8.22).

not up to them to bury Euctemon: If Euctemon had left legitimate sons by a second wife, it would have been their responsibility, not that of the first wife and her daughters, to conduct his funeral. Evidence that one party had (and the opposing party had not) conducted the funeral could be used in disputed inheritance claims; cf. the introductory note to 4.18–26.

42 take these documents and read them: See on 'please read', §7.

43–47. The illegality of Androcles's and Antidorus's actions (argumentation and testimony)

In these sections Isaeus's account of his opponents' litigation strategy is (no doubt deliberately) confusing. He presents their actions as not only irregular, because they followed the wrong procedure, but also inconsistent because their various claims are self-contradictory. Since there is no coherent chronology, it is difficult to assess the validity of the accusations, but the passage makes better sense if it is recognized that there were separate legal proceedings over Philoctemon's and Euctemon's estates.

43 did not dare to initiate a direct action but lodged a *diamartyria*: Again, Aristomenes criticizes Androcles for adopting the wrong procedure. (For the distinction between these procedures, see on 'direct action', §3 and *diamartyria*, §4.) The language ('did not dare') is tendentious, implying that Androcles avoided the correct procedure because he saw it as too risky.

44 as being the adopted sons of Philoctemon and Ergamenes: See on 'registered the two boys with the archon...', §36.

the law does not allow an adopted son to return to his natural family unless he leaves a legitimate son behind: This law is also mentioned at Isae. 10.11. (Cf. [Dem.] 44.21, 44, 46.)

45 not dared to submit a claim: Once more, Aristomenes repeats his criticism of Androcles's choice of procedure.

46 *epiklēros*: A woman whose father died leaving no sons (or descendants through a male line) was known as an *epiklēros*. The word is sometimes translated as 'heiress', but that is misleading because the woman did not have personal control over the property she inherited; she could be claimed in marriage, along with the property, by her father's next of kin, and her inheritance passed to her son(s) two years after puberty.

It becomes clear at §51 that the woman claimed in marriage by Androcles was the widow of Chaereas. While it was, in theory, possible for a married *epiklēros* to be forced to divorce her existing husband, this would not be necessary when she had an unmarried or widowed sister.

Isaeus, once again, is emphasizing the inconsistency of Androcles's behaviour: if, as Androcles asserts, Euctemon left legitimate sons, then his daughters would have no share in his estate and could not be claimed in marriage by his next of kin. Modern scholars have found it difficult to explain the timing of Androcles's intervention in relation to the rest of the litigation process. As Wyse (1904, 486) observes: 'The sequence and causal connection of the moves and countermoves of the combatants are not clearly explained. It would be interesting to know at what stage in the struggle Androcles made a claim on his own behalf.' Harrison (1968, 221, n.3) suggests that it was an alternative strategy: Androcles, intended to submit a claim to the *epiklēros* if he lost in the *dikē pseudomartyriōn*. But that is not consistent with the text, which makes it clear that Androcles has already made his claim to the *epiklēros*. The perfect tense ('has claimed'), which recurs at §57, implies that the claim was recent, and that the litigation was still continuing. The most satisfactory explanation is that there were separate legal proceedings over the estate of Philoctemon and that of Euctemon. Chaerestratus submitted his claim to Philoctemon's estate, and Androcles responded with his *diamartyria*, while Euctemon was still alive. Then, after Euctemon's death, Androcles initiated a new claim to his estate.

together with a fifth share of Euctemon's estate: It is generally thought that if a man with no sons left two daughters, his estate would be divided equally between them, to be divided, in turn, among their offspring after they died. On this basis there is no apparent reason why Androcles should have claimed only one fifth of Euctemon's estate with the *epiklēros*, so modern editors have assumed that the text is corrupt at this point but they have not been able to suggest an alternative reading. Jones (1779, 188) proposes a solution: that distribution among daughters and their children was *per capita*, immediately after the father's death. In that case, Euctemon's two daughters, two grandsons and one granddaughter would each be entitled to one fifth of his estate, since Androcles, who refused to recognize the adoption of Chaerestratus by Philoctemon, would have counted Chaerestratus as one of the five. Jones's solution, in the absence of corroborating evidence, is considered by Wyse (1904, 533) to be implausible, but since there is no evidence to the contrary (or a better explanation of the text) it should perhaps not be so lightly dismissed.

The clerk will read you the testimony: See on 'please read', §7.

47 since the archonship of Eucleides: On the Athenian system of dating by 'archon years', see on 'the archonship of Arimnestus', §14. Eucleides was archon in 403/2, the year in which the democracy was restored after the oligarchic rule of the Thirty Tyrants and a major revision and consolidation of Athenian law was enacted.

neither an illegitimate son nor an illegitimate daughter: Cf. [Dem.] 43.51, where the citation of Solon's law on the order of intestate succession (setting out the order in which collateral relatives would succeed to the estate of a man who had died without natural or adopted sons) ends with an identically worded clause excluding illegitimate children from inheritance rights since the archonship of Eucleides. The reason for the limitation is not entirely clear, because the exclusion of illegitimate children (or at least some restriction on their rights) certainly dates back to Solon. The most likely explanation (cf. Wyse, 1904, 536) is that the law had not been strictly enforced during the latter years of the Peloponnesian War, and was re-enacted in 403/2. There may be a link with Pericles's citizenship law of 451/450 BC, restricting Athenian citizenship to those of Athenian parentage on both sides, which apparently fell into disuse during the Peloponnesian War but was re-enacted in 403/2 and applied to anyone born subsequently. Cf. Blok (2017, 106) on 'the congruence in criteris for inheritance in the family and for sharing in the *polis*'.

As Leão and Rhodes (2016, 85) point out, 'This distinction between the rights of *gnesioi* [legitimate] and *nothoi* [illegitimate] ... emphasises very sharply the benefits of the official recognition of marriage and of legitimate birth.' In the present case, the distinction would not be strictly relevant unless Euctemon was in fact the father of Alce's sons, a point which Isaeus never explicitly concedes. (Cf. on 'who she said was the father of these boys', §20.) In any event, the reference to the law reinforces the speaker's critique of Alce's unacceptable behaviour.

kinship: The Greek word is *ankhisteia*, for the legal significance of which see on 'our degree of kinship', 1.4.

family cults and property: This wording follows the conventional interpretation of the Greek phrase *hiera kai hosia*, which occurs frequently in classical texts concerned with Athenian citizenship and inheritance and has normally been taken as denoting a distinction between the 'sacred' (*hiera*) and the 'profane' or 'secular' (*hosia*). But the precise meaning of *hosia* is controversial; most recently, Blok (2017, esp. 57–59) argues that it can never mean 'secular', and that the terms *hiera* and *hosia* represent different aspects of Athenian religion. While her thorough analysis of the sources is helpful, I am not persuaded by her conclusions, or by her more general emphasis on shared religious cults as the defining feature of Athenian citizenship.

both the estate of Euctemon and that of Philoctemon: The property on which Androcles has designs comprises two separate estates: that of Euctemon and that of Philoctemon.

depriving Euctemon's daughters and their children: In accordance with the principle of male precedence, Euctemon's daughters would inherit his estate only if he left no legitimate sons. The share of the wife of Phanostratus would, eventually, go to her sons: Chaerestratus and his younger brother. So, in addition to maintaining his status as Philoctemon's adopted son, Chaerestratus has a clear interest in excluding 'Alce's sons' from the succession to Euctemon. Cf. on 'not beneficial for the boys...', §30.

48–50. Alce's character

Aristomenes alleges that Alce, a former slave and prostitute, illegally attended the Thesmophoria, a festival reserved exclusively for Athenian citizen women. The accusation was clearly calculated to arouse the anger of the judges, and no doubt they would have agreed that the sons of such a woman were not fit to be confirmed as Philoctemon's heirs and successors. That presupposes, however, that Alce really was the mother of the claimants put forward by Androcles; if she was not, then her character has no relevance to the issues in the case.

48 shows her contempt not only for Euctemon's family but for the city as a whole: Isaeus elevates the significance of Alce's behaviour by claiming that she has transgressed in the public as well as the domestic sphere.

one single indication: On the meaning of *sēmeion*, here translated as 'indication', see on 'some significant signs', 1.31.

Please take and read the law: This law, presumably, concerned the Thesmophoria, an annual festival lasting three days and celebrated exclusively by the wives of Athenian citizens. (For a detailed description, see Parker, 2005, 270–82.)

49 these goddesses: Demeter and Persephone, to whom the Thesmophoria was dedicated.

gentlemen: Eight of Aristomenes's 18 addresses to the judges in this speech occur in the final 17 sections (§§49–65), where argumentation predominates over narrative and there is a heightened emotional intensity. The effect is particularly strong when the address is combined with one or more verbs of supplication (§§ 57, 62), or with an oath (§58), or when it forms part of an ironic rhetorical question (§54).

the mother of these young men: This, of course, begs the question whether the claimants put forward by Androcles really were Alce's sons.

51–59. The issues facing the judges (argumentation)
In these sections the speaker purports to remind the judges of the issues on which they are required to decide. His summary is highly tendentious, and the argumentation is characterized by the frequent use of stylistic and rhetorical features such as questions, addresses to the judges, apostrophe to the opponent, and invocations to the gods.

51 **that woman's son**: Again, this begs the question of Alce's relationship to the two young men claiming to be Euctemon's sons. The allegation that she attended the Thesmophoria illegally is clearly intended to blacken her character and prejudice the judges against her, but it has no relevance to the case unless the story about her seduction of Euctemon (§§17–26) is true. (Cf. Griffith-Williams, forthcoming b.)

Philoctemon's heir: This confirms that the estate at issue in the present litigation was that of Philoctemon. Cf. on 'Philoctemon's heir', §4 and 'Philoctemon's estate', §61; also 'Euctemon's heirs', §17.

and go to the family tombs to offer libations and sacrifices: Inheritance in classical Athens involved religious obligations as well as the transmission of property. A son and heir, whether natural or adopted, would not only inherit his father's material property but also continue his line of descent and perform the family cults. By focussing on the religious dimension of inheritance, Isaeus appeals to the emotions of the judges while avoiding any suggestion that Chaerestratus's motives for claiming the estate were materialistic.

who was married to Chaereas but is now a widow: This confirms that it was the widow of Chaereas whom Androcles claimed in marriage (cf. on 'who has claimed Euctemon's daughter as an *epiklēros*', §46).

adjudicated by you to marry whoever you think fit: Any claim from Euctemon's relatives to marry one of his daughters as an *epiklēros* would be subject to the adjudication of the court. The use of the second person plural to refer to the judges who might hear a hypothetical future case does not imply that the composition of the panel would be the same as at the present hearing; rather, it reflects the Athenian perception of a specific panel of judges as representing the citizenry as a whole, with its collective responsibility for the making and interpretation of laws and the dispensation of justice. Cf. on 'the laws which you made', 4.17.

52 **these are the issues on which you must now vote:** A pointed reminder to the judges that the the dicastic oath (cf. on 'vote in accordance with your oath', §2) required them to base their decisions only on the relevant issues.

(Cf. Harris, 2013b, 127, with n.72.) In this context, of course, the speaker's definition of those issues is highly tendentious. On the dicastic oath, see on 'vote justly, in accordance with the laws and your oath', 2.47, and cf. 'the oaths that you swore', 4.31.

the *diamartyria* gives them the advantage: If Androcles wins the *dikē pseudomartyriōn*, his *diamartyria* remains in force and his protégés will be able to take possession of the estate. If, on the other hand, he loses, the court will not have decided the substantive issue in favour of Chaerestratus, but merely found that the estate is subject to adjudication. Chaerestratus, therefore, will not be able to take possession without re-submitting his claim for *epidikasia*, which would put him at risk of a further challenge from Androcles or indeed other claimants. (For the scholarly debate about the effect of a decision in a *dikē pseudomartyriōn*, see Harrison, 1968, 156–57.)

***diamartyria* ... direct action:** See on 'direct action', §3.

a will that he had no legal right to make: Aristomenes had initially said, or at least implied, that the *diamartyria* included a statement that Philoctemon did not leave a will adopting Chaerestratus (cf. on 'falsely stated', §5 and 'it has been proved to you', §10). Now, he seems to anticipate a different argument from Androcles: that Philoctemon was not legally entitled to make a will (apparently because he owned no property separately from Euctemon; cf. on 'not entitled to make a will and the estate was Euctemon's', §56). It is impossible to know what Androcles really said; Isaeus may well be misrepresenting his point in order to strengthen his own accusation of procedural abuse.

53 'Androcles, how do you know that Philoctemon did not make a will or adopt Chaerestratus?' For Isaeus's sparing use of direct speech, see on 2.11. In this instance, Aristomenes is not recording a past conversation, but suggesting a question that the judges might like to put to Androcles.

when one was present: For the identification of witnesses as 'those who were present', see on 'those who were present will testify', §7.

testify by hearsay: The use of hearsay evidence in the Athenian courts was limited to events of which there were no living witnesses ([Dem.] 44.55).

54 But you have expressly testified: Aristomenes interrupts his address to the judges with a brief apostrophe to Androcles personally (cf. on 'For why did he need to marry, Androcles...?', §25). When the speech was delivered in court, the unexpected change of addressee would no doubt have been signalled by the speaker's tone of voice and body language, with Aristomenes placing strong emphasis on the second person singular pronoun 'you' (Gk. *su*), while turning to face Androcles and pointing an accusatory finger at him.

How on earth can he know this, gentlemen?: On Isaeus's use of irony to ridicule his clients' opponents, see on 'they are now treating us so well', 2.33.

55   his worst enemy: This is inconsistent with the narrative at §§27–29: it was only after Philoctemon's death that Androcles joined forces with Alce, so, if Philoctemon did regard him as his worst enemy, it cannot have been for that reason. Such a discrepancy may have been less obvious to the judges, who heard the speech once, than to a modern reader who has the opportunity to check the text.

all his other wickedness: If Androcles had really had a verifiable record of criminal or anti-social behaviour, Isaeus's allegations against him would surely have been more specific (cf. 4.28 on the criminal record of Chariades). As it is, this general slur intensifies Aristomenes's attack on Androcles for his alleged conspiracy to take control of Euctemon's property.

the only one in the family: Cf. on 'his relatives', §23.

56   not entitled to make a will and the estate was Euctemon's: See on 'a will that he had no legal right to make', §52.

to his daughters, who are acknowledged to be legitimate ... or to people who are not related to him at all: The antithesis is highly tendentious. There was certainly no dispute about the legitimacy of Euctemon's daughters, but they would still not be entitled to inherit their father's estate if he left legitimate sons, and the speaker prejudges the question whether 'Alce's sons' were indeed Euctemon's legitimate sons.

and us as their descendants: By using the first person plural, Aristomenes associates himself with Chaerestratus and his brother. Again (cf. on not beneficial for the boys...' §30) he reminds the judges that Chaerestratus has an interest in the case not only as Philoctemon's adopted son but also as a son of one of Eucetmon's daughters.

57   I earnestly beg and implore you, gentlemen: Cf. on 'So I ask you to have sympathy and listen with good will', §2. Here, the plea to the judges, using two verbs of supplication combined with a direct address in the vocative, heightens the emotional intensity of the speech as it approaches its conclusion.

he himself has claimed Euctemon's estate ... on his own behalf: See on 'who has claimed Euctemon's daughter', §46. Here, again, the perfect tense makes it clear that the claim has already been submitted.

58   by the gods of Olympus, gentlemen: See on 'But, by Zeus', 4.20.

Serafim (2020, 7) cites this instance as an example of the 'aggressive' use of oaths and invocations to the gods by the Attic orators, designed to 'add validity to the accusations levelled against the opponents'.

condemned not only by us but also by his own actions: Cf. on 'by their own conduct', §12.

59 it is open to him to initiate a direct action, but he is trying to deprive everyone else of their claim: Aristomenes repeats his allegation that Androcles has followed the wrong procedure by choosing the *diamartyria* instead of a 'direct action', thus gaining an unfair advantage (see on 'direct action', §3, *diamartyria*, §4, and 'the advantage of the *diamartyria*. §52). The specific point he makes here is that if Androcles had followed the correct procedure by submitting a *lèxis*, it would have been open to other claimants to do the same, whereas the *diamartyria* has blocked any further claims.

saying that my friends are rich but he is poor: This evidently anticipates an attempt by Androcles to incite the envy of the judges by suggesting that Chaerestratus does not deserve to inherit Philoctemon's estate because he and his family are rich enough already. (Cf. on 'so you should bear no grudge against them', §61.) The judges, who were normally among the poorer citizens, might well have been receptive to such an argument, especially if Androcles presented himself and Antidorus as the protectors of the poorer members of the family (cf. Humphreys, 2019, 193). So Isaeus, while pointing out that his clients' wealth is not relevant to the legal case, seeks to deflect a negative reaction by explaining how they have used it for the benefit of the city as a whole.

60–61. The character of the rival claimants
Like the speaker of Isaeus 4, Aristomenes follows the main part of his presentation with a comparison between the opposing parties in terms of character. In this case it appears that Androcles and Antidorus have no previous record of criminal or anti-social behaviour on which he could draw, so the emphasis is strongly on the impressive record of public services performed by Chaerestratus and his father Phanostratus: they have served the city well in the past, and if the estate is awarded to Chaerestratus he will use it for the benefit of the whole community. Unlike the speaker of Isae. 4, Aristomenes does not suggest that Chaerestratus's good character was a reason for Philoctemon to adopt him, presumably because the main focus in this speech is on the legitimacy of Euctemon's supposed sons rather than the circumstances of the adoption. (Cf. Griffith-Williams, forthcoming b.)

60 spent on the city rather than themselves: See on 'saying that my friends are rich but he is poor', §59.

acted as trierarch seven times, performed all the liturgies: Phanostratus's dedication to the service of the *polis* reflects well on his son, Chaerestratus. The speaker of Isaeus 4 made a similar point about Thrasippus, the father of the claimants Hagnon and Hagnotheus. (See on 'performed public services', 4.27.)

young as he is: In view of his youth, Chaerestratus had not yet had the opportunity to match his father's record of service to the city. There was a minimum age of 30 or 40 for some of the public offices in classical Athens.

the Three Hundred: The 300 richest Athenians, who were required to contribute to the city's war taxes (*eisphora*). By the time of Demosthenes, they had to pay the total amount of the tax in advance (*proeisphora*), later recovering the contributions due from other taxpayers. For details and primary references, see Wyse (1904, 545).

61 so you should bear no grudge against them: Cf. on 'saying that my friends are rich but he is poor', §59. The Greek verb *phthonein*, used here to express the concept of 'bearing a grudge', may convey, according to context, ideas of 'envy', 'indignation', or 'spite'.(Cf. on 'a matter of spite', 2.23.) *Phthonos* is essentially a negative emotion, but, as Sanders (2014, 43) observes, 'There are ... a number of passages in the Attic oratorical corpus in which orators openly call on their audience to feel *phthonos*. ... Jurors should not feel resentment for the true heirs to an estate, but rather for those contesting the will if they get what they do not deserve (Isae. 6.61)'. Spatharas (2019, 147) similarly explains this passage in terms of what he calls 'legitimate envy': 'Again, in his anticipation of dikasts' possible sentiments of envy towards a substantially rich man ... who claims the inheritance of his (allegedly) adoptive father, the *phthonos* script that Isaeus constructs revolves around considerations of justice. It is Chaerestratus' opponents rather than public-minded Chaerestratus who, through their selfishness, will eventually cause dikasts' legitimate envy'. Cf. Fisher (2003, 199–200) who cites Isae. 6.59–61 in discussion of the idea that 'Athenian jurors understood and accepted the distinction between unfair envy, yielding to the temptation of which might bring rebuke and shame on the people; and envy which was justified because the rich man concerned had not earned the right to any reciprocal consideration by displays of the good *philotimia*'.

by Zeus and Apollo: Cf. on 'by the gods of Olympus', §58, and see on 'But, by Zeus', 4.20.

If you award Philoctemon's estate to my friend: Again, this confirms that the subject of the present litigation was Philoctemon's estate, not Euctemon's. Cf. on 'Philoctemon's heir', §4 and §61; also 'Euctemon's heirs', §17. Arguing along similar lines to the speaker of Isaeus 4, Aristomenes reminds the judges of the public services carried out by Chaereas and Phanostratus, suggesting that if they award the estate to Chaereas he will put it to good use.

they will squander it and then conspire against others: There is no indication that Androcles and Antidorus, or either of them, had a previous record of fraud or mismanagement of estates, or any other criminal activity before their alleged behaviour in the present case. (Cf. on 'all his other wickedness', §55.) Nevertheless, if the judges believed Aristomenes's story about their conspiracy against Euctemon, they would probably accept that the conspirators would be likely to repeat this pattern of behaviour in the future.

62–65. Conclusion
Aristomenes concludes his speech by again directing the judges' attention to the terms of the *diamartyria*. After briefly recapitulating his arguments about the validity of Philoctemon's will, he challenges Androcles to prove his statement that the boys he has put forward as claimants are legitimate sons of Euctemon, reminding the judges again of the weakness of the evidence produced by Androcles about Euctemon's supposed second marriage. The emphasis is on the question of legitimacy, which has been the predominant topic throughout the speech, but the tortuousness of some of the argumentation (see, especially, on 'it is explicitly written...; §63) may perhaps suggest that Aristomenes was less confident in the validity of the will than he wanted the judges to think.

62   So I beseech you, gentlemen: The concluding paragraphs begin with another combination of an address to the judges with a verb of supplication (cf. on 'I earnestly beg and implore you, gentlemen', §57).
in order that you are not deceived: See on 'trying to deceive you', 4.1.
63   What else does it say? ...biological children? By framing this part of his argument in the form of questions, Aristomenes continues to speak to the judges directly, creating the impression of a dialogue with them.
that Philoctemon died childless: This might be taken as reinforcing the view that 'Hegemon' should be substituted for 'Philoctemon' at §44: if Androcles made this claim, after putting forward one of Alce's boys as Philoctemon's adopted son, why did Isaeus not point out the inconsistency? But the argumentation at this final stage of the speech is so tortuous that it is impossible to draw any firm conclusions from it.

left his own nephew as his adopted son ... just as it does to biological children?: While it is true that an adopted son had the same inheritance rights as a natural son, Isaeus's wording here overlooks the point that only a son adopted *inter vivos* was automatically entitled to take possession of his father's estate. A testamentary adoption did not come into effect until it had been ratified by the court.

it is explicitly written in the law that ... both inherit in the same way: If a man adopted a son but later fathered a natural legitimate son (or sons), the natural and adopted sons would share the father's estate equally. The existence of this law has been taken as an indication that an Athenian adoption *inter vivos* could not normally be revoked (Rubinstein, 1993, 56). In referring to it here, Isaeus apparently wanted the judges to think that Chaerestratus would still be entitled to a share in the estate, even if the claimants put forward by Androcles were legitimate. But it is difficult to see how the law could apply to any testamentary adoption, let alone to the particular circumstances of the present case. Someone who made a will adopting a son would presumably have been expected to revoke it if he subsequently fathered a legitimate son of his own, and in any event a testamentary adoption did not come into force until it had been confirmed by the court after the testator's death. And in the present case, the boys were said to be sons of Euctemon, not of Philoctemon. If Philoctemon's will was accepted as valid, Chaerestratus was entitled to the whole of his estate, regardless of whether Euctemon had left legitimate sons. If the will was not valid, Philoctemon's estate would go to his next of kin, in which case there were two possibilities: either the boys would share the estate between them as Philoctemon's legitimate half-brothers by the same father, or (if they were not recognized as legitimate) the estate would go to Philoctemon's sisters.

64 Let him therefore prove: Aristomenes reminds the judges of the need for proof, not merely unsubstantiated assertions.

simply because he tells you their mother's name: Again, the speaker reminds the judges that the information provided by Androcles at the *anakrisis* was inadequate

the relatives who know that she was married to Euctemon and the demesmen and phratry members: Cf. on 'all his relatives...', §10: Aristomenes knows that Androcles will not be able to meet this standard of proof, because he himself has already produced testimony from Euctemon's relatives, phratry members and fellow demesmen, none of whom had any knowledge of Euctemon's supposed second marriage.

that Euctemon performed liturgies on her behalf; also where she is

buried and in what kind of tomb: After complaining about the inadequacy of the information provided by Androcles at the *anakrisis* (§§10–16), Aristomenes now demands further proof that Euctemon had a second wife. (Androcles had, presumably, said that Callippe was dead, although that is not mentioned earlier in the speech.) This passage has been taken by Parker (2005, 29) as evidence that 'Mothers had the same right to honour as fathers; they would normally be buried in the same plot'.

65 a just and appropriate vote: This is one of the passages cited by Harris (2013b, 112) in arguing that the Athenians used the terms 'law' and 'justice' as 'virtual synonyms' (see on 'vote justly, in accordance with the laws and your oath', 2,47.

BIBLIOGRAPHY

Adamidis, V. 2017. *Character Evidence in the Courts of Classical Athens: Rhetoric, relevance and the rule of law*, London.
Avramovič, S. 1997. *Iseo e il diritto attico*, Naples. [Originally published Belgrade, 1988, as *Isejovo sudsko besednistvo I atinsko pravo*.]
Blok, J. 2017. *Citizenship in Classical Athens*, Cambridge.
Blundell, M. W. 1989. *Helping Friends and Harming Enemies: A study in Sophocles and Greek ethics*, Cambridge.
Brock, R. 2020. 'Civic and local identities in Athenian rhetoric', in *The Making of Identities in Athenian Oratory*, eds J. Filonik, B. Griffith-Williams, and J. Kucharski, London, 15–31.
Caillemer, E. 1879. *Le droit de succession légitime à Athènes*. Paris.
Cairns, D. 1996. 'Hybris, dishonour and thinking big', *Journal of Hellenic Studies* 116, 1–32.
Carey, C. 1996. 'Nomos in Athenian rhetoric and oratory', *Journal of Hellenic Studies* 116, 33–46.
Carey, C. 2017. *Trials from Classical Athens*, 2nd edn, London.
Christ, M. R. 1998. *The Litigious Athenian*, Baltimore.
Cobetto Ghiggia, P. 2002. *Iseo, Contra Leocare (sulla successione di Diceogene)*, Pisa.
Cobetto Ghiggia, P. 2012. *Iseo, Orazioni: introduzione, testo rivisto, traduzione, note e glossario giuridico attico*, Alessandria.
Cohen, D. 1995. *Law, Violence and Ccommunity in Classical Athens*, Cambridge.
Cox, C. A. 1998. *Household Interests: Property, marriage strategies, and family dynamics in ancient Athens*, Princeton.
Cudjoe, R. V. 2010. *The Social and Legal Position of Widows and Orphans in Classical Athens*, Athens.
Davies, J. K. 1969. 'The date of I. G. ii^2 1609', *Historia* 18, 309–33.
Davies, J. K. 1971. *Athenian Propertied Families, 600–300 BC*, Oxford.
Denommé, J. M. 1974. *Recherches sur la langue et le style d'Isée*, Hildesheim.
Dickey, E. 1996. *Greek Forms of Address from Herodotos to Lucian*, Oxford.
Edwards, M. 2002 'A note on Isaeus 4.7', *Mnemosyne* 55, 87–8.
Edwards, M. (trans.) 2007. *Isaeus*, Austin, Tex.

Edwards, M. 2008 'Isaeus and the Athenian inheritance laws', in *Symposion 2007,* eds E. Harris and G. Thür, Vienna, 41–53.
Ferrucci, S. 2005. *Iseo: La successione di Kiron,* Pisa.
Fisher, N. R. E. 1990. 'The law of *hybris* in Athens', in *Nomos: essays in Athenian law, politics and society,* eds P. Cartledge, P. Millett, and S. C. Todd, Cambridge, 123–38.
Fisher, N. R. E. 2003 '"Let envy be absent": envy, liturgies and reciprocity in Athens' in *Envy, spite and jealousy: the rivalrous emotions in ancient Greece,* eds D. Konstan and N. K. Rutter, Edinburgh, 181–215.
Forster, E. S. 1927. *Isaeus, with an English Translation* (Loeb Classical Library) Cambridge, Mass.
Foxhall, L. 1989. 'Household, gender and property in classical Athens', *Classical Quarterly* 39, 22–44.
Friedman, L. M. 2009. *Dead Hands: A social history of wills, trusts, and inheritance law,* Stanford.
Gagarin, M. 2003 'Who were the *kakourgoi*? Career criminals in Athenian law' in *Symposion 1999,* eds G. Thür and F. J. Fernandez Nieto, Böhlau, 183–92.
Gernet, L. 1917. *Recherches sur le développement de la pensée juridique et morale en Grèce: étude sémantique,* Paris.
Glazebrook, A., 2005 'The making of a prostitute: Apollodoros's portrait of Neaira', *Arethusa* 38, 161–87.
Glazebrook, A.. 2014. 'The erotics of manumission: prostitutes and the πρᾶσις ἐπ' ἐλευθερίᾳ', *Eugesta* 4, 53–80.
Golden, M. 2015. *Children and Childhood in Classical Athens,* 2nd edn, Baltimore.
Griffith-Williams, B. 2008. '"Those who know the facts": witnesses and their testimony in Isaios 9', *Acta Antiqua Hungarica* 48, 235–61.
Griffith-Williams, B. 2012. '*Oikos,* family feuds and funerals: argumentation and evidence in Athenian inheritance disputes', *Classical Quarterly* 62, 145–62.
Griffith-Williams, B. 2013. *A Commentary on Selected Speeches of Isaios,* Leiden.
Griffith-Williams, B. 2017. 'Would I lie to you? Narrative and performance in Isaios 6', in *The theatre of justice: aspects of performance in Greco-Roman oratory and rhetoric,* eds S. Papaoioannou, A. Serafim, and B. da Vela, Leiden, 42–56.
Griffith-Williams, B. 2018. 'Isaios 6: a case of procedural abuse (and scholarly

misunderstandings)', in *Use and Abuse of Law in the Athenian Courts*, eds C. Carey, I. Giannadaki, and B. Griffith-Williams, Leiden, 95–109.

Griffith-Williams, B. 2019 'Families and family relationships in the speeches of Isaios and in Middle and New Comedy', in *Poet and Orator: A symbiotic relationship in democratic Athens*, eds A. Markantonatos and E. Volonaki, Berlin, 375–87.

Griffith-Williams, B. 2020a. 'The two Mantitheuses in Demosthenes 39 and [Demosthenes] 40: a case of Athenian identity theft?', in *The Making of Identities in Athenian Oratory*, eds J. Filonik, B. Griffith-Williams, and J. Kucharski, London, 32–46.

Griffith-Williams, B. 2020b. 'Social norms and the legal framework of forensic narratives in disputed inheritance cases', in *Forensic Narratives in Athenian Courts*, eds M. Edwards and D. Spatharas, London, 55–70.

Griffith-Williams, B. 2022. 'ὁ γὰρ ἀγὼν οὐ μικρὸς αὐτοῖς, ἀλλὰ περὶ τῶν μεγίστων: Competition for inheritance in ancient Greece', in *The Agōn in Classical Literature: Studies in honour of Chris Carey*, eds M. Edwards, A. Efstathiou, I. Karamanou and E. Volonaki (BICS Supplement 145), London, 175–82.

Griffith-Williams, B. (forthcoming a) 'Blood is (usually) thicker than water: kinship and friendship in ancient Greek inheritance disputes' in *Philia: Friendship in ancient Greek thought and literature, in honour of Chris Carey and Mike Edwards*, eds A. Efstathiou, J. Filonik, C. Kremmydas, and E. Volonaki, Leiden.

Griffith-Williams, B. (forthcoming b) 'Character evidence in Isaeus's speeches from inheritance disputes, in *Keeping to the Point: Law, Character, and Rhetoric in Athenian Forensic Orator*, eds E. M. Harris and A. Esu, Edinburgh.

Hall, E. M. 2006. *The Theatrical Cast of Athens: Interactions between ancient Greek drama and society*, Oxford.

Hansen, M. H. 1976. Apagoge, endeixis *and* ephegesis *against* kakourgoi, atimoi *and* pheugontes: A *study in the administration of justice in the fourth century BC.* Odense.

Harris, E. M. 2006a '*Apotimema*: Athenian terminology for real security in leases and dowry agreements', in Harris, E. M., *Democracy and the Rule of Law in Classical Athens*, Cambridge, 207–39.

Harris, E. M. 2006b 'In the act or red-handed? *Apagoge* to the Eleven and *furtum manifestum*' in Harris, E. M., *Democracy and the Rule of Law in Classical Athens*, Cambridge, 373–90.

Harris, E. M. 2013a. 'Feuding or the rule of law?', in Harris, E. M., *The Rule of Law in Action in Democratic Athens*, Oxford, 60–98.

Harris, E. M. 2013b. 'The judicial oath', in Harris, E. M., *The Rule of Law in Action in Democratic Athens*, Oxford, 101–37.

Harris, E. M. 2013c 'Open texture in Athenian law: the approach of the litigants', in Harris, E. M., *The Rule of Law in Action in Democratic Athens*, Oxford, 175–212.

Harris, E. M. 2018 'Trials, private arbitration and public arbitration in classical Athens or the background to [Arist.] *AthPol* 53, 1–7', in Athenaion Politeiai tra storia, politica e sociologia: Aristotele e Pseudo-Senofonte, eds C. Bearzot, M. Canevaro, T. Gargiulo, and E. Poddighe, 213–30, Milan.

Harrison, A. R. W. 1968. *The Law of Athens, Volume 1: The Family and Property*, Oxford.

Harrison, A. R. W. 1971. *The Law of Athens, Volume 2: Procedure*, Oxford.

Hatzilambrou, R. 2018a. *Isaeus' On the estate of Pyrrhus (Oration 3)*, Cambridge.

Hatzilambrou, R. 2018b. 'Abuse of inheritance law in Isaios?', in *Use and Abuse of Law in the Athenian Courts*, eds C. Carey, I. Giannadaki, and B. Griffith-Williams, Leiden, 336–51.

Humphreys, S. C. 2019. *Kinship in Ancient Athens: An anthropological analysis*, 2 vols, Oxford.

Hunter, V. J. 1993. 'Agnatic kinship in Athenian law and Athenian family practice: its implications for women', in *Law, Politics and Society in the Ancient Mediterranean World*, eds B. Halpern and D. W. Hobson, Sheffield, 101–21.

Johnstone, S. 1999. *Disputes and Democracy: The consequences of litigation in ancient Athens*, Austin, Tex.

Jones, W. 1779. *The Speeches of Isaeus in Causes Concerning the Law of Succession of Property at Athens, with a prefatory discourse, notes critical and historical, and a commentary*, London.

Just, R. 1989. *Women in Athenian Law and Life*, London.

Kamen, D. 2000. *Isaeus' Orations 2 and 6*, Bryn Mawr.

Kamps, W, 1938. 'Une affaire de fraude successorale à Athènes', *Annuaire de l'Institut de Philologie et d'Histoire Orientales et Slaves* 6, 15–27.

Kapparis, K. 2017. *Prostitution in the Ancient Greek World*, Berlin.

Kapparis, K. 2021. *Women in the Law Courts of Classical Athens*, Edinburgh.

Karabélias, E. 1992. 'L'acte à cause de mort (diathèke) dans le droit attique', *Recueils de la Société Jean Bodin* 59 (Actes à cause de mort), 47–121.

Konstan, D. 1996. 'Greek friendship', *American Journal of Philology* 117, 71–94.

Kremmydas, C. 2013. 'The discourse of deception and characterization in the Attic orators', *Greek, Roman, and Byzantine Studies* 53, 51–89.

Kremmydas, C. 2018. '*Anakrisis* and the framing of strategies of argumentation in Athenian public trials', in *Use and Abuse of Law in the Athenian Courts*, eds C. Carey, I. Giannadaki, and B. Griffith-Williams, Leiden, 110–31.

Kucharski, J. 2020. 'Prosecutorial identities and the problem of relevance', in *The Making of Identities in Athenian Oratory*, eds J. Filonik, B. Griffith-Williams, and J. Kucharski, London, 171–90.

Labarbe, J. 1953. 'L'âge correspondant au sacrifice du Koureion et les données historiques du sixième discours d'Isée', *Bulletin de la Classe des Lettres de l'Academie Royale de Belgique*, 39, 358–94.

Lambert, S. D. 1993. *The Phratries of Attica*, Ann Arbor, Mich.

Lanni, A. 2006. *Law and Justice in the Courts of Classical Athens.* Cambridge.

Leão, D. R. and Rhodes, P. J. 2016. *The Laws of Solon: A new edition with introduction, translation and commentary*, London.

Lentzsch, R. 1932. *Studien zu Isaios,* Weida i. Thür.

MacDowell, D. M. 1976. '"Hybris" in Athens', *Greece & Rome* 23, 14–31.

MacDowell, D. M. 1978. *The Law in Classical Athens*, Ithaca, NY.

MacDowell, D. M. 1989. 'The *oikos* in Athenian law', *Classical Quarterly* 39, 10–21.

Martin, G. 2006. 'Forms of address in Athenian courts', *Museum Helveticum* 63, 75–88.

Ogden, D. 1996 *Greek Bastardy in the Classical and Hellenistic Periods.* Oxford.

Papachrysostomou, A. 2019 'Ctesias of Besa', in *The Encylopedia of Greek Comedy* ed. A. H. Sommerstein, Hoboken, 333.

Parker, R. C. T. 1996. *Athenian Religion: A history*, Oxford.

Parker, R. 2005. *Polytheism and Society at Athens*, Oxford.

Raubitschek, A. E. 1954. 'Philinos', *Hesperia* 23, 67–81.

Rhodes, P. J. 1981. *A Commentary on the Aristotelian Athenaion Politeia*, Oxford.

Roebuck, D. 2001. *Ancient Greek Arbitration*, Oxford.

Roussel, P. 1926. *Isée: Discours*, Paris. (repr. 2003)

Rubinstein, L. 1993. *Adoption in IV Century Athens*, Copenhagen.

Rubinstein, L. 2000. *Litigation and Co-operation: Supporting speakers in the Athenian courts*, Stuttgart.

Rubinstein, L. 2018. 'Clauses out of context: partial citation of statutes in Attic forensic oratory' in *Use and Abuse of Law in the Athenian Courts*, eds C. Carey, I. Giannadaki and B. Griffith-Williams, Leiden, 165–80.

Sanders, E. 2014. *Envy and Jealousy in Classical Athens*, Oxford.

Sawyer, C. and Spero, M. 2018. *Succession, Wills and Probate*, 3rd edn. London.

Scafuro, A. C. (trans.) 2011. *Demosthenes, Speeches 39–49*, Austin, Tex.

Schaps, D. 1977. 'The woman least mentioned: etiquette and women's names', *Classical Quarterly* 27, 323–30.

Schulthess, O. 1886. *Vormundschaft nach attischem Recht*, Freiburg im Breisgau.

Schweigert, E. 1940. 'The Athenian cleruchy on Samos', *American Journal of Philology* 61, 194–98.

Serafim, A. 2020. *Religious Discourse in Attic Oratory and Politics*. London and New York.

Sommerstein, A. (ed.) 2013. *Samia (The woman from Samos)/Menander*. Cambridge.

Sommerstein, A. H. and Torrance, I. C. 2014. *Oaths and Swearing in Ancient Greece*. Berlin.

Spatharas, D. 2019. *Emotions, Persuasion, and Public Discourse in Classical Athens*. Berlin.

Tartaglia, G. M. 2019. *Alkenor-[Asklepiodo]ros: introduzione, traduzione e commento (Fragmenta comica, 16.1)*. Göttingen.

Thomas, R. 1989. *Oral tradition and written record in classical Athens*, Cambridge.

Thompson, W. E. 1970. 'Isaeus VI: the historical circumstances', *Classical Review* 20, 1–4.

Thompson, W. E. 1981. 'Athenian attitudes toward wills, *Prudentia* 13, 13–25.

Todd, S. C. 1993. *The Shape of Athenian Law*, Oxford.

Usher, S. 1999. *Greek Oratory: Tradition and originality*, Oxford.

Wevers, R. F. 1969. *Isaeus: Chronology, prosopography and social history*, The Hague.

Whitehead, D. 1986. *The Demes of Attica, 508/7–ca. 250 BC*, Princeton.

Whitehead, D. 2000. *Hypereides: The forensic speeches*, Oxford.

Wohl, V. 2010. *Law's Cosmos: Juridical discourse in Athenian forensic oratory*, Cambridge.

Wyse, W. 1904. *The Speeches of Isaeus, With Critical and Explanatory Notes*, Cambridge.

INDEX

The index is selective, focusing on significant people, places and topics mentioned or discussed in the introductions and commentaries. The translations of the speeches are not indexed.

Acharnae (deme) 94–95
addresses (to the judges) 42, 43, 45, 47, 48, 51, 54, 59, 62–63, 64, 92, 103, 119, 142, 151, 154, 160, 200, 208, 211, 216, 228, 229, 230, 231, 234
see also apostrophe (rhetorical figure)
adoption
　inter vivos 3–5, 6, 7, 22, 65, 92, 100–101, 103–104, 105–106, 148, 166, 202, 205, 222, 235
　posthumous 148, 222
　testamentary 3–4, 15–16, 103, 204, 205, 214, 222, 235
　see also wills
affection *see* friendship/affection
age *see* old age
anger 14, 17–18, 29, 43, 47, 48, 49, 53, 54, 61, 106, 228
apostrophe (rhetorical figure) 216, 229, 230
　see also addresses (to the judges)
arbitration/arbitrators 8, 21, 51, 68, 70, 72, 111, 114–15
betrothal 97, 99, 209–10, 215
　see also dowry, marriage
blood relationship *see* kinship
burial of the dead *see* funeral and commemorative rites

Cephale (deme) 93, 95, 108, 115, 118
Cephisia (deme) 95, 163, 202, 204, 205, 207, 218
Cerameicus (district of Athens) 164, 214
character 110, 112, 117, 148
character evidence 10, 125, 127–28, 150, 156–57, 158, 228, 232
childlessness 67–68, 93, 97–98, 101, 103, 105, 109, 110–11, 115, 117, 119, 204, 205
circumstantial evidence *see* evidence (in legal cases)
citizenship 2, 3, 42, 94, 104, 147, 148, 157, 171, 172, 207, 208, 213, 214, 219, 227
Cleisthenes 94, 104
comedy 69, 74, 106, 107, 119, 126, 145, 147, 148, 211
commemorative rites *see* funeral and commemorative rites
common knowledge (topos) 57, 158, 200
Corinthian War (395–86 BC) 204
customary rites *see* funeral and commemorative rites
deception (of judges) 143, 151, 154, 174, 208, 234
demes/demesmen 3–4, 7, 67–68, 70, 72–73, 93, 94–95, 99, 100,

Index

demes/demesmen *contd.* 103–104, 106–108, 113, 117, 118, 202, 207, 235
  see also Acharnae, Cephale, Cephisia, Pithus, Sphettus
demotics 94, 99, 113, 114, 202
deposit (in legal proceedings) 144–45, 149, 154, 208
depositions *see* witnesses/witness testimony
dicastic oath 120, 128, 160, 201, 229–30
dicasts *see* judges (Athenian)
direct speech 74, 102, 230
divorce 3, 67, 69, 94, 95, 97, 98, 100, 102, 171, 215, 225
  see also betrothal, dowry, marriage
dowry 7, 67, 69, 71–72, 95, 96, 97, 100
  see also betrothal, divorce, marriage
emotions *see* anger, envy, friendship/affection
enmity 14, 46, 50, 56, 114, 231
envy 110, 111, 112, 151, 232, 233
Euclides (archon, 403/402 BC) 4, 226–27
evidence (in legal cases) 7, 10, 18, 42, 48, 49, 56, 57, 70, 104, 112, 117, 125, 142, 149, 150, 151, 156, 159, 205, 210
  see also character evidence, probability, relevance, witnesses/witness testimony
false testimony 6, 66, 92, 151, 161, 168, 200, 201, 203, 205, 208
friendship/affection 9, 10, 44–45, 47, 52, 55, 56–57, 58, 61, 63, 67, 71, 72, 73, 94–96, 101, 102, 152, 156, 202
funeral and commemorative rites 8, 9, 10, 47, 68, 72, 93, 95, 101, 105, 106, 116, 124, 145, 152, 153, 217, 225
guardians/guardianship 14, 46, 47, 48, 60, 100, 146, 221–22, 223
  see also orphans
identity 7, 8, 94–95, 99, 122, 143, 144, 146, 164, 168, 173, 200, 202, 207, 213
illegitimacy *see* legitimacy/illegitimacy
intestate succession 4–5, 16–17, 22, 42, 44, 52, 56, 57, 59, 61,151, 173, 227
irony 9, 54, 74, 108, 109, 111, 115, 145, 153, 154, 155, 228, 231
judges (Athenian) 6, 8, 10, 18, 20, 49, 53, 57, 58, 59, 64, 70, 73, 74, 105, 109, 112, 116, 120, 127, 128, 149, 157, 167, 174, 213, 214, 228, 229, 231, 232
  see also addresses (to the judges), dicastic oath
juries (Athenian)
  see judges (Athenian)
kinship 10, 17, 20, 44, 45, 51–52, 54, 55, 56–57, 58–61, 64, 71, 123, 126, 128, 142, 144, 146, 148–49, 151, 154–55, 227
  see also intestate succession
legitimacy/illegitimacy 2–4, 6, 7, 8, 104, 147–48, 164, 166, 171–73, 206–207, 208, 210–11, 213, 216–17, 219–20, 227, 231, 234

Index

Lemnos 208
liturgies *see* public services (liturgies)
marriage 3, 59, 67, 71, 94–96, 97–100, 107, 108, 164, 166, 171, 207, 208, 209–10, 215, 220, 225–26, 227
see also betrothal, divorce, dowry
mercenary soldiers 97, 118, 121, 122, 157
military service (official) 67, 68, 97, 102, 118, 155, 157, 161, 163, 168, 204–205
mourning *see* funeral and commemorative rites
names/naming 7, 94, 114, 116, 122, 143, 145–47, 202, 207, 208, 212–13
see also demotics, patronymics
oaths 72, 93, 115, 118, 153, 207, 214, 228, 231–32
see also dicastic oath
old age 3, 58–59, 67, 69, 98, 101, 102, 106, 164, 211–12, 215
orphans 46, 68, 100, 112, 113, 221, 222–23
see also guardians/guardianship
patronymics 94, 143
Peloponnesian War (431–404 BC) 208, 227
personal names *see* names/naming
phratries 3–4, 7, 67, 72, 93, 100, 103–105, 106, 164, 169–70, 207, 211, 214–16, 235
Pithus (deme) 113
posthumous adoption *see* adoption
probability (in legal argumentation) 9, 20, 51, 73, 108, 125, 127, 152, 156, 158
prostitutes/prostitution 3, 161, 164, 171, 211, 212–13, 228
public services (liturgies) 118, 119, 127, 157, 158, 201, 224, 232, 233, 234
see also trierarchs/trierarchy
relevance (of evidence in legal cases) 9, 10, 127, 228, 229
repetition (of key words and phrases in speeches) 9, 45, 73–74, 92, 109, 118
rhetorical questions 9, 54, 74, 108, 109, 110, 111, 112, 119, 145, 153, 208, 216, 228, 229, 234
Samos 169, 170, 201, 218
senility *see* old age
Sicilian expedition (415–413 BC) 164, 168, 200, 209
slaves 147, 164–65, 172–73, 210–13
Solon 3–4, 17–18, 20, 43, 44, 53, 54, 57, 60, 64, 65, 69, 71, 92, 101, 103, 150, 151, 204, 206, 208, 214, 219, 227
Sphettus (deme) 99
style/stylistic features *see* direct speech, irony, repetition, rhetorical questions
supporting speakers 6, 45–46, 65, 121, 124, 145, 161, 165, 200, 211
testamentary adoption *see* adoption
testimony *see* witnesses/witness testimony
Theban War (378–71 BC) 169, 204
Timotheus (Athenian general) 164, 168, 169, 201, 209, 218

trierarchs/trierarchy 157, 170, 200, 201, 204, 217, 218, 233
wills 3–4, 5, 7, 8, 10, 14–21, 43, 47, 49, 52, 53, 54, 57, 59–60, 103, 123, 125, 126, 142–43, 144, 146, 148–49, 150, 151–52, 154, 155, 161, 201, 205–206, 214, 217, 219–20
see also adoption, testamentary
witnesses/witness testimony 6, 7–8, 16, 23, 42, 48, 50, 51, 56, 57, 65, 71–74, 96, 97, 99, 102, 104, 106–107, 108, 115–16, 117, 122, 124–26, 142, 143, 149, 159, 151, 152, 154, 155, 156, 159, 173, 201, 206, 207, 210, 217, 218, 220, 221, 223, 230
see also false testimony
women 5, 65, 69, 70, 92, 95, 99, 171–72, 207, 210, 211–12, 225, 228

Printed and bound by CPI Group (UK) Ltd, Croydon, CR0 4YY
12/05/2024

14500776-0003